China's New Business Elite

China's New Business Elite

The Political Consequences of Economic Reform

Margaret M. Pearson

UNIVERSITY OF CALIFORNIA PRESS

Berkeley / Los Angeles / London

University of California Press
Berkeley and Los Angeles, California

University of California Press, Ltd.
London, England

© 1997 by The Regents of the University of California
Earlier versions of parts of this book were published previously:
Chapter 3: "Breaking the Bonds of 'Organized Dependence': Managers
in China's Foreign Sector," *Studies in Comparative Communism* 25, no.
1 (1992): 57–77. Reprinted by permission of Elsevier Science Ltd., The
Boulevard, Langford Lane, Kidlington OX5 1GB, United Kingdom.
Chapter 5: "The Janus Face of Business Associations in China: Socialist
Corporatism in Foregin Enterprises," *Australian Journal of Chinese
Affairs*, no. 31 (January 1994): 25–46.

First Paperback Printing 1999

Library of Congress Cataloging-in-Publication Data

Pearson, Margaret M., 1959–
    China's new business elite : The political consequences of economic
reform / Margaret M. Pearson.
        p.   cm.
    Includes bibliographical references and index.
    ISBN 0-520-20718-1 (cloth : alk. paper)
    ISBN 0-520-21933-3 (pbk. : alk. paper)
    1. Businessmen—China—History.   2. Entrepreneurship—China—
History.   3. China—Politics and government—1976-.   4. Elite social
sciences)—China—History.   I. Title.
HC427.92.P39   1997
338.951—dc20   96-26088
                                                                    CIP

Manufactured in the United States of America

9   8   7   6   5   4   3   2   1

The paper used in this publication meets the minimum requirements of
American National Standard for Information Sciences—Permanence of
Paper for Printed Library Materials, ANSI Z39.48-1984. ∞

For Benjamin

Contents

Acknowledgments

This book, though mostly a product of my own sweat, could not have been completed without the help of many others. I owe my greatest research-related debt to interviewees from the foreign and private sectors of China's economy who, in both 1991 and 1995, shared with me their time and their insights as to the evolving place of the "new business elite" in China. These interviewees represent an extremely impressive group of people, and I come away from this project feeling hope that they will be instrumental participants in China's future. I also thank Jan Borgonjan, Li Zhaoxi, and John Child of the China-EC Management Institute in Beijing for helping me in 1991 to get started with interviews.

Once I had committed to paper my initial ideas, a number of friends and colleagues generously commented on the text, either in whole or in part. These friends and colleagues included Steve Goldstein, David Kang, Bill Kirby, Kenneth Lieberthal, Jean Oi, and anonymous readers for the University of California Press. While none of these commentators will agree in all (or even most) respects with what I have written here, their input and support were nevertheless invaluable. Many other people and institutions also were involved in the process of writing this book. At the University of California Press, Sheila Levine, Tony Hicks, and Sue Heinemann ably and with great professionalism guided this manuscript through the review and editing process. For this, I am extremely grateful. Financial support crucial for conducting the research for this book was provided by a Burke Research Initiation Grant, a

Dartmouth College Junior Faculty Fellowship, Dartmouth College Professional Development Funds, and University of Maryland (College Park) Research Funds. Over the course of several years, Mobena Hashmi, Sanjay Natarajan, Matt Trusch, and Steve Tseng, all of Dartmouth College, and Mike Turner of the University of Maryland provided valuable research assistance. A fellowship during the 1991–92 academic year at the Mary Ingraham Bunting Foundation at Radcliffe College provided a wonderful place for doing some early writing on the project.

I wish to thank members of my family who, too, were involved in this endeavor. My father, Justus R. Pearson, Jr., put back on his college professor hat in order to at least try to put the manuscript in its most readable form. My husband, Steve Gunby, kept urging me along in both subtle and not-so-subtle—but always supportive—ways. Lastly, I wish to thank my son, Benjamin. He was an infant and toddler when most of this book was written, and so had no direct influence on its content, and yet the happiness he has brought us has made the months of writing much, much more pleasurable. I dedicate this book to him.

Introduction

The transition from planned to market economy that was initiated in China in the late 1970s unleashed one of the most rapid economic transformations ever to have occurred, with changes that have spilled over into the social and political realms. Among the most important social and political results of the economic reforms is the emergence of new economic strata, including the group that is the subject of this book: China's new business elite. Reflecting the central government's perception that it depends increasingly on members of the new business elite to promote industrialization, it has granted members of this elite greater economic authority and control over economic resources. Moreover, the government has revitalized business "associations" (*xiehui*) to act as intermediaries with enterprises.

It would seem that China's new business elite is poised to use its economic position to play an important role in China's political life. That such a role is possible is suggested by the example of parallel groups in other developing countries. In these countries, members of the "national bourgeoisie" have helped to drive the conversion to markets and integration into the world economy. Members of the business elite, including those who have ties to international firms, have influenced government policy in a direction favorable to international economic cooperation. Members of the business elite also have a potential role to play in the political realm. Indeed, although the premise is questioned in this book, it is often assumed—particularly by U.S. policy-makers—that the Chinese business elite will be the carrier of democracy or "civil society" in China, much as its counterparts were in the development of the Western industrial nations.[1]

The growing command of resources and autonomy on the part of China's new business elite, plus a consciousness of the role its counterparts have played elsewhere, raise the core problem addressed in this book: whether *economic* reform alone can, or inevitably does, lead to significant *political* change, even if the regime in power is unwilling to initiate such change. The very appearance of a new business elite suggests the possibility that its members and their associations may not be mere "transmission belts" of the Leninist state but, rather, harbingers of a new and unintended pattern of state-society relations.[2] But have the members of the post-Mao business elite in fact translated their greater economic autonomy into pressure for political change, carving a new pattern of interaction with the state at either the central or local levels?[3] Is the new pattern that has appeared, if any, "democratizing,"[4] or does it

---

1. Such an assumption has surrounded the annual debate in U.S. policy circles over the renewal of China's most favored nation status. To wit: "Policy makers argue that [suspending China's most favored nation status] would set back political freedom in China, because economic expansion results in a growing middle class that in other countries has supported political liberalization" (Blustein and Smith [1996]). The notion that economic reforms will lead to political liberalization also is argued in parts of the academic literature on China (e.g., Glassman [1991]). Indeed, it would appear that policy-makers and scholars writing about China's reforms use as their reference the common understanding that, in the West, the bourgeoisie (interacting with peasants and workers and the state) was the carrier of liberal democracy. Three classic works in this vein are Moore (1966); Habermas (1989); and Lindblom (1977). In addition, a "preconditions" school of political development has identified industrialization and the emergence of a middle class as a prerequisite for democratization (Lipset [1981]). Interestingly, the assumption made in much of the literature on the role of the national bourgeoisie in Latin America, particularly the literature on dependency (e.g., Evans [1979]) and bureaucratic authoritarianism (e.g., O'Donnell [1973]), suggests that this group will be anti-democratic. (As will be discussed in chapter 1, recent scholars [Payne (1994)] have begun to challenge this latter view.)

2. The totalitarian model depicted societal groups in the Maoist era as "transmission belts" of state policy. See Friedrich and Brzezinski (1961) and Townsend (1967).

3. The political outcome of economic reform this book considers is primarily the emergence of new social groups and how they relate to the state, i.e., the evolution of state-society relations. I do not consider the full impact of economic reforms on the political elite or bureaucratic politics. Nor do I consider second-order effects of economic reform on the political environment, such as the rise of corruption that undermines the ideology and the moral legitimacy of the Party-state. Some of these issues are discussed in Gordon White (1993).

4. By "democratizing" I refer to changes characterized by the two processes identified by Dahl (1971) as central to the creation of polyarchy: contestation, or an increase in genuine competition among political elites; and inclusion of citizens in political decision-making, perhaps by voting but not necessarily. This definition is used, implicitly or explicitly, in much of the literature on democratic "transitions" from authoritarian rule.

reflect an alternative type of transition? What forces have shaped the emerging relationship between new business groups and the state?

In short, this book represents an attempt to understand how the creation of a new elite as an outgrowth of economic reform has shaped state-society relations in the most advanced sectors of the Chinese economy, and to understand whether the popular assumption that economic reform leads inevitably or easily to democracy holds in the case of China. An examination of two segments of China's new business elite provides the empirical basis for addressing these issues. The group that receives primary emphasis is the topmost stratum of "foreign-sector managers"—Chinese nationals who manage the foreign-backed businesses that have been allowed to operate in China since the late 1970s. The other segment of the new elite this book examines is private entrepreneurs. Together, members of these two groups have been granted a considerable degree of autonomy from the state, and through their jobs command considerable economic resources. They seem positioned, more than other economic groups in post-Mao China, to convert their autonomy and resources into a new pattern of state-society relations. If we find that these two relatively autonomous groups have *not* made such a conversion, or if any conversion they have made is not democratizing, it is unlikely that other, less well positioned groups will be able or willing to do so.

Chapter 1 establishes a framework for exploring the link between economic reform and the emergence of new state-society relations by examining three models of state-society relations that might be expected to emerge from China's economic reforms. The chapter begins by considering arguments that economic reform will lead to civil society or democratization. It uncovers significant flaws in the logic underlying such a scenario and suggests that, contrary to conventional assumptions, market reform by itself is highly unlikely to lead directly to democratization. Rather, there is ample reason to expect that the relationship between China's new economic elite and the state will be complex and shaped by a multitude of factors, and that extensive democratization by this path is unlikely. Chapter 1 then examines two alternative models of state-society relations that, prospectively, seem to offer more plausible alternatives: clientelism and a version of state corporatism.

Although it is part of a broader worldwide "national bourgeoisie," China's new business elite has appeared in its own historical context. It is easy to recall images of a Chinese nation hostile to merchants, as in the derogation in Confucian thought of merchant and trade activity and the elimination of the national capitalist class by Mao in the 1950s. Yet these signs of hostility must not be allowed to overshadow an equally important legacy of merchant dynamism, significant independence from the state, and a *de facto* influence in political life. These two legacies blend to create a dominant historical pattern that can best be described as a dualism. In this dualism, merchants and their associations possess a degree of autonomy and yet, at the same time, are closely tied to and often dominated by the state. This pattern, which remains important for the present era, is the subject of chapter 2.

The three chapters which then follow examine the specific cases of foreign-sector managers and private entrepreneurs in the post-Mao era. Each chapter tells a part of the story of the pattern of state-society relations that has emerged as a result of reforms. Chapter 3 demonstrates why China's new business elite has the potential to carve out a new pattern of state-society relations by describing how, as a result of the economic reforms, foreign-sector managers and, to a lesser degree, private-sector entrepreneurs have obtained a striking degree of structural autonomy from the state compared to other economic groups. It also shows how the views of members of the business elite toward economic reform and politics are firmly pro-market and, to a large extent, anti-regime and anti-communist.

Chapter 4 goes on to address directly the question of whether this new elite has converted its privileged economic position, structural independence, and ideological predilections into a force for democratization. A seeming paradox arises, for, in spite of the advantages they possess, members of China's business elite have shown few signs of becoming an independent, activist political force. They desire to escape from politics, not to engage in it or to create a "civil society." Individual foreign-sector managers, and private entrepreneurs even more so, use means familiar in Chinese political life to shape their situation: personalistic, clientelist efforts designed to influence officials. Having gained structural independence, they try to *rebuild* informal ties to the state. Members of the business elite are characterized by neither strong horizontal ties to each other, nor strong links to other societal actors, both of which we expect in an emergent civil society.

Although the structural autonomy and ideological antipathy of foreign-sector managers and private entrepreneurs have not been channeled into strong pressures against the state, a new pattern of state-society relations *has* appeared around these groups. The continued use of clientelist ties is one element of that new pattern. The analysis in chapter 5 brings to light an additional element. Business associations have been established to represent the new elite. In these new associations can be seen the strongest attempts to date by representatives of the business elite to influence the state in an organized way and, more generally, to turn these state-initiated institutions into more independent societal organizations. But unlike in "civil society," where the associational realm is a central forum for establishing and maintaining political autonomy, post-Mao business associations are established by the state and are dominated at the top by retired officials from relevant ministries. The state has attempted—albeit with only limited success—to use these organizations to co-opt potentially autonomous social forces. This strategy, which may be termed "socialist corporatism," echoes what has occurred in other developing countries where the state remains strong.[5]

Chapter 6, in closing this study, concludes that new patterns of state-society relations have indeed emerged in the leading sectors of the post-Mao economy as a result of economic reforms. But this pattern is not what many expect; while inklings of civil society have appeared, structural, historical, and international factors have thwarted a link between economic reform and democratization and, instead, have created a hybrid pattern of state-society relations. This hybrid pattern contains both "socialist corporatism" and clientelism. These characteristics have roots in China's socialism and, at the same time, are strongly reminiscent of pre-revolutionary China. The hybrid pattern is likely to endure, not least because it serves the interests of members of both the business elite and the central and local governments. Chapter 6 also observes that China's hybrid pattern bears some similarities to the "statism" found in the East Asian countries of Taiwan and South Korea. But China's socialist legacy has meant that the corporatist institutions, which ideally would help coordinate business-government relations and foster effective policy-making, are significantly weaker than elsewhere in East Asia, making China's situation different enough to preclude its firm inclusion in the "East Asian statist" mold.

Defining China's "New Business Elite"

China's new business elite is part of a broader international stratum: a modern, often influential business class, a portion of

---

5. The establishment of corporatist structures by the state has been used elsewhere as a strategy for state survival in the face of an anticipated or actual challenge from society. Egypt under Nasser and Mexico under Cardenas, for example, have used such strategies—with better results in the latter than the former. See Migdal (1988), pp. 231–234.

which is supported by foreign capital. This elite has been termed, depending on its precise makeup, the national bourgeoisie, the comprador elite, the managerial bourgeoisie, or, in this study, the "new business elite."[6] As used here, the term "business elite" denotes a group defined primarily according to its position in the hierarchy of the economy and its members' income, education (primarily formal), and prestige.[7] In terms of their position in the economy, members of China's new business elite work in the most advanced sectors of the reform economy.[8] Consistent with the orthodox Leninist definitions of the "national bourgeoisie," they are sometimes property owners (as in the case of private entrepreneurs). But, departing from the rather simplistic Leninist definition, members of the new business elite are also professional and technocratic *managers* of modern companies. Many members of China's new business elite have gained their position by managing assets belonging to others, including foreign companies. These managers possess "property rights"—in the sense of having substantial latitude to acquire, use, and dispose of assets—and hence possess authority on a par with or near to that of owners.[9]

6. Under the socialist regime, it is only since the late 1980s that demarcation of groups other than the Marxist standards—worker, peasant, intellectual, bourgeoisie, etc.—has been politically and popularly accepted in China. Yet even as of the 1990s, the term "elite" carries a negative connotation when applied to social status. The preferred term often is "professionals" or "white-collar" (*bailing*) workers. Although the latter term has gained considerable popularity, it is too broad because it includes low-level professional staff and support staff who might work in offices, in addition to elite professionals.

7. This definition based on socio-economic variables is consistent with the spirit of "elite" as used in Ding Xueliang's (1995, pp. 10–13) study of China's "political elite" and "counterelite." Ding adopts a sociological definition (from Mosca) that includes those in the stratum just below the narrow elite at the very top and who possess one or more of the variables of power, prestige, authority, influence, and wealth. This book's definition is also consistent with views of members of the Chinese business elite, as expressed in a survey of 1,100 Shanghai employees of joint ventures, banks, trading companies, hospitals, news media, and universities (United Press International [1995]).

8. That the non-state sectors are at the leading edge of the economy is reflected in the fact that by 1992 they were responsible for over half the output value of industry, as follows: collective (38.3%), private (6.7%), and foreign (6.6%) (*Guojia Jingji Tizhi Gaige Weiyuanhui* [1994], p. 605). For the reasons noted below, however, members of the business elite in the collective are not studied here.

9. The orthodox view of the national bourgeoisie as owners is from Lenin (1939). Management as a basis for significant authority has also long been recognized in the mainstream literature on business organization. See Berle and Means (1932). More recent class-based theories have adopted a "control of resources" definition, most notably the theory of post-imperialism. See Sklar (1976) and Becker (1983). On property and management rights in China, see Granick (1990). It is either ironic or prescient that some of the earliest efforts to argue that the bourgeoisie was constituted by managers as well as property owners grew out of criticisms that *socialist* countries were becoming dominated

The business elite is also defined by its members' relatively high income. Its members are compensated at a level many times the average wage in the PRC. Usually this difference reflects legitimate salaries, although some members become wealthy through illegitimate means such as kickbacks or smuggling. Regardless of the source of their funds, members' higher income translates directly into a better standard of living, as measured by owning modern conveniences, purchasing luxury consumer items, dining out, and sometimes living in more spacious surroundings or even owning an apartment.[10]

The general educational level of members of the business elite is similarly high, consistent with the profile of the national bourgeoisie in other developing countries. As education and expertise are once again officially valued in China, they have become stepping-stones to business opportunities, especially for the generation in their twenties and thirties.[11] Although, as a whole, members of the business elite tend to be extremely well educated, there are Horatio Alger–style exceptions of those who have succeeded by virtue of their business acumen. A quirk unique to the PRC is that the disruption of education during the Cultural Revolution has meant that the portion of the population who would have entered a university between 1967 and 1969 could not do so. Many in this cohort, who in the mid-1990s were in their mid-forties and have been labeled *laosanjie* ("three old ranks"), did not return to school after they were sent to work in villages and factories, and yet they have risen to the top on the basis of their intelligence and determination.

Their position, education, and income level have translated into considerable prestige for the new business elite in urban society. In recent years, as consumerism has gripped China, business is seen as increasingly legitimate and desirable work, and those who are successful in business are respected and/or envied. One measure of this evaluation was the increasing attention paid to professionals and white-collar workers in the mid-1990s on television, in the print media, and in fiction. Yet, the high regard in which many Chinese hold members of the business elite is not universal. Disapproval from older people and those who are

---

by a class-like group of managers operating in government bureaucracies and state-owned enterprises. This concern was the essence of Djilas's (1959) famous critique of the "new class" and was a precipitating rationale for the Cultural Revolution in China.

   10. Specific data on salaries are presented below. A survey of private entrepreneurs reported that their families owned on average 1.36 color television sets compared to the average of .75 for urban families. Cai (1994), p. 59.

   11. Davis (1992), pp. 1075–1076.

politically conservative reflects in part the historically low status of merchants in Chinese culture, a view accentuated by Marxist-Leninist and Maoist disdain for market-related activities and consumerism. Moreover, the fact that many of the post-Mao era's first entrepreneurs were from groups not generally respected (notably the unemployed and ex-convicts) and operated on the fringes of "socialist legality" also hurt the image of business.[12] More recently, corruption scandals involving members of the business elite, particularly those who are former government officials, also have taken a toll. To counter this image, the government initiated a campaign in the official press in the early 1990s emphasizing the contributions and good behavior of entrepreneurs. Perhaps in part because of such campaigns, but most directly as a result of its financial success, the business elite has continued to gain considerable status and prestige in post-Mao society, especially among young people.[13]

Research Focus

Building on the broad definition of China's new business elite just presented, it is necessary to describe in greater detail the segments of the business elite examined in this book, and the research methodology used to study them. As noted previously, managers in the foreign sector are the primary focus of this book. Foreign-sector managers were chosen as the basis for study because they appeared, prospectively, to be the group granted the greatest autonomy by the state, and therefore better positioned than any other economic group to engage in organized efforts to influence the state from outside the state. In order to expand our confidence in the generalizability of findings based on managers in the foreign sector, this book examines whether the experiences of foreign-sector managers are replicated elsewhere within China's new business elite. Specifically, it examines the literature on members of the elite in the other sector that is most formally autonomous from the state, that is, the private sector.

Insofar as foreign-sector managers and private entrepreneurs are the groups most involved in market reforms, these groups serve as "critical cases" in the study of post-Mao state-society relations. By the critical case logic, if we find that members of these most autonomous segments

---

12. On entrepreneurs' backgrounds, see below.

13. On the government's campaign, see Sabin (1994), p. 961. One survey indicated that young people consider "entrepreneurship" as their first job choice. See Kristof (1993).

of the business elite have *not* in fact converted their economic position to political influence, or have done so under very limited conditions, then it is unlikely that other members of the business elite who are *more* bound to the status quo of the state, or other non-elite economic groups, will be able or willing to do so either.[14] A study of China's private and foreign business elite therefore delimits the boundaries of what we can expect to find in other sectors.

Before looking more closely at these two groups, it is important to point out that other segments of the business elite are not studied here. These other segments include entrepreneurial managers of state-owned enterprises and of collective township and village enterprises (TVEs). Many TVE managers have successfully navigated their enterprises into competitive export markets, while some state enterprise managers have striven to list their enterprises on the Chinese or foreign stock exchanges.[15] Managers in quasi-governmental investment organs such as the China International Trade and Investment Corporation (CITIC) and its provincial equivalents also qualify as members of the business elite. Most important among these other segments of the new business elite, perhaps, are former government officials (who are said to have resigned their posts to "jump into the sea," or *xiahai*) and children of high-level government or Party cadres (so-called "princelings," or *taizidang*). Both are able to use contacts gained through official channels to their advantage in making business deals.[16] The personal connections of former officials and *taizidang* are impressive and give them entree, in many cases, to leadership circles.[17] But, consistent with the

14. On the "critical case" method in comparative politics, see Harry Eckstein (1975).

15. Many TVEs also owe much of their success to managers and local officials who act as "chairmen of the board" to guide localities to greater wealth. See Oi (1992); Zweig (1991); and Walder (1991).

16. Sabin (1994, p. 963) notes a 1987 survey in Beijing that reports that 25% of all private ventures were owned by people who had left their state-sector jobs or who kept their positions formally but actually worked in private business (*tingxin liuzhi*, or "stopping wages but maintaining the position"). The State Council has issued circulars to try to define the legitimate business scope of officials. See Tan (1993).

17. Usually, former officials who have gone into business had been fairly well established and successful in their previous work. Former officials' connections to established government figures, as with the family connections of *taizidang*, in an important sense give them an even higher status than foreign-sector managers and private entrepreneurs without official backgrounds. According to Du Wei-ming (in conversation, 7 February 1996), these people have a growing sense of themselves as a group. They are increasingly taking leadership in cultural affairs and are funding cultural projects. Their political role, based on connections with the leadership, is "assumed but unspoken," according to Du. These groups remain important subjects for further field study of the questions motivating this volume, and for testing the conclusions raised in it.

"critical case" logic, because such people are formally tied to the state, they are prima facie less useful as initial tests for understanding the question of whether economic marketization generates new groups that readily convert their economic position to pressures for democratization. In other words, because these groups are already closely tied to the state, we would expect them to be a source less of change than of conservatism.

CHINA'S FOREIGN SECTOR
AND ITS MANAGERS

China's foreign business sector appeared first during the late 1970s and became established as an important force in the economy in the mid-1980s. Whereas the Maoist government had long rejected the idea that foreign businesses should be allowed to operate and profit on Chinese soil, the post-Mao reformers actively encouraged such activities, hoping that foreign businesses would bring in not only capital but also technology and managerial skills. Since the late 1970s, foreign-backed companies have been established across a wide range of industries in China, including manufacture of computers, chemicals, pharmaceuticals, automobiles, consumer goods (notably toys, bicycles, televisions, and textiles), together with trading companies and, in the early 1990s, financial services and real estate. Although the growth of foreign investment in China was small in the early 1980s, and erratic in the mid- and late 1980s, dramatic growth began in the first half of the 1990s. (See appendix 1.) Total pledged foreign investment was reported to be nearly $400 billion (in more than 258,000 enterprises) by the end of 1995.[18]

Foreign-sector businesses take several forms, the three most common of which house the elite of foreign-sector managers examined in this study.[19] First, Sino-foreign joint ventures (JVs), of both the equity and contractual varieties, represented approximately 85% of the total num-

18. Note that all dollar figures in the text refer to U.S. dollars. It is likely that this figure is inflated, reflecting a channeling of PRC funds through Hong Kong and back into China in an effort to gain the privileges of foreign investors. (For more on such "false" joint ventures, see appendix 2.) Nonetheless, it is beyond dispute that there has been a significant increase in investment during the 1990s. For an analysis of foreign investment trends in the 1980s and early 1990s, see Pearson (1991), pp. 69–78; Pearson (1994); and Lardy (1995).

19. Joint oil development projects were a large source of foreign capital early in the 1980s, but their importance as a percentage of foreign capital has since declined. This study does not consider managers who work in these enterprises.

ber of foreign direct investments (and 75% of the total pledged value) by the early 1990s.[20] Second, wholly foreign-owned enterprises (WFOEs) involve no Chinese investment and are often preferred by foreign investors because they can maintain a greater degree of control over their operations and technology. The number of WFOEs has grown dramatically since the mid-1980s, yet they represent just under 15% of all foreign direct investment. In all, there were approximately 70,000 JVs and WFOEs registered in China by the end of 1992.[21] The third type of foreign-sector businesses included in this study are representative offices (ROs). These are not technically direct investments but, rather, operate as agents for large foreign companies, and tend to be located in Beijing and Shanghai. There were an estimated 13,000 ROs in China as of mid-1993.[22]

Members of China's business elite who are employed in the foreign sector are PRC nationals who work alongside expatriates. Many foreign-owned enterprises have hired Western and Asian managers, often from Hong Kong. By doing so, these enterprises have attempted both to inject Western managerial methods into their operations and to maintain some level of foreign control. The lack of access to a supply of trained Chinese managers—due to the upheaval of the education system during the Cultural Revolution, to poor labor mobility, and to political disincentives for Chinese managers' taking responsibility for foreign-backed enterprises—has discouraged extensive use of Chinese managers in many foreign-funded enterprises. Yet both Chinese and foreign participants in these businesses have preferred to promote high-quality PRC nationals to middle- and senior-management levels. The presence of expatriates, who tend to hold high positions and who make much higher salaries than their Chinese counterparts, causes tensions within companies.[23] Many Chinese officials and managers are also sensitive to the circumstance that extensive foreign control recalls experiences of foreign imperialism of the nineteenth and early-twentieth centuries.

---

20. Equity JVs are limited liability companies established by two or more firms that each contribute assets to be owned by a new legal entity. Contractual JVs are similar to partnerships in which no separate legal entity is formed. In both forms, the foreign partner usually contributes capital, technology, and perhaps some equipment, and the Chinese partner generally contributes land, facilities, and some equipment. Equity JVs make up approximately 70% of the number of all JVs.

21. FBIS-CHI-93-094 (18 May 1993), p. 37.

22. "Over 13,000 Foreign Enterprises Established" (1993).

23. Local managers' salaries run between 25% and 100% of expatriate salaries. The average is about 50%. See Frisbie and Brecher (1992), p. 25.

Management by local personnel is also desirable for effective communications within the firm. The recent rapid growth in numbers of foreign-backed enterprises has intensified the demand for talented indigenous managers. Thus, early on, efforts were made in JVs to set up management structures that paired Chinese and foreign managers at equal levels in so-called "shadow" management structures. Explicit efforts at management training, both inside and outside of China, have also been made.[24]

The foreign sector has three types of managers, only one of which can be considered part of the business "elite." The first type of manager was dominant in foreign-sector companies in the first part of the 1980s. These are "old-line" managers who work in medium and large joint ventures, most of which have been formed with Western or Japanese partners. Such managers most often have been transferred to JVs from the Chinese state-owned parent company. They often have many years of on-the-job experience (and hence seniority) and tend to be in their late forties or fifties. They generally have not received either university degrees or schooling in Western managerial methods except, perhaps, for traveling to the foreign parent company for short-term technical training.[25] Rather, they have obtained their position in the foreign-sector enterprise because of their status in the parent Chinese company, through personal ties with others involved in the venture, or by virtue of their political "reliability" or their ability to offer good connections on behalf of the enterprise. Their political "reliability" and lack of formal managerial training too often has meant that they are unwilling to take bold initiatives or accept responsibilities that might contravene standard practice in state-owned enterprises.[26] Because of these problems, foreign participants often have been dissatisfied with their performance. Increasingly, these "old-line" managers have been eased aside or have transformed themselves into more effective managers.

The second type of manager in the foreign sector is clustered in the majority of Hong Kong– and Taiwan-funded investments. Most of these investments are small factories involved in value-added manufacturing

24. Many JV contracts specify that foreign partners are responsible for training Chinese managers, and explicitly require the sinification of management. See Pearson (1991), pp. 177–182.

25. These managers generally survived earlier campaigns and shifts in management models to be able to gain a privileged position in the foreign sector in the 1980s. On the background of the older of these managers, see Schurmann (1968). On the lack of extensive management training for this group, see Vermeer (1988); Brown and Jackson (1991).

26. These characteristics also are common to managers in state-owned enterprises. See Child (1994).

or processing, or in producing goods using fairly low-level technologies. Their managers tend to be recruited through family or clan networks rather than through merit-based processes.[27] Anecdotal evidence suggests that their salaries are lower than in Western- and Japanese-funded enterprises, and that their status is not as high. This characterization does not diminish the importance of Hong Kong and Taiwanese investments in China's economic development; both Hong Kong and Taiwan firms have contributed enormously to China's export capacity and to rural industrialization, and much of the success of these factories can be attributed to the entrepreneurial behavior of their Chinese managers. Yet despite their success, these factories are not the major source of the foreign sector's new business elite.

A third type of manager forms the core of the foreign-sector business elite. Consistent with the meaning of "elite," the number of foreign-sector managers in this category is quite small—not more than 50,000 as of the mid-1990s.[28] In contrast to the overall profile of the origin of foreign capital, in which more than half the reported foreign investment in the PRC has come from Hong Kong investors, members of the foreign-sector business elite are disproportionately concentrated in Western and Japanese firms.[29] These firms offer managers the highest salaries and status, and tend to hire at their middle and upper tiers managers with the highest educational credentials.[30] Because investments by Western and Japanese firms are more likely to incorporate advanced

27. Redding (1995).

28. This figure is estimated as follows: there were an estimated three foreign-sector managers (FSMs) at senior- and middle-management levels in each of the approximately 70,000 equity and contractual JVs and WFOEs actually registered by the end of 1992, and in the estimated 13,000 in ROs set up by mid-1993. This totals 250,000 FSMs in all three types of firms. Members of the foreign-sector business elite tend to be found in the Western and Japanese enterprises that make up about 20% of the overall number of foreign-sector firms, generating the figure of 50,000 elite managers. Although the fact that a portion of managers in Western and Japanese firms are "old line" would reduce this figure, this gap is compensated for by the fact that (a) there may be more than 3 FSMs in the largest Western and Japanese investments, and (b) some members of the foreign-sector elite are found in Hong Kong and Taiwan firms.

29. In 1994, Hong Kong and Macao firms made up 60% of all actual foreign investment funds, and Taiwan firms invested another 10%, significantly more than investment from the U.S. (7.3%), Japan (6.1%), and Europe (estimated at 5%). Other countries that contributed significant amounts of investment (at least 2% of the total) included Singapore and South Korea. Percentages are calculated from data in "$82.68 Billion Foreign Investments Approved Last Year" (1995).

30. Managers in some Asian firms—such as sophisticated Hong Kong investment firms—do have a small presence in the business elite, but do not form the core of the group (Redding [1995]). See appendix 2 for a further discussion of the issue of firm nationality.

technology and appropriate management skills, these firms tend to be most interested in hiring managers with advanced training. Such training occurs in a variety of venues. The most advanced management training is in Western-style M.B.A. programs located in China or abroad. Despite strong interest in M.B.A. degrees in China, government quotas on the number of M.B.A. degrees have kept the number awarded by foreign-run programs at 60 per year, and the number awarded by Chinese programs at 150.[31]

The number of Chinese students enrolled in M.B.A. programs located overseas is increasing. Yet, although some of these students return to China to work in foreign companies because of the emerging work opportunities as well as for family reasons, the number overall remains small. Management training for most members of the elite foreign-sector managers is therefore provided in Chinese-government-run universities, particularly those sponsored by the Ministry of Foreign Trade and Economic Cooperation (MOFTEC), or in special training centers (such as those established in Shekou and Wuxi) that are financed by foreign governments or universities or by the World Bank.[32] Alternatively, many large foreign companies choose to recruit directly from China's premier universities (though there are some government restrictions on this practice), and then provide in-house management training either in or outside of China.[33] In part as a result of their training, members of the business elite tend to be less cautious in their management style compared to their "old-line" counterparts.[34]

31. These programs have been set up in conjunction with, and with financial support from, foreign governments. For example, the School of Management at the Dalian University of Technology was established with aid from the U.S. Department of Commerce, and the China-EC Management Institute was established with aid from the European Community. These programs have been vulnerable to the foreign origin of their funding, as many of them were closed following the government crackdown of 1989. In 1991, the Chinese government approved domestic M.B.A. programs on a trial basis in nine universities. See Borgonjon and Vanhonacker (1992); "China Pledges Reform to Join GATT" (1993); and Treacy (1988). Reflecting the educational bias of the system, even those trained in "modern management" tend to be more oriented toward "hard" knowledge (e.g., quantitative techniques based on engineering approaches) rather than "soft" concepts (e.g., marketing and organizational behavior).

32. MOFTEC is the former Ministry of Foreign Economic Relations and Trade (MOFERT). On these Chinese and foreign-sponsored training programs, see Borgonjon and Vanhonacker (1992), pp. 15, 18; Vermeer (1988); Treacy (1988), p. 40; and Dalton (1990).

33. For example, the Motorola JV's "Cadre 2000" program rotates senior management recruits through the firm's operations worldwide. See Engardio (1993).

34. Bjorkman (1992).

Employees of Western and Japanese businesses are the highest tier of foreign-sector managers in terms of status as well. This is in large part a result of the international prestige of many of their firms. It is also a result of the higher salaries they are paid, particularly for managers who work in the U.S. financial and other professional services offices that began operating in the early 1990s.[35] According to one survey, managers in joint ventures and wholly foreign-owned enterprises earned about 850 yuan ($160) per month (including pay, bonuses, and subsidies) in 1992. Chinese managers in representative offices earned even more, generally making between 1,000 and 3,500 yuan ($190 to $670) per month, plus benefits, in the early 1990s.[36] These salaries compare favorably with other typical salaries, including those of managers in state-owned companies. In some cases, the salaries of RO managers are astronomical by Chinese standards; the manager of a U.S. financial house located in Shanghai reportedly earned $60,000 to $80,000 per year. In Shanghai, Chinese JV managers were ranked fourth among categories of the "richest people," after private entrepreneurs, entertainers (actors and singers), and government bond traders.[37]

The foreign sector's elite managers are a self-selecting group. They have striven to reach beyond the rigidly prescribed stations of socialist society to apply for highly competitive schools, perhaps abroad or in some distant location within China. They are attracted to jobs in the foreign sector because these positions allow them to use their skills and to have more responsibility at a younger age. Indeed, being young can present a problem in a society that respects age and seniority. Talented young people often have difficulty finding positions in state enterprises commensurate with their skills and ambition, where promotion to management positions is more often based on seniority and personal ties than skill. Young managers without firmly established contacts in state enterprises or government see foreign companies as offering them more

35. According to one study, JVs with European or U.S. partners or WFOEs (the top choice) are viewed as more favorable places to work in terms of wages, benefits, and opportunities than are Sino-Japanese joint ventures, although the latter ranked higher in terms of job stability. See Ling Wenli et al. (1993).

36. In JVs, some of the salary goes to the Chinese JV partner or to the government, or is fed into special welfare funds in the JV. Still, the take-home pay remains higher than it would be in a comparable Chinese enterprise. On JV and WFOE salaries, see Frisbie and Brecher (1992). On RO salaries, see McGregor (1991). See also Bulman (1994).

37. "Shanghai's Richest" (1993). The rankings following JV managers were: managers of township and village enterprises, managers of new companies, managers of profitable state-owned enterprises, tour guides for foreigners, and taxi drivers.

chance for upward mobility.[38] Many are attracted, moreover, by the opportunity to gain international experience and travel abroad. Working for a foreign company may enhance their chances for emigration, although this does not appear to be a primary motive for taking a job in the foreign sector. As we shall see, young people's risk-taking nature has tended to accompany a more independent attitude about the state and a willingness to break the bonds that tie them to it. At the same time, many find in the foreign sector the opportunity to escape the "politics" that pervades jobs in government and state enterprises.

PRIVATE ENTREPRENEURS

Examination of the literature on private entrepreneurs, the second segment of the business elite considered in this book, allows us to test whether what has been learned about members of the elite in the foreign sector is generalizable to other leading-edge sectors of the economy. If China's most successful private entrepreneurs are found to behave similarly to members of the foreign-sector elite, then we can be more confident of the conclusions based on the foreign sector.[39]

The government in 1979 sanctioned China's first private businesses since the 1950s in the form of individual (*geti*) or small family enterprises. By mid-1993, the official number of such businesses was 15 million.[40] Small enterprises have been seen as a means to solve two chronic problems: unemployment and the lack of a service sector. Regulations limit *geti* businesses to a maximum of seven employees and to ownership only by farmers, retirees, or unemployed persons. *Geti* businesses have operated mostly in commerce, handicrafts, restaurants, repair, and service businesses, and are restricted from operating in finance and military sectors. Other owners, particularly those who entered the private sector early, are of lower-status backgrounds (ex-convicts, the unem-

38. American companies also have a reputation for promoting PRC nationals to higher positions. Nonetheless, interviewees, even in U.S. companies, frequently expressed disappointment that middle- and high-level management positions were monopolized by Hong Kong or expatriate managers.

39. Conclusions drawn about entrepreneurs are based primarily on a review of the primary and secondary literature, and have been supplemented by a small number of interviews in the PRC and Hong Kong with entrepreneurs and overseas Chinese who are in contact with them. Key studies of the private sector include Bruun (1995); Gold (1989, 1990a); Kraus (1991); Liu (1992); McEwen (1994); Odgaard (1992); Sabin (1994); Shi (1993); Solinger (1992); Wank (1991, 1992, 1995); and Young (1991).

40. Bangsberg (1993).

ployed, or semi-skilled workers), although by the mid-1980s school graduates had come to make up a larger portion of the roster of *geti* entrepreneurs.[41]

In early 1988, the government sanctioned a second type of non-state business: private (*siying*) enterprises. Even in the early 1980s, government reformers recognized that many individual enterprises had expanded to outgrow the *geti* restrictions on numbers of employees, and allowed *siying* enterprises to employ eight or more people. For the most part, private enterprises have remained relatively small, despite the absence of a mandated cap on their size. As of the late 1980s, most such businesses employed an average of sixteen people. Although the largest enterprises, such as the Stone (Sitong) Group, have received the most attention, fewer than one percent employed more than one hundred workers. In contrast to the *geti* sector, private enterprises are less oriented to consumer services; their customers tend to be state enterprises and local government agencies. Most private enterprises have been established in manufacturing, mining, transportation, and construction industries, and many have leased land and equipment from small and medium state-owned firms. More recently, however, private enterprises have been established in the nascent professional services sector in the major coastal cities; indeed, the most risky and speculative areas of private business—especially finance (interbank lending and securities trading) and real estate—have grown rapidly in the 1990s.[42] In 1994, the government news agency reported that there were a total of 420,000 private enterprises, although the number is undoubtedly much higher.[43] The majority (60% in the mid-1990s) are located in the south and eastern coastal regions of China.[44]

41. Sabin (1994), p. 963.

42. On finance businesses, see Karmel (1994).

43. Xinhua (1995). Together, the *geti* and *siying* enterprises were estimated in the mid-1990s to employ more than 30 million people (Bangsberg [1993]). Sabin (1994) makes clear the extreme difficulty of obtaining a true accounting of the numbers of *geti* and *siying* enterprises and their employees. Not only do official estimates vary, but official figures undercount, probably dramatically; private enterprises register as collectives in order to protect themselves against potential political problems and to avoid difficulties obtaining financing, permits, etc. Sabin estimates that at least one-half of all urban "collectives" are privately owned, and argues that many Sino-foreign JVs are essentially private enterprises, as state enterprises operating at the behest of private firms set up "false" joint ventures. See appendix 2. On counting private firms, see also Kraus (1991), pp. 63–66, 96–114; and Young (1991), pp. 117–120.

44. Cai (1994).

Although the backgrounds of the earliest *siying* enterprise owners resemble the early entrants to the *geti* sector (i.e., older or of lower status), there has been an influx of new types of people to the *siying* enterprise ranks. These newer entrants have been less often studied, but it is they who constitute the elite of the private sector. They number 5,000 or less.[45] Although they face financial risks, many private enterprise owners have found their work to be quite lucrative. According to one survey, the annual income of private entrepreneurs (including salaries and bonuses) averaged $10,600 (92,000 yuan, or $883 per month), a figure twenty times greater than the average individual's salary.[46]

The private-sector elite is more diverse in background than are elite members of the foreign sector. Nonetheless, they increasingly share the foreign-sector elite's characteristics of good formal education and high salaries. Members of the private-sector elite have essentially succeeded on their own. As with the foreign sector, some, particularly members of the "*laosanjie*" in their forties, who were frozen out of higher education during and after the Cultural Revolution, have no university education, and have developed their businesses "out of their kitchens." In general, however, private entrepreneurs have a higher level of formal education than the average worker; more than 70% in a 1994 survey had earned a high school degree, and 17% had gone on to higher education.[47] Indeed, a significant number of established academics and other educated technical experts have gravitated toward *siying* enterprises. An increasing number of them are in their twenties and thirties, and have university educations. Despite this level of education, these younger private entrepreneurs are usually not well connected to the existing state-owned or bureaucratic sector, and they often eschew the traditional assignments upon graduation from university.[48]

45. Estimates based on 1995 interviews.
46. Cai (1994). Although the entrepreneurs included in this study earn money through legitimate means, some entrepreneurs earn "black money" (*heiqian*) through illegal activities such as gambling and prostitution, or "gray money" (*huiqian*) from practices such as arbitrage, which skirt the edges of legality. See Kristof (1992).
47. Cai (1994). Sabin (1994) reports a 1993 survey showing that at least 25% of private firm owners had an above-high-school education. (In contrast, the majority of workers in private firms have little formal education.) Even if the entrepreneurs themselves do not have good educations, they often pay huge sums for their children to enroll in the best schools. See Bruun (1995).
48. In other words, they are not the well-connected former officials or *taizidang* described earlier. This summary of characteristics is derived from 1995 interviews, and Sabin (1994), p. 963.

To some degree, members of the *siying* elite fit well the Western image of what it means to be an entrepreneur. As one interviewee put it, "They aren't related to Party members; they are nobodies, and have only their guts." Echoing the tendency of foreign-sector managers, moreover, elite entrepreneurs tend to enter the private sector in order to make better use of their talents and have more control over their careers. Over the course of the 1980s, as academics and state-sector managers saw the benefits of their stable salaries being eaten away by inflation, the private sector appeared to talented young people as an even more attractive alternative.[49]

• • • •

The business elite in post-Mao China is a far cry from the compradors of the late Qing, and nearly as distant from the state enterprise managers of the Maoist era. A theoretical basis for understanding the potential political role of this new business elite is presented in the next chapter.

49. See Xinhua (1994c); Chen Cui (1992); and Gold (1990a), p. 172.

CHAPTER I

China's New Business Elite

A Framework for Study

Reform in socialist countries has often been characterized by simultaneous economic and political liberalization, both of which are initiated by the ruling regime.[1] In contrast, the hallmark of the post-Mao reform strategy has been the intentional decentralization of economic authority by the state and the introduction of market mechanisms, but without permission for extensive reforms in the political system, much less democratization.[2] The questions which drive this study arise from the Chinese government's attempt to limit reforms to the economic sphere. Do the new economic groups that have been created through marketizing reforms attempt to convert their new economic status into political advantage, even though the latter has not been approved by the state? Does political change grow simply and directly out of economic reform and pressures from societal groups that are created by such reform, or do other factors intervene to influence the relationship between economic and political change? Is the new political format that arises out of economic reform, if any arises at all, likely to be a form of democratization, or another type of state-society relation?

1. This was true, for example, of Lenin's New Economic Plan in the 1920s and the Yugoslav reforms of the 1950s. Gorbachev's strategy in the former Soviet Union emphasized political reform before economic reform. See Goldman and Goldman (1987–1988).

2. This is not to say that no political reforms have been carried out in the PRC. There have been efforts, for example, to routinize inner-Party life and to upgrade the role of the National People's Congress and the Chinese People's Political Consultative Conference (CPPCC). But these cannot be considered "democratizing" reforms, as would be the termination of the Party's monopoly and the sanctioning of opposition.

0842271

The present chapter provides a framework for beginning to answer these questions. The chapter's primary goal is to set forth three alternative models of state-society relations that might be expected to result from China's economic reforms—civil society, clientelism, and state corporatism—and to assess their prospective utility for understanding developments in state-society relations in post-Mao China.

Three Models
of State-Society Relations in China

A number of models have been put forth by Western scholars of China to describe state-society relations over the last four decades. Yet no consensus has emerged. Two of the most common models of communist politics during the Maoist and early post-Mao eras, totalitarianism and pluralism, have been rejected for the most part. Popular during the 1950s, 1960s, and early 1970s, the totalitarian model's assumption of a monolithic Chinese state that allowed no autonomy for societal actors and was immune to internal dissension was belied by the divisions within society and within the leadership that erupted during the Cultural Revolution. Similarly, attempts in the late 1970s and 1980s to apply a pluralist image to China failed to gain adherents because that model underemphasized the interests and authority of the state and focused almost exclusively on the group as the key unit of society. Pluralism was unable, moreover, to account for such aspects of Chinese politics as patron-client networks. Totalitarianism and pluralism do not answer the problems posed here.[3]

Three alternative models of state-society relations appear more likely to shed light on the study of the business elite in contemporary China. One of these alternatives, neo-traditionalism/clientelism, was developed in the 1980s in an explicit attempt to overcome the shortcomings

3. On totalitarianism, see Friedrich and Brzezinski (1961). A pluralist model for communist systems (also called institutional pluralism or interest group models) was developed for the Soviet Union in Skilling and Griffiths (1971) and in Hough and Fainsod (1977). A small literature has examined whether groups in post-revolutionary China have behaved in a manner analogous to Western "interest groups." See, e.g., David S. G. Goodman (1984) and Falkenheim (1987). This literature is valuable for suggesting where the totalitarian model falls short, and tries to keep the limits of the pluralist perspective in view, but it fails to offer a cohesive alternative model. Useful critiques of the application of pluralist approaches to communist systems are: Janos (1979); Shue (1988), pp. 12–19; and Walder (1986), ch. 1.

of pluralism and totalitarianism.[4] Two additional models, "democratization" models (including "civil society") and state corporatism, have only recently been examined seriously with respect to China. An examination of these three models of state-society relations suggests that, as appealing as models of democratization may be, they are highly problematic in the post-Mao context. In contrast, clientelist and state corporatist models provide a much better framework for explaining the pattern of state-society relations that has emerged as a result of China's economic reforms.[5]

"DEMOCRATIZATION" AND "CIVIL SOCIETY" MODELS

Democratization models tend to the view that economic reform invariably gives rise to pressures for, and eventually the realization of, political liberalization, and that those people at the cutting edge of economic reform will also lead political reform. Consistent with this view, democratization models start with the observation, drawn from modernization theory, that economic development and growth of a middle class are highly correlated with democracy. They assume that a middle class will arise that has an interest in pressing for greater freedom from state control and, ultimately, democratization—or, at the very least, that freedoms won to protect markets will provide defenses against the state's curtailment of political freedoms.[6] Taken as a whole, this literature views the linkage between economic reform and democratization as direct, proceeding through two interrelated sets of steps. The first set of steps involves the devolution of economic power away from the state and the creation among economic actors of greater (though not necessarily

4. Walder (1986).

5. Still another model of contemporary state-society relations has been developed for rural China by Shue (1988). On the difficulty of generalizing Shue's model of the "honeycomb polity" to urban China, and therefore to China's new business elite, see Perry (1989).

6. A causal link between economic reform and democratization in the academic literature is made in Burks (1983) and Glassman (1991). A popular example of this reasoning is Maibach (1995). Although ultimately skeptical of these arguments, Brus (1983, pp. 122–129) states a version of them elegantly. The absence of a middle class is considered a major structural reason for the failure of democratizing reforms in the former Soviet Union. See Bova (1991). This assumption about the democratizing role of the middle class is often associated with the literature on "preconditions" for democracy as well as literatures on the role of the bourgeoisie in the emergence of liberal democracy. See introduction, n. 1. A more sophisticated, and plausible, literature on democratization is the "transitions" literature, discussed below.

expansive) space in which to press for political change. Successful economic reform, it is suggested, requires that both resources and decision-making be put in the hands of non-governmental actors, especially owners and managers outside the state sector, thereby weakening the power of the central bureaucracy. Economic reforms further foster autonomy from the state in that markets create an alternative source for goods (such as housing) that previously have been guaranteed by the state. These processes provide economic actors with somewhat greater autonomy to express their diverse interests in the marketplace. Once decentralization and the growth of market alternatives have freed economic actors from dependence upon the state, these people have more opportunity to develop horizontal relationships with their counterparts in society, and to strengthen intra-societal bonds.[7]

If these structural changes are to translate into actual political change initiated from below, a second set of steps involving consciousness and political behavior must occur. Strengthened horizontal relationships will lead to a greater consciousness on the part of societal actors that they can determine their own economic fate. This realization, it is posited, will in turn stimulate involvement in political activity at the same time that the reform's emphasis on economic values undermines the legitimacy of the unifying ideology. Not only will new economic groups act readily, they will act toward certain ends. New economic groups will be motivated to act by the unlikelihood that the existing state will protect these groups' emerging interests in free markets, or that the state will establish laws to protect the new structures. Ultimately these new groups will press for extensive liberalization and democratization of the polity, since political freedoms will be seen as necessary to protect economic freedoms.

Recent efforts to apply the concept of "civil society" to communist systems undergoing reform are consistent with this vision of democratization. Until the eighteenth century, philosophers defined "civil society" as coterminous with the state. But, gradually, theorists such as Hegel, Kant, Voltaire, Paine, Tocqueville, Marx, and, most recently, Habermas divorced the two realms, and linked civil society to specific historical phenomena.[8] Hegel included the role of the market economy

---

7. This kind of reasoning is evident in McCormick and Kelly (1994), pp. 813–814.

8. On the origins and evolution of the term, see Keane (1988); and Pelczynski (1988), pp. 363–364. Even after the eighteenth century, some philosophers, notably Gramsci, characterized civil society as both part of and separate from the official realm (Pelczynski, pp. 367–368).

as a crucial component and guarantor of the autonomous spheres. In turn, Marx narrowed the definition of "civil society" to include almost exclusively the capitalist market economy. As a result of this evolution, the term is commonly understood today to describe a society "comprising a complex of autonomous institutions—economic, religious, intellectual and political—distinguishable from the family, the clan, the locality and the state." It is, moreover, a society that possesses "a distinctive set of institutions which safeguard the separation of the state and civil society and maintain effective ties between them."[9] In the economic arena, civil society guarantees "the rights of individuals and particularly the right of property," and forms "a constellation of many autonomous economic units or business firms, acting independently of the state and competing with each other."[10] For most scholars, civil society also refers to non-economic limits on the state. Such constraints include the pillars of liberal democracy, for example, competing political parties, an independent judiciary, and a free press. Thus, the term "civil society" broadly conceived refers to bourgeois society of the sort that emerged in seventeenth- and eighteenth-century Western Europe, in which social forces, economic and non-economic, act separately from and often against the state.

Many Eastern European scholars appropriated this vision, particularly those writing on the economic reforms in Hungary in the 1970s and on the emergence of the Solidarity trade union movement in Poland in the late 1970s and early 1980s. To analyze the reform of and, ultimately, disintegration of twentieth-century communist regimes, these scholars have focused on the capacity for a repressed civil society to rise against the state. In the case of Hungary, for example, private entrepreneurs formed horizontal alliances with other societal groups in order to extract concessions from the state.[11] To these writers' voices have been added those of some scholars of China who find in the post-Mao era signs of a nascent civil society.[12] When applied to reforming socialist countries

9. Shils (1991), p. 4. A third criterion of Shils, a widespread pattern of refined or civil manners, is idiosyncratic and less relevant to the present discussion.

10. Shils (1991), p. 7. The concept of civil society is distinct from that of pluralism, though, for it avoids the latter's nearly singular emphasis on the group as the sole valid unit of analysis, and encompasses a notion (albeit vague) of transition.

11. On Hungary, see Szelenyi (1988). On Poland, see Arato (1981) and Pelczynski (1988).

12. The application of civil society to China is made, in a variety of ways, in Gold (1990); Strand (1990); Gordon White (1993, 1993a); Whyte (1992); and Yang (1989). White and Yang argue that civil society is emerging as a result of economic reform.

(including China), "civil society" refers to the emergence of a realm of activity outside and independent of the hegemonic communist Party-state. This usage suggests the growing autonomy not only of individuals but also—and this point is key for understanding China, where a tradition of individualism is weak—of civic groups or associations. Civil society is seen either to creep or to burst through the gap left open by a lax or reforming state, a state which does not or cannot stop social forces from bubbling up from below. Activities judged to constitute signs of civil society include the appearance of underground newspapers, the organization of discussion groups outside of state boundaries, the politicization of private entrepreneurs, and the effective conveyance of societal interests within collective enterprise. The end result is seen to be the establishment of liberal political institutions.

Judgments that economic reform will readily produce societal pressures for and, ultimately, the realization of democratization and civil society have clear normative appeal. They also capture empirically the decentralization of authority away from the state, the growing marketization of the economy, and the rise of independent business interests (i.e., the first set of steps discussed above). Such judgments appear, moreover, to capture some of the socio-political trends of China's reform era, particularly the student protests and appearance of associations. They further appear to find support in examinations of Taiwan's economic and political reforms during the 1970s and 1980s, examinations which have pointed to the rise of the middle class as a contributing force to democratization. Data from patrimonial regimes in Africa, too, suggest that the emergent middle class supports democratization because that process usually is dedicated to establishing property rights, rights that are missing in the existing pre-capitalist regime.[13]

But this model of democratization or civil society as a direct outcome of economic marketization is fraught with problems. One difficulty is that the concepts of democratization and civil society in the context of socialist systems remain too vague. While the civil society model describes the general trend toward societal autonomy from the state, upon closer reflection it is not specified clearly enough to offer much guidance as to the details of the evolution of state-society relations, or of the process of democratization. To the extent that democratization models suppose that the rise of a middle class is a precondition for lib-

---

13. On Taiwan, see Tien (1989, 1992) and Cheng and Haggard (1992), pp. 10–11. On Africa, see Bratton and Van De Walle (1994), pp. 467–468.

eralization, they fail to see that the emergence of a middle class may not be a sufficient condition for the emergence of democracy.[14]

A kindred difficulty lies in how well a concept, civil society, that has been developed with reference to the emergence of pluralist institutions in (pre-) capitalist Western society can explain movements in twentieth-century socialism. Keane has alluded to Hegel's view that civil society emerged from *both* capitalist and anti-capitalist forces that coalesced in opposition to the state, thereby implying that the roots of civil society can be diverse.[15] Similarly, some scholars of Eastern European politics argue that civil society can emerge through paths other than that pioneered in the West. For example, a second path was evident when reform that was imposed from above sparked mass social movements in Czechoslovakia during the 1960s, while in Poland the structural reform initiated from below by Solidarity in the late 1970s and early 1980s constituted a third path.[16] Other writers have countered that civil society is bound too inextricably to the simultaneous growth of liberal political institutions and private property to be useful in describing movements in societies where there are few concrete signs of such institutions. The most restrictive analyses are Marxian ones, which argue that the concept can refer only to the development of the substructure of capitalism.[17]

The possibility that the concept of civil society cannot travel across cultures or between economic systems requires us to question carefully whether core definitional features of civil society (particularly its institutions, horizontal structures, ideologies, and behaviors) actually appear in socialist countries, or whether analyses positing the emergence of civil society in post-Mao China are merely wishful thinking. Even though economic reforms may empower new groups, spur them to realize diverse interests, and create somewhat greater opportunity for activism, it is questionable whether these phenomena ensure the will to act, the form that political action takes, and the ends for which action occurs.

14. This problem with democratization models is pointed out by Karl (1990).

15. Keane (1988), pp. 63–65. Pelczynski (1988) concurs with Keane on this point.

16. The distinctive mark of Poland's structural reform from below, according to Arato (1981, pp. 24–27), was that it was, of necessity, carried out in cooperation with the state and was not pro-capitalist, though it was liberal in its politics.

17. See Marx (1958); and Szelenyi (1989), pp. 222–223. Habermas concludes that the related idea of the "public sphere" is temporally and culturally tied to the industrial West. Drawing on Habermas, Strand (1990, p. 2) defines the "public sphere" as "the presence of a critical public willing and able to hold government accountable for its actions." See also Rowe (1990), pp. 314–318. For a brief argument from within the China field that the concept cannot travel to China, see Chevrier (1990), pp. 126–127, and p. 344 n. 82.

Stated somewhat differently, although economic reform may set forth certain conditions conducive to democratization, the processes leading to political liberalization are multi-faceted. Economic reform can be one relevant variable but, even when it favors liberalization, liberalization can nonetheless be thwarted. Several examples help illustrate why we must be skeptical of assuming an easy or unfettered link between marketization and democratization. Occasionally a direct link does exist between groups that have grown out of economic reforms in socialist countries and political activism. This occurred, for example, in the financial support given by Chinese entrepreneurs to private, pro-democratic institutions during the 1980s.[18] But such examples are exceptional and, usually, marginal. More often, economic reform has occurred alone, without generating significant pressures for political change. Neither East Germany's New Economic System nor the Kosygin/Khruschev reforms in the Soviet Union (both in the mid-1960s) spurred significant political activity from below; both programs were tightly controlled by their respective governments and, after several years, abandoned.[19]

Even where economic reform succeeds in generating pressures on the state from below, the will to act and the goals of societal actors are easily influenced by non-economic factors. Sometimes, of course, these other factors may support democratization. Such favorable pressure was present in the student protests in China in the 1970s and 1980s, when economic reform bolstered protesters' confidence in the gains to be had from political action. But it should be observed that factors *unrelated* to economic reform, particularly the declining emphasis in the early 1980s on class struggle and the greater tolerance for a plurality of views, were all more important for opening up political space and motivating students to protest than was economic reform. Attitudes about political participation formed during the previous decades, particularly by the Cultural Revolution, further shaped the manner in which protests occurred.[20]

At other times, non-economic variables may *hinder* any pro-democracy tendencies arising from economic reforms. In particular, the political *interests* of new economic actors cannot be assumed to support

---

18. Bonnin and Chevrier (1991), p. 585.

19. Brus (1983), p. 112. These economic reforms occurred in a very different time, of course. For one, a "wave of democratization" around the world was not present to support political protest by actors in socialist countries, nor was there a worldwide breakdown of socialism.

20. Halpern (1989).

democratization. The established wisdom on members of the business elite in Latin American is that they have been a major force in favor of military or authoritarian rule, particularly insofar as they fear that democratization will set the stage for increased influence by labor, and hence threaten their interest in stability and labor docility.[21] Such a dynamic has also occurred in East Asia. In Korea, business interests have long colluded with the authoritarian regime to protect against unruly protests against the state. In Taiwan, the business elite has promoted its own interests, and has gained influence as a result of democratization, but it has not been at the forefront of democratization the way middle-class intellectuals have.[22] The absence of a deep interest in democratization also was evident in the early post-Mao reform era. Unlike students, newly independent entrepreneurs in China in the early 1980s evinced little interest in becoming politically active: "economic opportunities appear to have served as an alternative to, not a motivation for, political action."[23]

Yet it cannot always be assumed that members of the business elite will automatically support authoritarian governments. It is true that business elites, even when interested in democratization, are seldom at the forefront of revolution, and tend to put business interests above political activism. Nevertheless, under certain conditions they may join in political movements favoring democratization after others, particularly students and intellectuals, have made the first moves, or when it is clear they will be supported by other sectors of society. In contrast to the standard wisdom that business interests support authoritarian governments, Payne found that Brazil's business elite contained a highly diverse set of ideologies during the 1980s, including industrialists who were both quite authoritarian and quite liberal in their views.[24] In turning the conventional wisdom on its head, Payne's study further implies that no easy assumptions can be made about the interests of groups emerging as a result of economic reforms in socialist countries.

A recent and more sophisticated theory of democratic "transitions" supports the view that the link between economic reform and political change is complex. Though the transition literature addresses broader

21. This was a key assumption behind the literature on bureaucratic authoritarianism. See O'Donnell (1973).

22. Chu (1994) and Cheng and Haggard (1992), p. 4.

23. Halpern (1989), p. 150.

24. Payne (1994). See also Becker (1983), p. 331. It also should be kept in mind that existing studies of the interests of business elites concern exclusively capitalist economies.

dynamics of transition than are under consideration here, and does not focus empirically on the business elite, this literature nevertheless is useful for considering the question of the link between economic reform and political change because it suggests that the outcome of a move toward democracy in any particular case is far from determined (as we have just seen with regard to the ideologies and interests of business groups), and will be much influenced by non-economic variables.[25]

Transitions to democracy, in the view of this literature, tend to result from negotiated pacts between elites in an authoritarian government and the societal forces of opposition. In particular, leaders of both the state and the opposing forces must be able to make correct strategy choices and to negotiate pacts. Although not a unified literature, the core works find two major factors to be most important for successful democratization through pact-making. Success requires, first, substantial organization on the part of societal actors. But such organization is not automatic, and depends much upon the context. For example, the well-organized Solidarity movement in Poland benefited from its links with the Catholic Church and pressed for democratization, while a fragmented business elite in Brazil was able to come together to support democratization in that country in 1988 (after having supported military governments in the 1960s and 1970s). In contrast, newly emergent business or middle-class interests in democratization are rendered ineffectual by poor organization, as was the case with East Germany.[26] Tran-

25. This growing literature has focused on democratization in Latin America, Southern Europe, and, most recently, Eastern Europe. Core works include O'Donnell and Schmitter (1986) and Przeworski (1991). Another feature of this literature that is broadly supportive of the argument made here is that it is skeptical of simple determinism of outcome; successful transition is path dependent and undetermined (O'Donnell and Schmitter, p. 3). It should be noted that much of the literature on transitions is not directly relevant to the issue of the link between economic and political change that is the major consideration here, for it often focuses on *either* economic reform *or* political reform, not the causal connection between them. On political transitions alone, see, e.g., Huntington (1992). On economic reform, see the debates over "shock therapy" versus gradualism nicely summarized in Adams and Brock (1993). Those writings that *do* discuss the link between economic and political reform (such as Przeworski's) tend to assume that the state explicitly intends democratizing reform at the same time as it carries out economic reform, something that, as is pointed out above, is not the case in China. The other major impetus for democratic transition is regime collapse, but this leads to a more insecure and often short-lived democracy.

26. On these cases, see Friedheim (1993), p. 505; and Payne (1994). The earliest "transitions" literature has been rightly criticized by Friedheim and others (Zhang [1994] and Bratton and Van De Walle [1994]) for focusing on the choices of elites and individual agency, without an eye toward institutional structures that constrain the path. As with the civil society model, early contributions to this literature tended to draw vague pictures of the emergence of civil society. See Levine (1988), pp. 388–389.

sitions theory emphasizes, second, the actions of the state, which can influence the potential for democratization in a variety of directions. Successful transition most often occurs when the state has chosen to negotiate with an opposition, a choice that usually follows a breaking off from the authoritarian leadership of a "reformist faction" that is willing to negotiate, as well as the availability of societal elites with whom negotiations actually can occur.[27]

Transitions theory therefore suggests the importance of focusing on these two conditions, societal organization and state strategy, in China. As to the latter, we can say fairly certainly that, although a leadership faction with reformist leanings exists, it is unprepared to engage in serious negotiation with societal elites. This circumstance further suggests the necessity to consider *other* possible strategies on the part of the state.[28] The state can design institutions to pre-empt the growth of organized pressure from new economic actors, even while it encourages these actors in other areas. This was the explicit strategy of the Guomindang informing peak business associations in Taiwan in the 1970s, for example.[29]

A state can more decisively attempt to halt the growth of political pressure that might arise by eliminating the economic reforms that it believes are causing unrest. This was done successfully in Hungary in the late 1960s and 1970s, where the New Economic Mechanism that was launched by the Hungarian Socialist Workers' Party was reversed when economic reform seemed to threaten central control.[30] Whereas state intervention occurred in this case in a relatively gentle fashion, intervention need not be gentle. This was true, of course, of the government crackdown on student protesters in China in 1989, which effectively destroyed strong political pressures from below. Whether gently or highly repressive, then, central state action can break the link between economic and political reform.

In sum, the lack of theoretical and empirical support for the assumption of a direct and simple causal link between economic reform and democratization from below means the application of civil society or democratization models to post-Mao China should be approached with

27. Friedheim (1993).

28. Zhang (1994) argues that, in addition to elite choice, institutional conditions that favor pact-making in corporatist authoritarian regimes do not exist in socialist countries such as China.

29. Cheng, Haggard, and Kang (1995). See also Przeworski (1991, p. 58) on co-optation as a common strategy of liberalizing regimes facing pressures for democratic transition.

30. Comisso and Marer (1986), pp. 256–273.

caution. It is true that market reforms may produce new groups with greater autonomy, greater opportunities for, and even possibly interest in political change. The market, moreover, may create "an economic environment more propitious for the maintenance of polyarchal elements" and "reduce the *area* of political authority and hence [provide] greater independence for the individual" as well as the group.[31] But we must take care that the assumption that these changes will dictate inevitably the emergence of civil society not distort the lens through which we examine actual processes in late-twentieth-century China.

Rather, the deficiencies in the civil society and democratization models highlight the need to be aware of other variables that intervene between economic reform and political change.[32] Not only must the concrete interests of societal actors and the translation of these interests into action be carefully scrutinized, but it must be recognized that pressures from below, if they occur at all, will interact with other forces that can influence the will to act and the type of pressure they produce. The ability of the state (at both central and local levels) to shape the whole process and the degree of organization of newly emergent economic actors seem particularly important.[33] In highlighting these factors that are absent in China as crucial to the success of democratization, the "transitions" literature, too, seems to suggest prospectively that democratization as a result merely of economic reform is unlikely in the PRC.

CLIENTELISM AND NEO-TRADITIONALISM

A factor ignored by the various democratization theories (including the rational-choice-based transitions theories) is the intertwining of state and society in personal networks. Inattention to ways in which state and society are closely yet informally connected is precisely

---

31. Brus (1983), pp. 127–128.

32. Other writers have focused on still other intervening variables. Chirot (1992) argues that, while the economic reforms in the 1980s in Eastern Europe led to the rise of new urban and professional classes and set the context for change, the decisive stimulus for action was the popular recognition—unrelated to the economic processes—of the *moral* illegitimacy of the regimes. A broader argument about the role of attitudes is suggested by works on political culture in China: anti-democratic Confucian political culture may hinder democratization even in the context of marketization. See Pye (1967). Others, however, argue that the political culture does not prevent democratization. See, e.g., McCormick and Kelly (1994); Nathan and Shi (1993).

33. In the judgment of Chinese intellectuals, Ma (1994, p. 192) argues, the growth of civil society "presupposes the active involvement of the state."

the problem addressed by clientelism and the related model of neo-traditionalism. It is useful to highlight two dimensions of clientelism. The first is clientelism based on formal organizational structures versus informal linkages between actors. The second is vertical clientelism, with ties up and down the hierarchy, versus horizontal, with rhizomic ties within society and among relative equals in status and power (such as between classmates or fellow villagers). This study is primarily concerned with vertical clientelism in both its formal and informal dimensions.[34]

Jean Oi states the basic premise of informal, vertical clientelism: "In developing countries, where the formal channels for meaningful partic-ipation and interest articulation are weak, individuals regularly pursue their interests through the use of informal networks built upon person-al ties."[35] Informal, reciprocal ties, based on personal relations (*guanxi*), are a crucial link between state and society. Because political behavior concerns primarily the distribution of economic resources, especially at local levels, clientelist behavior appears when those with neither author-ity nor autonomy from local officials, and hence with few alternative sources for resources, develop strategies based on personal ties to influ-ence the state's distribution decisions.[36] Clientelism is a strategy on the part of those subordinate to the (central or, especially, local) state to use a subculture of instrumental personal ties to influence what on the sur-face appears to be a rigid authority system.

Andrew Walder's "communist neo-traditionalism" model of author-ity relations for state-owned enterprises expands on the informal aspect of vertical clientelism by including an additional, formal and official aspect. Rather than seeing clientelism as an informal structure in systems with weak states, Walder argues that "Party-clientelism" was established in China in the 1950s by a strong Party-state as a way to control soci-ety (especially workers).[37] In the neo-traditional model, managers in the

34. Although not a primary focus of this book, horizontal ties are considered insofar as they create class cohesiveness (i.e., formal ties) within the new business elite. The impor-tance of these four dimensions of clientelism in post-revolutionary China has been docu-mented in Gold (1985); Hwang (1987); Nathan (1973); Oi (1985); Walder (1986); Whyte and Parish (1984); and Yang (1986, 1989, 1989a). On clientelism more general-ly, see Schmidt et al. (1977). The clientelism discussed in this book occurs among citizens and at the lower level of politics. Though not incompatible, it must be distinguished from patron-client ties and factionalism at the very elite levels of politics. The debate about elite factionalism has been rekindled in *The China Journal* (1995).

35. Oi (1985), p. 238. Similar arguments about vertical ties are made by Shue (1988).

36. In rural areas, clientelist practices surround the distribution of grain rations, relief funds and goods, loans, and private plots. See Oi (1985), pp. 241–243.

37. Walder (1986), pp. 24–25, 170–175, 180–181. Walder's view that clientelism can be a formal strategy of a strong state is a revision of the standard definition of clientelism,

enterprise, who are either Party members themselves or are responsible to them, wield broad personal discretion over employees. Like rural team leaders, factory leaders have controlled key decisions, such as promotions, job mobility, and the distribution of material benefits (e.g., food coupons and housing), that in China have been allocated by the enterprise rather than the market or the central state. This authority over distribution has created an "organized dependence" that has forced Chinese employees to rely upon personal relationships with cadre-managers and, through them, with the Party-state.[38] Thus, clientelism in urban China grew out of the specific pattern of authority set up explicitly by the Leninist state.

The concepts of clientelism and neo-traditionalism as set forth by Oi and Walder have provided tremendous insight into Chinese communist politics through the early reform era. But China has changed dramatically since these approaches were found applicable to a non-market system in which a Leninist state has denied significant autonomy to societal actors. The post-Mao reforms raise the question of whether vertical clientelism, in either its formal or informal aspect, remains relevant. An implication of neo-traditionalism is that, when the authority of the Party breaks down at the factory level, so too will formal Party clientelism. As the reforms have brought societal actors increased autonomy from the Party-state, neo-traditionalism would lead us to expect that relations of dependence too have weakened.[39] In theory, moreover, the expansion of market relations should obviate the need for both horizontal and vertical personal relations, as impersonal market signals substitute for informal, localized personal ties.

Although the relatively extensive autonomy of China's new business elite can be expected to undermine many of the formal aspects of neo-traditionalism, there is reason to believe that informal clientelism remains a viable and important strategy in post-Mao China. We can expect informal relations in the political realm to continue as long as formal channels for business-government relations remain poorly institutionalized; if policy interests on the part of a new and relatively

---

which is typically applied to historically weak states such as Italy. Although Oi's and Walder's models have been set forth separately, they overlap in assumptions and conclusions. On the link between the two models, see also Pearson (1992), pp. 61, 76.

38. Walder (1986), pp. 8–27. Party leaders and managers in the factory also cultivate the loyalty of "activists" among workers upon whom they can rely. See also Walder (1983). "Organized dependence" is described further in ch. 3.

39. Walder (1991, 1991a, p. 339) agrees that authority relations of organized dependence and the behaviors associated with it have evolved with the post-Mao reforms.

autonomous economic elite grow, yet are not given effective voice in existing political institutions, then personal ties as a means of interaction with officials can be expected to remain attractive.

An equally important reason to expect the continuing salience of clientelism is economic, namely, the absence of full marketization. Partial marketization fosters informal clientelism in two ways. First, the state is still important in such a system; economic authority has been partly transferred to the market, but local officials have kept some types of authority and gained many more. Although the distribution of economic resources is no longer as rigidly defined as previously, local officials still retain tremendous authority, which has created incentives for them to maximize personal ties to the non-state sector and to be sure personal ties remain useful for economic actors who need to gain resources still controlled by local officials.[40] A second result of partial marketization is that the market relations are poorly defined and surrounded by uncertainty. This uncertainty can be expected to lead societal actors to try to attach themselves to more defined authority (officials)—if not formally then through informal means. Even as market relations deepen, the fact that personal networks are a key currency of business-government relations elsewhere in East Asia raises the possibility that the reliance on personal ties in China is unlikely to be reduced to the comparatively low level of the U.S.[41]

CORPORATISM AND
EAST ASIAN "STATISM"

The concept of corporatism has been explored less frequently with regard to China than for many other regions of the world. Yet one variant of corporatism, state corporatism, has more potential than civil society to offer insights into state-society relations in post-Mao China, at least when modified for China's socialist context. The classic, ideal-typical definition of corporatism has been offered by Philippe

40. Although local officials who previously had significant distributional power over resources provided by the center now have fewer resources handed to them from the center, they have gained much decision-making authority (such as over investment) as well as resources (e.g., tax revenues). On the change in central local fiscal relations and incentives for local officials, see Shirk (1993), Oi (1992), and Zweig (1991). That *guanxi* is compatible with some marketizing reforms is shown in Nee and Su (1990).

41. Importance of networks in East Asian capitalism is discussed in, e.g., Gerlach (1992); Dore (1986); and Redding (1995). As ch. 2 will suggest, this personalism is not unique to the socialist era of China; it has traditional roots as well.

Schmitter: "Corporatism can be defined as a system of interest representation in which the constituent units are organized into a limited number of singular, compulsory, noncompetitive, hierarchically ordered and functionally differentiated categories, recognized or licensed (if not created) by the state and granted a deliberate representational monopoly within their respective categories in exchange for observing certain controls on their selection of leaders and articulation of demands and supports."[42]

Schmitter delineates two subtypes of corporatism, "state corporatism" and "societal corporatism." The statist subtype, which has often been used to depict business-government relations in Latin America, is the more applicable to late-twentieth-century China since, whereas societal corporatism evolves as a bargain struck from below, state corporatism is foisted upon society by the state. Although in state corporatism some autonomy is allowed within functional realms, state-formed organizations serve state interests broadly and the ultimate authority of the state is not challenged. Hence, state corporatism emphasizes the dominant role of the state in each dimension of Schmitter's ideal-typical definition. The state deliberately restricts the number and multiplicity of associations, officially decrees their legitimacy, and protects their monopoly. It centralizes the organization, frames the associational categories, requires its own sanction as a condition for formation and operation, and imposes controls on leadership selection and interest articulation.[43] The state that is most likely to succeed at establishing state corporatist institutions is the one with considerable organizational strength and ideological unity, and which has extensive control over resources.[44]

A handful of scholars have found state corporatism to be useful for analyzing post-1949 China. Lowell Dittmer has suggested very generally that united front politics in China is "neocorporatist" and is consistent with the deeper and traditional "corporate concept of interest" in which "[g]roup or individual interests may be acknowledged, but the public interest occupies a position of sacrosanct priority, and other interests may be tolerated only within this latitude of some plausible interpretation of public interest."[45] Scholars who have attempted more concrete applica-

---

42. Schmitter (1974), pp. 93–94.
43. Schmitter (1974), pp. 103–104. See also Stepan (1978), pp. 30–45, and chs. 2 and 3. In societal corporatism, interests are organized from below and in a more liberal initial political setting.
44. Stepan (1978), pp. 83, 88.
45. Dittmer (1987), pp. 17, 20. He does not examine specific corporatist institutional structures, however.

tions of state corporatism in the post-Mao context have fallen into two (not mutually exclusive) categories. In the first category are scholars who, drawing at least implicitly on Weber's discussions of "corporate groups" and patrimonialism, examine the relationship between leaders and individuals within Chinese work units and villages. These scholars emphasize the ways in which work unit leaders, although sanctioned by the upper echelons of the state, have obligations to the constituents of the work unit. These obligations encourage unit leaders to protect their constituents, often in conflict with government interests.[46]

A second category of writings on state corporatism in China focuses on the relationship between societal units and the state. Consistent with Schmitter's definition, these works emphasize the socialist state's licensing of intermediary associations in order to better carry out state goals. The state organizes and co-opts into associations key functional groups, such as trade unions, industry, and entrepreneurs. Co-optation serves a regime-maintenance function but also allows the regime to harness these groups' initiative. At the same time, these groups are granted a degree of autonomy within their own functional sphere.[47] A number of analyses in this second category have also been made of the Soviet Union and Eastern European countries prior to the implosions of their socialist regimes. These states, it is argued, restructured segments of their economies along corporatist lines in an effort to rally the nation behind economic development. Particular attention has been focused on Poland, where a corporatist "solution" was seen to have emerged prior to the ouster of General Jaruzelski. First the Catholic Church, and then the Solidarity trade union movement, developed a degree of autonomy from the state in economic and social/religious realms. Yet this autonomy did not go so far as to threaten the political authority of—and was

46. See Weber (1947), pp. 145–147. Works on China that fall into this category include Yang (1989a) and Oi (1992). This kind of relationship is echoed in Shue's (1988, pp. 95–116) analysis of both the Qing gentry and Mao-era rural work teams, and in Walder's (1989) study of factory managers, although these scholars do not apply the term "corporatism." Clientelism complements some of these scholars' understandings of corporatism, as they often see clientelist relations operating within the context of these corporate work units. Interestingly, Yang (pp. 35–38) has folded the concepts of both corporatism (in this first sense) and civil society into one analysis, arguing that a framework which places at its center the growing opposition of society and the state—civil society—is the most useful way to understand the tensions expressed in the printing factory she studied.

47. See Whiting (1991) and Unger and Chan (1995). Fewsmith (1985) applies state corporatism in this sense to Republican-era China. Although elements of the first, Weberian definition appear in his work, this second use of corporatism also is suggested in Peter Nan-shong Lee (1991), esp. p. 162. The analysis of business associations presented in ch. 5 fits with the works in this second category.

even sanctioned by—the Party-state. Romania has been argued to have established corporatist structures in agriculture and industry in its drive for national construction by the late 1970s. Corporatism in this second sense also has been seen to have characterized the Brezhnev era in the Soviet Union, under which major functional interests were included in the policy process while the Soviet Party's authority was maintained.[48]

State corporatism has been justly criticized for failing to specify clearly what differentiates it from other forms of authoritarianism or even totalitarianism.[49] But if these problems of specification can be overcome (as the following analysis attempts to do), the concept can provide significant insights into core elements of the evolving state-society relations in post-Mao China, elements that render the emerging system distinct from Leninism. Some of these insights are explicitly included in Schmitter's construction of state corporatism. State corporatism recognizes the existence of interests that are defined by society rather than the state, particularly in the economy. As China's reforms have deepened, the existence of interests other than those of the proletariat, and interests outside the Party, has been legitimated at the highest levels. This legitimation occurred most clearly at the 13th Party Congress with Zhao Ziyang's deliberate attempt to legitimate a greater diversity of interests than had been permitted under Maoism, even in its liberalized, united front form.[50] At the same time, state corporatism is consistent with the post-Mao reformers' emphasis on coordination and harmonization of legitimate societal interests with state goals.[51] State corporatism also envisions that the main goal for which societal interests will be coordinated is rapid national economic development. In China, rapid industrialization is indeed at the core of the state's agenda. Moreover, unlike civil society conceptualizations, by assuming the existence of a strong state at its core, state corporatism does not obscure the fundamental hierarchy of power between state and society.

The concept of state corporatism can also be a catalyst for insights that are not envisioned by Schmitter. Schmitter did not see state corporatism as applying to socialist countries in transition. But in just such a

---

48. On Poland, see Ost (1989), esp. p. 159; and Arato (1981), pp. 23–47. On Romania, see Chirot (1980). On the Soviet Union, see Bunce and Echols (1980). Three analyses of non-socialist countries that generally fit this second category of state corporatism are Stepan (1978); Robinson (1991); and Bianchi (1984).

49. See Cohen and Pavoncello (1987); and Goldstein (1995).

50. See Zhao (1987). These ideas were reiterated in Luo, Zhu, and Cao (1987) and Zhao (1987a).

51. This has been true in much of Chinese history. See ch. 2 and Nathan (1985).

context, we see state corporatism combining with elements of the socialist structure in a format we can call "socialist corporatism."[52] The concept of socialist corporatism helps capture the rationale, the flow of authority, and the institutional structure inherent in the efforts of socialist reformers to permit societal autonomy and yet simultaneously control the growth and range of that autonomy. Schmitter envisions the origins of state corporatism to be in the context of the "rapid, highly visible demise of nascent pluralism," that is, where the state in a delayed, dependent capitalist country, substituting for a weak bourgeoisie, attempts to enforce social peace through repression of demands of the subordinate class.[53] Yet it makes sense that a variant of state corporatism would be used by a reforming socialist regime that is attempting to *prevent the emergence of* autonomous societal groups rather than to capture existing groups. The dynamic of Schmitter's state corporatism, moreover, is to *gather in* social forces in order to increase national power in the world economy.[54] (This was true, for example, in Brazil and in Republican China.) The trend of socialist reforms, on the other hand, is to *devolve* power from a bureaucracy that has been in place for four decades. Socialist corporatism emphasizes a dispersion of power to extra-state bodies, albeit those the government itself has had a hand in creating.[55]

Socialist corporatism also meets the commonsense expectation that China's Leninist background—specifically, the weight of an expansive state and of a large planning bureaucracy coupled with the historical weakness of societal institutions—will influence the new corporatist institutions that reform produces. The socialist corporatist strategy may take parts of the existing Party or state bureaucracy and make them significantly more autonomous, even if formal organizational links remain.

---

52. Schmitter (1974, pp. 88, 94) dismisses the possibility that his ideal type is extant anywhere; even as he develops the concept in light of the Iberian peninsular countries and the authoritarian regimes of Latin America, he suggests that no actual system completely fits the ideal. Stepan (1978, pp. 68–69) concurs. Gordon White (1993) also has adopted the term "socialist corporatism" to describe the trends he sees in state-society relations. His meaning differs from that employed here, however, in that he sees socialist corporatism as consistent with the eventual emergence of civil society.

53. Schmitter (1974), p. 106.

54. Schmitter (1974), p. 120.

55. These features of socialist corporatism contrast with the Leninist and united front models, in which the state's jurisdiction is unambiguous. Jowitt's concept of "inclusion" captures a part of the devolution of the sort we see in China. However, his focus on regime values (manipulation, persuasion, expertise, etc.) offers little guidance on the concrete institutional results of shifts in state-society relations. Moreover, Jowitt's emphasis—consistent with the Leninist paradigm—is on the inclusion of voices into the state itself. See Jowitt (1975).

Still, while the ideal socialist corporatist institution would be located formally outside of the Party-state organizational structure, the context in which socialist corporatism is evolving is one in which institutions encompassing society may be slower to come out from under the Party-state. It is therefore unlikely that *all* post-Mao socialist corporatist institutions would be fully outside of the state.[56] Moreover, rigid distinctions between what is within the Party-state and what falls outside of it are extremely difficult to make in the post-Mao environment; a second-order effect of the reforms has been to blur both the juridical and the practical reach of the state.[57]

Socialist corporatism appears to be equipped to take us a good distance in our attempt to understand the evolution of socialist systems away from a highly penetrated, Party-dominated Leninist system to one in which a degree of autonomy for economic interests outside the Party-state structure is deemed by the state to be necessary for industrialization (and therefore legitimate), at the same time that the state finds it desirable to prevent the independent organization of the societal groups that might undermine the state. As promising as the socialist corporatism model appears, several caveats are necessary. First, it is unlikely the *whole* of state-society relations in post-Mao China can be understood through the socialist corporatist lens alone. As we will see, other modes of state-society relations, particularly clientelism, have been shown to coexist alongside corporatism elsewhere.[58] Second, explicit acknowledgment or even consciousness of corporatism is absent from socialist doctrine. The post-Mao government's revitalization of functional associations, for example, is framed as part of a united front strategy. (Nor

56. As will be shown in ch. 5, some socialist corporatist institutions clearly fall outside of the state's organizational structure, such as the business association of the new foreign sector. At the other extreme, the association for small private entrepreneurs (the Self-Employed Laborers Association) is clearly under the formal jurisdiction of the Bureau of Industry and Commerce.

57. This is true, for example, of the post-Mao version of the All-China Federation of Industry and Commerce (ACFIC) which was formerly part of the United Front Work Department of the Party and still has some ties to that department, but whose formal status as part of the state is extremely fuzzy.

58. Schmitter (1974, p. 92) himself suggests that corporatism may be part of a mixed system. The criticism has been made that state corporatism cannot be a "partial" system, that it is intended to describe a whole system. Although system-encompassing concepts should perhaps be a goal of comparativists, it may be that systems are in reality mixed. This criticism therefore seems to me to be unjustified. A similar argument for the non-exclusive use of models is made for Turkey and Mexico, where corporatist and pluralist business associations coexist. On Mexico, see Levy and Szekely (1987). In Turkey, corporatism often has clientelist patterns embedded in it. See Bianchi (1984, 1989).

was the development of corporatism a conscious strategy in Poland or Romania—or in Republican-era China.)[59] Most importantly, even though the central government in China may intend, in certain realms, to set up institutions that we can call "socialist corporatism," there is no guarantee that these institutions will be effectively established. The fact that they will evolve from an extremely state-dominated environment in which ties to society are, in recent history, weak and institutionalization is poor also will be likely to render them less potent.

The role of state-dominated institutions established to coordinate government and business is a subject that has been considered by the literature on East Asian "statism." The East Asian statist model has argued that state coordination of the economy has been responsible for the astounding growth in that region's "newly industrializing countries." The literature on East Asian statism does not always employ the term "corporatism," and its main purpose is to explain economic performance rather than state-society relations. Yet its effort to explain performance leads to an investigation of the institutions shaping state-business relations in the East Asian context, an investigation that can offer support for the view that some version of state corporatism may be appropriate to understanding evolving state-society relations in China.[60]

Specifically, the conventional East Asian statism model draws a picture of business-government relations in which business is subordinate to the state and depends heavily on ties with the "technobureaucracy" to accomplish its goals. Institutions, including peak associations and industry conglomerates, coordinate ties between business and government. Although their exact character varies from country to country, business associations are seen as heavily influenced or co-opted by the state, even if not directly controlled by them.[61] Several recent studies

59. On these cases, see Ost (1989); Chirot (1980, p. 368); and Fewsmith (1985). Schmitter (1974) argues that absence of explicit corporatist doctrine in a given system does not preclude the existence of corporatism.

60. The question driving the East Asian statism model is: what explains the phenomenal economic growth in the newly industrialized countries of East Asia (Taiwan, South Korea, Singapore, and Hong Kong)? In reaction to neoclassical economic arguments that attribute these countries' economic growth to purely market forces, the statism literature contends that the state has facilitated growth by augmenting or directing the market (although the exact nature of intervention varies across countries). A major reason that this strategy has been effective, it is argued, is that the states involved are highly autonomous (i.e., shielded from private interests of business and labor) and have capable bureaucracies. On East Asian statism, see Amsden (1985, 1989); Deyo (1987, 1990); Haggard and Moon (1983); Johnson (1982, 1987); and Wade (1990).

61. See Deyo (1987), pp. 232–233; Gold (1986), pp. 71, 140 n. 21; Park (1987), pp. 906–907, 915–917; and Tien (1989), p. 46. A somewhat more ambiguous picture of

have modified this depiction of complete business subordination to the state. It has been pointed out, for example, that although the governments of Taiwan and South Korea routinely have pressed business toward certain goals, business has agreed to cooperate only when it has been confident of the state's genuine commitment to economic goals.[62] Associations have been shown, moreover, to use lobbying to influence how government capital or resources are channeled, rather than serving solely as pawns of the government. More generally, efforts by business to pressure government appear to have increased in tandem with East Asian regimes' moves away from authoritarianism.[63]

Debates over the precise degree of state domination of business in East Asia suggest a range of possible relationships between business and government that can exist. Yet the idea that state domination of business (even if imperfect) through corporatist-style institutions is a common pattern in East Asia (particularly in the earlier stages of rapid industrialization) alerts us to a broad regional pattern that may be relevant for China as well.

Looking Forward

It would be convenient if one of the three models of state-society relations described in this chapter could be expected to be fully explanatory of relations between the state and the leading-edge sectors of the post-Mao economy. But, in fact, none of the models paints a holistic picture. Indeed, in subsequent chapters we will find that, of these three models, a hybrid pattern of state-society relations most accurately describes the direction in which business-government relations are evolving in post-Mao China. "Socialist corporatism" proves to be most

---

South Korea (in the 1960s), but one in which the state still appears basically dominant over business, is Haggard, Kim, and Moon (1991).

62. See Kang (1995); Lew (1992).

63. On these patterns, see Doner (1992). In Southeast Asia, the end of military domination in Thailand in the early 1970s coincided with a growing assertiveness and effectiveness on the part of business associations (Anek Laothamatas [1992], ch. 7). The rise in activity by business associations operating in authoritarian regimes has been even better documented in studies of business-government relations in Latin America. See Becker (1990); Levy and Szekely (1987, p. 61); and Bennett and Sharpe (1985, p. 235). It is also to be expected that, as in Latin America, business associations also can be expected to achieve a degree of influence through intra-elite circulation in which the bureaucracy both supplies staff to and draws staff from private-sector associations. See Cleaves and Stephens (1991); and Becker (1983), pp. 334–335.

useful for describing a key aspect of the institutional structures that the government has attempted to set up to control economic interests that have arisen from the reforms. Clientelism, in addition to signaling an important aspect of how these new institutional structures work in practice, best characterizes how individual members of the business elite interact with the state. Indeed, despite the government's corporatist efforts, clientelism has much greater relevance for how members of the business elite actually navigate through their environment. Civil society, which we might expect to have progressed furthest in the leading economic sectors, is in fact not at the core of state-society relations there, although it is operative around the edges.

A number of important intervening factors will be shown to shape this hybrid form of state-society relations. One important factor is the concrete interests and behaviors of members of the new economic elite. The interests and behaviors of the state are another. The precise character these forces have taken on in the post-Mao era will be spelled out in more detail in subsequent chapters. Yet these intervening factors, as well as all three of the models, have roots in pre-1949 Chinese history. This historical legacy is the subject of the following chapter.

CHAPTER 2

The Janus-Faced Role
of the Business Elite
in Chinese History

China's post-Mao business elite is part of a contemporary international phenomenon—the emergence of an international managerial bourgeoisie—but it also has its own long and rich legacy. That legacy as it manifested itself in the middle and late Qing, early Republican, Nationalist, and Maoist eras is the subject of this chapter. We can discern in the historical record an enduring tradition in the relationship between merchants and the state at both the central and local levels. The essence of that tradition is a pattern in which the merchant elite was neither wholly autonomous nor state-dominated but instead sat, Janus-like, between state and society, and at times even blended socially with the official class and carried out "public" (*gong*) works. This pattern contrasts with the Western tradition in which the bourgeoisie, "civil society," fought for and gained a lasting independence from the state. In China, the precise nature of the relationship between merchants and the state varied over time, depending on specific conditions. But excepting two extreme conditions—either near total disintegration of central authority (as after the fall of the Qing government) or state attempts to completely eradicate private business (as during the Maoist era)—the Janus-faced pattern endured. As subsequent chapters will demonstrate, the core elements of this pattern have regained their salience in the post-Mao era.

Merchant Life in Qing China

Formal Confucian doctrine disdained merchants (*shang*) and placed them in the lowest rank in the social order. The ranking of merchants in last place after scholar-officials (*shi*), peasants (*nong*), and artisans (*gong*) reflected the view that agriculture, not trade, was the basis of a strong economy. This view was bolstered by the deeply root-ed belief that trading activities that redounded to private (*si*) gain were selfish and illegitimate, and that a private "society" did not exist autonomously from the state. The lower three categories lacked author-ity to oppose the state on the basis of autonomous or private interests, and certainly posed no alternative source of authority.[1] Yet doctrinal dis-dain for merchants, and the state control of them that this disdain implied, failed to fully reflect actual practice. A flourishing private econ-omy with an expansive local rural market system was tolerated and, indeed, was vital to the well-being of the imperial state. Vigorous com-mercialization in local markets depended on merchants, who "had to be protected and freed as far as possible from the confines of bureau-cratic control and taxation to keep trade flowing."[2] Trading guilds also flourished. Originally, guilds were organized along lines of local origin to provide shelter and aid for travelers from the guild's home region, to carry out traditional rites, and to serve as intermediaries between merchants and officials. By the eighteenth and nineteenth centuries, small guilds had grown into larger networks, including regional guilds (*huiguan*), and trade or professional guilds or associations (*hanghui, gongsuo, fatuan*) organized around production or processing of a specific commodity such as tea and salt. With their origins in native-place or clan-based associations, they operated largely according to norms of personalism, yet without eschewing these norms, they grew into multi-functional and, often, large and complex anchors of the community.[3]

The coexistence of doctrinal disdain of economic activity and a flour-ishing merchant and guild life meant that the role of merchants was fraught with complexity. In essence, merchants had a dual position com-

---

1. On this formal view of merchants in China, see Mann (1987), pp. 18–21; and Wellington Chan (1977), pp. 15–18. Chan finds the roots for a tradition of state inter-vention and, more generally, an anti-merchant stance in the Legalist (as opposed to Con-fucian) tradition of the Former Han dynasty (202 B.C. to A.D. 8).

2. Mann (1987), p. 20. See also Hao (1986).

3. Guilds, which have been documented as early as the Song period (960–1279), existed alongside a wide variety of societal groups, such as benevolent halls (*shantang*), study societies (*xuehui*), and agricultural societies (*nonghui*). On the development of guilds, see Wellington Chan (1977), pp. 214–216; Elvin (1973), pp. 172, 268; Fewsmith (1985), ch. 1; Gernet (1973), pp. 86–88; Mann (1987), pp. 23–25; and Rowe (1984), esp. chs. 8 and 9.

prised of both autonomy and elements of state control. This dual role was reflected in the juridical framework in which they operated. Guilds were allowed to regulate a good deal of their own trading activity; officials did not interfere, for example, in efforts by guilds to protect their monopsony power or to prevent the formation of competing guilds.[4] Yet even as the court permitted sufficient autonomy for an effective economy, it tried to regulate certain forms of commercial activity, particularly where it involved commodities of geographically widespread (as opposed to local) importance. The court intervened, for example, to regularize the transportation of grain from south to north, and it monopolized important commodities such as salt. The Qing state also baldly discriminated against wealthy merchants, believing that they "privatized public wealth for selfish ends."[5]

The dual role was also reflected, and in an important sense reconciled, in the social blending of the merchant and official (literati) classes. Sons of wealthy merchants moved, via the exam system or the purchase of titles, into the ranks of the literati, while merchants and officials joined common native-place (*tongxiang*) clubs. Moreover, because of the risk that literati sons would not pass the exams necessary to preserve their families' rank in the next generation, literati families tried to hedge against the future by amassing wealth. Even though literati families usually tried to mask money-earning activities by using other individuals, companies, or halls (*tang*) as "fronts," this blending of literati and merchant classes helped legitimate merchants who followed Confucian codes.[6]

The dual merchant role was also reflected in the growth, as early as the sixteenth-century Ming, of a "public" (*gong*) realm.[7] Although some scholars have depicted China's "public" realm as paralleling the growth of the "public sphere" which in Western Europe led to "civil society," that is not the meaning intended here. Unlike the "public sphere" that emerged in Western Europe via the articulation of private interests through public opinion, the *gong* realm in China arose in the context of management by members of the local elite of essentially official functions. Thus, the *gong* realm can be conceived of as sitting between the private and official (*guan*) spheres; it is "best conceptual-

---

4. Rowe (1984), chs. 8–10.
5. Mann (1987), p. 20.
6. Mann (1987), pp. 21–23, and Wellington Chan (1977), p. 21.
7. See, e.g., Mann (1987), ch. 2; Rankin (1990); Rowe (1984, chs. 8 and 9; 1990); and Strand (1990).

ized as an intermediate area of interaction between state and society in which the two sides meet and which neither can claim as completely its own."[8] The Qing court did not formally sanction the *gong* realm, yet the court at times relied heavily upon it and fostered *gong* activities to serve its own ends. Lacking the resources to regulate the market economy from within the "official" sphere, the court often devolved responsibility for regulation to merchant elites and their organizations. Using their own resources, merchants performed—and often benefited from—public services on behalf of the state. A regional association might assume responsibility for public works such as the upkeep of canals, fire fighting, or town or port planning.[9] *Gong* activities by guilds were intended to complement the state's needs; they were not a legitimate center of authority. Through their relations with guilds, officials could informally check on guild members' behavior and call on their help in times of local crisis. Moreover, although on occasion local merchants operating in *gong* functions did express criticism of the government,[10] the *gong* realm never connected to an emergent civil society as it did in Europe.[11] Guilds, instead, used *gong* activities to receive the sanction and patronage of officials. Guilds were not required to register with either central or local authorities, and no laws governed associational life, and yet guilds "regularly applied to local and regional officials to have their corporate existence made a matter of public account."[12] Public recognition legitimated the right of guilds to exist and to operate according to their own bylaws, and provided guilds with allies among officials.

8. This definition, and an excellent discussion of the meaning of *gong*, can be found in Rankin (1990).

9. See Wellington Chan (1975); Mann (1987), pp. 12–21; and Rankin (1990). Rankin (p. 55) cautions that private actors carrying out public taxation were not *always* working primarily for the state. Rather, the public sphere was "an arena in which elites performed public services on behalf of their localities, and usually, but not necessarily, in cooperation with the state."

10. Rankin (1986), pp. 147–169.

11. The concept of the *gong* realm has been attacked on similar grounds as leveled against "civil society," as discussed in ch. 1. One such attack is Wakeman (1993). Although many of the authors writing on the *gong* realm draw some inspiration from Habermas's ideas of the "public sphere," most do not argue that it was linked to the emergence of a bourgeois "civil society" in China.

12. Rowe (1984), pp. 257–258, 334–337. On a similar dynamic during the Song, see Gernet (1973), p. 88. Song guilds, however, were "too numerous and too varied to allow their influence to be felt . . . and the State gave every assistance towards maintaining the requisite sense of duty and obligation" (Gernet, p. 94).

Late-Qing Merchants and Guilds: 1840 to 1911

During the late-Qing period—reaching from the mid-nineteenth century to the fall of the Qing empire in 1911—the place of merchants evolved. Foreign military incursion and domestic rebellion weakened Qing authority, and at the same time the authority of merchants and their organizations increased. Despite the burgeoning merchant power, however, the government continued to try to supervise business in order to harness industrialization and strengthen the state. These trends put a new, more modern face on the merchant-state relationship. Yet the traditional dualism, as seen in the state's regulation of business, the social blending of merchant and official classes, and the separate existence of the *gong* realm, remained basically intact.

Defeat upon defeat by foreign militaries over the Qing army paved the way for a growing foreign economic presence in China's Treaty Ports. In the Treaty Ports, foreign traders for the first time were free to carry on transactions with whomever they pleased. This development in turn created a new segment of merchants: the comprador bourgeoisie (*maiban zibenjia*).[13] Compradors who began as clerks and purveyors under the earlier Cohong (*gonghang*) system became guarantors for business transactions between their new foreign employers and Chinese businesses. Increased foreign trade presented the opportunity for compradors to trade exclusively for their own accounts, and as a result many amassed substantial private wealth.[14] Compradors and other prominent Chinese merchants also introduced a distinctive lifestyle into urban

13. A "comprador" (literally "purchaser" in Portuguese) was head of a foreign firm's Chinese staff, and performed a multitude of functions: house steward, business assistant, salesman, treasurer, interpreter, freight broker, and intelligence provider. Members of this class came primarily from the coastal regions of Ningbo, Shanghai, Jiangsu, Zhejiang, and Guangdong. See Bergère (1989), pp. 38–40; Wellington Chan (1977), pp. 43–44, 236; and Hao (1970), ch. 4. Classic works on the Treaty Ports include Feuerwerker (1976) and Murphy (1970).

14. During the early- and middle-Qing periods, Chinese merchants who handled trade with foreigners had been organized into the "merchant guild of Cohong" that was centered in Guangdong. The guild was "licensed by and responsible to the officials, and had a monopoly over all trade with Western merchants" (Hao [1970], p. 2). Bergère (1989) notes that compradors made money not only from their high salaries and business investments, but also from commissions from their foreign employers, interest from their Chinese clientele, and other benefits that accrued from their position.

coastal China. Whereas, previously, merchants had been anxious to blend into the traditional gentry mold, they became more confident in asserting a more cosmopolitan lifestyle. For example, compradors in Shanghai generally preferred, for reasons of convenience, comfort, and prestige, to live in the International Settlement. They chose Western-style houses and clothing (exchanging their blue, floor-length, silk gowns for jackets and suits). Often, they spoke in pidgin English and converted to Christianity or Catholicism (depending upon the religion of their foreign employers).[15]

Business guilds also became more prominent in the late Qing, and they became politically engaged. The decline of Qing authority led them increasingly to participate in the keeping of social order and in major *gong* works, and at certain times (such as during the 1850s Taiping Rebellion) guilds assumed the powers of municipal government. They resisted efforts by city and provincial governments following the Taiping Rebellion to take over functions that by custom had been the prerogative of guilds. New guilds were founded to resist local officials' demands for payments.[16] During the waning years of Qing rule, merchants also increased their contacts with members of Sun Yat-sen's Revolutionary Alliance (Tongmenghui), and after the 1911 revolution, many merchants, including many compradors, participated in the new but short-lived municipal governments. The nationalism of the business elite was also aroused, though not to the degree of the later May Fourth era. Still, many merchants, including some increasingly nationalistic compradors, protested against the foreign presence in China, particularly (after 1905) the Qing court's heavy reliance on foreign development of railways.[17]

15. Bergère (1989), pp. 46–51. Bergère argues that the fact that compradors and other members of the business elite were anxious for "modernity"—and that "modernity" was equated with Westernization—is responsible for much of this transformation. Still, she notes that their assimilation of things Western was accompanied by nationalism, leading to a "hybrid culture." The size of the comprador class grew from a few hundred in the mid-nineteenth century to 20,000 by the beginning of the twentieth (see Bergère, pp. 39–40).

16. On the evolving role of guilds in the late Qing, see Wellington Chan (1977), p. 215; Elvin (1973), pp. 292–293; Fewsmith (1985), ch. 1; Mann (1987), pp. 12–21; and Rowe (1984), pp. 285–286. Guilds also continued to attend to the "three great concerns" (*san da shi*) of travelers: food, funerals, and sacrificial rites.

17. The Railway Rights Recovery Movement (1906–1909) created privately run provincial railway companies in Guangdong, Zhejiang, and Jiangsu provinces. See Liao (1984), pp. 128–146, 240. The United States government's Exclusion Act forbidding

The decline in Qing strength and the concomitant rise of merchant authority forced government reformers in the late nineteenth century to reappraise China's economic strategy and the role of merchants in it.[18] If China were to industrialize, they reasoned, the country would need to engage the participation of industrialists and other commercial experts. A 1903 imperial edict proclaimed it time to eradicate the attitude of superiority toward merchants and the accumulation of wealth. The anti-merchant tendency was challenged and effectively (if temporarily) eroded. The lifting of restrictions on the participation of scholar-officials in commerce and industry in the second half of the nineteenth century further legitimated the merchant role. In a pattern strikingly prescient of the post-Mao era, some officials-turned-industrialists even relinquished their government posts and created successful businesses using ties to their former colleagues, while merchants were encouraged to participate more in official projects. By 1903, the newly established Ministry of Commerce had announced it would grant titles and ranks to merchants to reward capital investments in modern enterprises. These changes continued to blur the social distinction between literati and merchant ranks. By the early 1900s, a local leadership class of "gentry-merchants" (*shenshang*) had emerged.

The view among reformers of that period that China required modern industry (in part to ward off foreign military and economic competition) was accompanied by an agreement that industrialization should strengthen the nation and occur within the framework of state supervision. There was considerable difficulty, however, resolving exactly what form that supervision should take. Late-nineteenth-century proposals for "government supervision and merchant management" (*guandu shangban*) and "official-merchant joint management" (*guan-shang heban*) both emphasized state control and did not produce successful industries. The officials-turned-entrepreneurs who emerged in the early

---

Chinese laborers from entering the country was another trigger for anti-foreign protests and boycotts. On the politicization of merchants during this period, see also Fewsmith (1985), pp. 40–45; and Bergère (1989), pp. 48–51.

18. Reform efforts began in the conservative Tongzhi Restoration (1862–1874), and at first were limited to borrowing foreign military technology. The scope of reform gradually came to include innovation in other core industries (such as textiles and shipping) and to emphasize industry and commerce as crucial sectors. The newly proclaimed attitudes nonetheless distinguished among merchants; smaller merchants involved in domestic commerce were still held in disrepute, while industrial entrepreneurs and international traders gained respect. See Wellington Chan (1977), pp. 25–57, 239.

1900s occasionally were able to gain the confidence of private investors, as well as to institute a "merchant management" (*shangban*) system that was comparatively free of direct bureaucratic supervision but retained official links, used state funds, and received political protection. Some connection with the state remained the norm.[19] In conjunction with the continued state supervision, and even as modernization and industrialization became watchwords of the day, clientelism and personalistic or native-place networks remained salient. As the son of one prominent official-turned-industrialist commented, "In Chinese society, you cannot accomplish anything without having close ties with officials. They can help you or break you."[20]

If the effort to carve out a new role for officials in supervising the economy was not particularly satisfactory, an innovative proposal for using merchant organizations in initiatives to strengthen the state proved more successful. Arguing that members of the local elite, including merchants, possessed expertise that could unleash China's commercial power, reformers proposed that the government create new commercial associations that would both prevent bureaucratic meddling in commerce and promote the trickling up of ideas from merchants to the state. They pointed to the powerful foreign chambers of commerce in the Treaty Ports as models of strength and unity within the business community. A newly formed Ministry of Commerce, supported by a 1904 imperial decree, directed that chambers of commerce (*shangwu hui*, or *shangyi*) be set up in all provincial capitals and major commercial cities, with branches in smaller commercial areas. By 1908 there were chambers in thirty-one major cities.[21] Like merchants and their guilds, these new chambers possessed a dual character. On the one hand, the reformers in the central government had a strong influence in the setting up of these chambers and clearly intended to put them to their

---

19. Wellington Chan (1977), pp. 237–241. Most post-1949 Chinese (and Western) scholarship on this era has been critical of its enterprise managers because they came from bureaucracy or government rather than private business, and lacked technological, managerial, and financial skills. Recently, however, historians inside and outside China have come to see more positive features in the earlier period. See Tim Wright (1988); Cochran (1980). It should be noted that a struggle between the central and provincial governments complicated the search for an effective form of state supervision, as the desire of the center to wrest control of industry from provincial governments underlay efforts in the first decade of the twentieth century to set up ministries at the center.

20. Wellington Chan (1977), p. 57.

21. See Wellington Chan (1977), pp. 32–33, 216–234; Fewsmith (1985), pp. 25–36.

own purposes; the new bodies were created under rules dictated by the government, usually by co-opting existing groups. The functions of these new bodies, also defined by the ministry, were to improve commercial matters, conduct surveys and channel information to the ministry, sponsor exhibitions, run training programs, notify the ministry of undue interference by local authorities, and pass merchant opinions to the local and central government authorities.[22] On the other hand, once legitimated, these organizations strove for greater independence. Particularly in Shanghai and Canton, the government was forced to allow some autonomy to the chambers in return for their cooperation in promoting modernization.[23] The Shanghai General Chamber of Commerce (SGCC) soon after its founding became active in the nation's political life, as exemplified by its effort to participate in the writing of the constitution promised by the Qing court in 1906. The SGCC, in conjunction with gentry representatives, organized an association devoted to constitutionalism, lobbied for procedural changes in the constitutional process, and participated in drafting provincial assembly regulations.[24] These political moves presaged the short-lived and yet remarkable activity of this and other chambers after the collapse of the Qing government.

During the late Qing, then, industrialization and the foreign threat generated a more sophisticated role for merchants and the creation of new institutions to guide industrialization. Even so, the essence of the old dual pattern—state supervision coupled with limited merchant autonomy, the social blending of official and merchant groups, and the existence of a "public" realm—remained.

The "Golden Age" of 1911–1927: A Push toward Merchant Autonomy

Merchants and their associations, particularly those based in Shanghai, made a strong move toward autonomy and activism during

22. Once again, an unsuccessful aspect of this plan was a strategy to circumvent the power of provincial bureaucracies that were resisting the court's last-ditch efforts at reform. See Wellington Chan (1977), p. 217 and, generally, ch. 11; Schoppa (1982), pp. 6–7, 34–35.

23. Bergère (1989), pp. 36–37, 53–55.

24. The constitutional association was the Association for the Preparation of Constitutionalism (Yubei Lixian Gonghui). See Fewsmith (1985), pp. 43–44.

a "golden age" of the bourgeoisie that followed the fall of the Qing in 1911. Marie-Claire Bergère claims that this era in Shanghai "saw the emergence of the nearest thing to an autonomous society in Chinese history—an urban society dominated by the united front of business circles, well structured and inspired by a modernist and pro-Western intelligentsia."[25] If it was a dramatic era for merchants, it was also exceptional, for merchant autonomy and activism were contingent upon the collapse of central authority in 1911 and, at the same time, upon the appearance of economic conditions under which merchants flourished. The era also failed to usher in a permanent system of merchant autonomy.

The advent of World War I meant that foreign powers, and foreign businesses operating in China, could not keep up with the demand for imported goods. Chinese entrepreneurs, particularly those in the coastal area surrounding the Treaty Port of Shanghai, moved in to fill the niche. War also strengthened the Chinese currency, and opened new export markets. A post-war wave of industrialization concentrated on the production of consumer goods, such as textiles, foods, cigarettes, and confections. As imports and investment into China dropped off, squeezing the traditional functions of compradors, those who survived became increasingly independent, and tended to blend with the rest of the merchant elite.[26] They used their understanding of Western business practices to seize new opportunities in the booming coastal cities. In short, the business class grew wealthier and more professional.

The autonomous organization of merchants and professionals also reached a peak. In Shanghai alone, eighty professional associations existed in 1912.[27] As in the past, these associations very often were formed

25. Bergère (1989), p. 240. She also argues that the bourgeoisie "was gradually constituting itself as a specific and coherent class" during the 1920s (p. 140). Although merchant groups became more autonomous, other groups, such as students, remained more firmly under government supervision. See, e.g., Strand (1990), p. 4. Moreover, provincial governments continued to exert significant control over business. See Schoppa (1982), p. 7.

26. The growth of banks, which reduced dependence on comprador guarantees, further curtailed compradors' role. Compradors were replaced in foreign businesses with professional Chinese managers who were responsible for actual administration rather than simply providing guarantees. The term "Chinese manager" (*Hua jingli*) was used in part to distinguish the new style of employee from the more discredited—given the nationalist environment—"comprador." See Hao (1970), pp. 59–63.

27. Shanghai merchants were particularly well organized; compared to their counterparts in, for example, Tianjin, merchant organizations in booming Shanghai grabbed

along native-place lines, and personal ties continued to be central to their operation.[28] These groups did not remain aloof from domestic politics. While previously they had been somewhat marginal to major political movements such as the 1911 revolution, their political participation intensified to such a degree that they were often at the forefront of movements. They espoused a commitment to modernization and, until the mid-1920s anyway, believed that modernization required vigorous ties to international business. Although strong ties to the foreign community and the Treaty Ports sometimes moderated their ideology, in keeping with the ideology of the May Fourth movement many merchant organizations—even those organized along "traditional" native-place lines—nevertheless became highly nationalistic.[29]

The immediate events of the May Fourth movement sparked several types of political activism. The announcement in May 1919 that the Chinese government had agreed to transfer German rights in Shandong Province to Japan stimulated merchant protests alongside those of students, intellectuals, and workers. Trade groups publicly reprimanded the Beijing government, and promoted "patriotic products" (*aiguohuo*). Stores were closed, boycotts of Japanese goods were initiated, and many businesses (especially banks) refused to deal with Japanese companies. The events were condemned in announcements of chambers of commerce and in the specialized press (such as the Shanghai Bankers' Association's *Banker's Weekly* [*Yinhang zhoubao*]).[30] Many of the efforts of the merchants were quite effective. For example, the merchants were partly successful in their demand to participate in the foreign-dominated Shanghai Municipal Council during the height of May

the opportunity created by the weak governing structure to further their own interests. See Bergère (1989), pp. 131–139, 145, 185–186, and 213–216.

28. These organizations were "new" in part because they opened their memberships to more than just the merchant elite. See Bryna Goodman (1992).

29. Bergère (1989), pp. 125, 131–133, 210–211, and 243–268; Bryna Goodman (1992). Bergère argues that those with the strongest foreign ties were not very different from others in the business class in their ideology, and implies that they cannot be distinguished as a separate group during this period (p. 217). Still, it must be kept in mind that the May Fourth and later movements embodied many diverse ideological strands—liberalism, nationalism, and communism—not all of which merchants could be expected to embrace. Nor were merchant groups unified in their actions; infighting (such as within the SGCC) surfaced, while in Shanghai smaller merchants began to organize into even more radicalized street associations and challenged the older chamber of commerce.

30. See Fewsmith (1985), pp. 51–60; Bergère (1989), pp. 207–217; Cochran (1980), ch. 5; Liao (1984), pp. 73–79; and Remer (1933).

Fourth activities.[31] The actions of business organizations could also be audacious and bizarre: the Federation of Chambers of Commerce, a body established in 1907 to link up chambers from different provinces, called for a national convention (*guomin huiyi*) of provincial assemblies and professional and educational societies that would choose a new, largely liberal, governmental regime and reorganize military and financial affairs. When the convention's meeting in 1922 failed to produce results, and a military coup in Beijing ejected the Republic's president in 1923, the Shanghai Chamber of Commerce declared its independence and its intent to organize a government of merchants (*shangren zhengfu*), despite the fact that it had no territorial basis or military forces. As dramatic as this move was, it ultimately failed.[32]

Nationalist Suppression and the Return to Dualism

The movement toward a genuinely autonomous business elite that had characterized the exceptional "golden age" was quashed with the coming to power of the Nationalists in 1927. Contrary to historical accounts, on the one hand, of an enduring and friendly alliance between "comprador" capitalists and the Guomindang or, on the other hand, of a complete suppression of business interests, more balanced accounts indicate that Chiang Kai-shek's government brought back the dualism of the merchant associations.[33] There were a number of ways in which business interests were met or shared by the new regime, and

31. Fewsmith (1985), p. 136.

32. Bergère, (1989), pp. 219–225. This was a time of great intellectual ferment. Some critics advocated Swiss- or American-style federal systems. John Dewey's "guild socialism" was an influential source for ideas of the broader autonomist movement of which this incident was a part.

33. The question of government-bourgeoisie relations during the Nationalist era has been much debated. PRC historians have argued that comprador capitalists were in full alliance with the Nationalists. This view is described in Tim Wright (1988, p. 189) and is endorsed in Moore (1966, pp. 189–192) and Giesert (1979). Other historians, however, argue that business interests were nearly completely suppressed. See Coble (1986), pp. xii–xiv, 61–65; Eastman (1984); and Fewsmith (1984). More balanced accounts showing both some business autonomy but also strong efforts at state suppression and/or co-optation of business are Fewsmith (1985) and Henriot (1993). Other useful treatments of the relations between government and capitalists are: Bergère (1989), pp. 227–240; Bush (1982); Coble (1986), pp. 25–41; and Cochran (1980), pp. 185–188.

in which the two groups were linked. The Nationalist government was less anti-capitalist than its rhetoric implied, and Nanjing was slow to nationalize key industries. Shanghai's most influential capitalists provided the political and financial backing Chiang needed to rise to power. The capitalists used personal ties—as in the person of Finance Minister T. V. Soong, a member of one of Shanghai's most prominent capitalist families—to influence government decisions. In Shanghai, "local notables" from the old bourgeoisie dominated the municipal councils and had particularly strong influence in their area of business and expertise, namely, finance.[34] Turning increasingly conservative over the course of the 1930s, many in the bourgeoisie relied upon Chiang to restore social order and reduce foreign economic competition.

Yet there was no happy bourgeoisie-Nationalist alliance. The Nationalist government was willing to tolerate neither significant merchant autonomy nor manipulation by the business class. Instead, reflecting the state's effort to re-establish its own pre-eminence, the links between private business and the Nationalist government were tinged with coercion by the latter, and the interests of many in the bourgeoisie, particularly those of medium and small merchants and of those who opposed the Nationalist government, were driven underground. Beyond the voluntary contributions it solicited, the government soaked the capitalist sector for funds, sometimes engaging the services of the underground Green Gang thugs.[35] Merchants engaged in some activism, such as anti-Japanese boycotts, but not without the government's sanction. The regime co-opted much of the technological and professional class into its ranks, most notably through the recruitment into the technocracy of Western-trained economists, engineers, and scientists.[36] Some who were at the very pinnacle of the bourgeoisie retained influence (such as through appointment to Shanghai's Municipal Council), but their influence resulted from their close ties to Chiang and/or their rather full support of the government.[37] Under pressure of the anti-Japanese conflict and subsequent civil war and the increasingly restrictive Nationalist policy, a significant portion of the merchant elite emigrated to Hong Kong and elsewhere.

The government also reorganized merchant organizations to facilitate its control of them. Guomindang branches, beginning in 1925, had

34. Henriot (1993), pp. 52–54.
35. Martin (1995).
36. Kirby (1989).
37. Henriot (1993), pp. 62–63.

established numerous local, mass-based federations for small and middle merchants as well as workers, peasants, students, and women. Later in the decade, these Guomindang-established federations and some of the still independent federations of small business were merged into the older chambers, while more radical street associations that had spontaneously sprung up were abolished.[38] The more established business chambers, particularly the SGCC, were brought firmly under Nationalist government control by 1929. Key laws governing trade associations and chambers of commerce were revised to limit the functions of these groups to merely assisting the state in management of the economy (primarily by stabilizing the market in tense times) and to submitting suggestions to the government and gathering commercial data.[39]

By the close of the 1920s, then, the associations born of the "golden age" were once again tied closely to and supervised by the state, though not incorporated into it. The reorganization of merchants under the umbrella of the SGCC created a "unitary, noncompetitive, hierarchical structure of interest organization which was, on the one hand, largely self-governing . . . but was, on the other hand, subordinate to (and indeed brought into being by) state authority"—in other words, a form of state corporatism.[40] The Nationalist government was not fully effective at establishing corporatism; its repression of merchants alienated many to the degree that they ignored Nationalist laws and continued to rely upon traditional family business structures and ties.[41] However, despite the flaws in the implementation of the Nationalist strategy—something we will see again in the post-Mao era—key elements of corporatism appeared. Only one segment of the merchant class, the members of the SGCC, was granted a representational

---

38. On the Guomindang-based federations, see Fewsmith (1985), pp. 103–159. The radical Shanghai Federation of Street Associations (and its branches), formed in 1919, was dissolved outright in 1928. The precise interpretation of these events has been disputed by scholars. To Fewsmith (1985, ch. 6, esp. pp. 161–168), the folding in of the small federations to the central chamber was part of a plan to rein in the authority of *local* Guomindang branches that had sponsored them. It therefore reflected a victory for the older merchant elite over more radical merchants, and a triumph of the central organization, led by Chiang Kai-shek, over the local party branches. Coble (1986, pp. 62–63) argues, in contrast, that the central Guomindang and its Shanghai branch emerged victorious because they were able to dilute the power of the elite SGCC by blending it with associations controlled by local party branches. In both interpretations, though, central political bodies clearly manipulated small merchant organizations to their own ends.

39. Fewsmith (1985), pp. 159–166.

40. Fewsmith (1985), p. 163. See also Martin (1995).

41. Kirby (1995).

monopoly by the state. The Nationalist government left the merchant organizations intact, but it removed much of the associations' ability to act in the vigorous, self-interested manner of the previous years. The state pre-empted the further emergence of competing, autonomous organizations and demobilized what previously had been a politically active constituency.

The Fate of China's Business Elite during the Maoist Years

The coming to power of the communist regime in 1949 shifted the balance between the business elite and the state to the opposite extreme from that of the "golden age." The Confucian assumption that private interests must be subordinated to state-defined interests was deepened by the Marxian notions of commerce. Profit-taking and "commodity circulation" (activities that produced no "use-value") were to be eliminated gradually, and industrialization was to be supervised by the state under state ownership. Maoist ideology recognized that some individual interests existed but denied that these separate interests could exist validly as a long-term aspect of communism. These Maoist views implied that even the *gong* realm that had been so useful to past regimes could not be tolerated. Rather, under the united front policy, the state defined the interests of those groups or classes whose interests might be distinct from those of the Party. Under the united front, moreover, the Party-state brought extra-Party groups such as merchants within its organizational structure and put them to the purpose of industrialization, or of other Party goals.[42] Hence, politically "reliable" members of the merchant elite were invited to join the Chinese People's Political Consultative Conference (CPPCC) and such "democratic parties" as the China Democratic League. Federations and professional associations for merchants were established after 1949, or were retained (in form) from pre-revolutionary days. Capitalists who had belonged to Nationalist trade organizations were organized into the All-China Federation

42. On Marxian notions of commerce, see Solinger (1984), pp. 12–16. On individual interests and the united front, see Burns (1988), pp. 21–22 and ch. 2; Dittmer (1987), pp. 18–23; and Seymour (1987). Prior to 1949, the united front was primarily a wartime strategy for alliance of the weak Communist Party and the Guomindang against the Japanese. However, it also sanctioned Party overtures to non-communist groups, including urban elites. See Stranahan (1992).

of Industry and Commerce (ACFIC). This federation became the cap-italists' main link with the new regime and provided a means to harness their expertise. There was no question that this and other such federa-tions were neither equal to the Party nor autonomous from it; the unit-ed front policy explicitly dictated leadership by and full loyalty to the Party. United front groups were legitimate only insofar as they mobi-lized the expertise and support of members on behalf of statist goals. The federations were controlled largely by members of the Party bureau-cracy. Potential opposition from these groups was defused further by granting them a highly limited "consultative role" in policy delibera-tions. Only occasionally were they a forum for the genuine expression of views and complaints.[43] Thus, ACFIC meetings became venues at which Party and state officials transmitted information on policies and mobilized the obedience of business representatives. By the time of the Cultural Revolution, bodies such as the ACFIC appeared to have been transformed fully into "mass organizations" that were firmly within the grasp of the regime and could be manipulated for the purposes of top leaders.

Despite its adherence to a new ideology, then, the socialist regime continued the tradition, established with the chambers of commerce of the late Qing, of sanctioning trade associations and attempting to guide and supervise their activities. By this time, however, there was room for even less autonomy than those earlier organs had possessed, and their form ran closer to totalism than corporatism.[44] Whereas the rather mod-erate strains created by the united front policy, as well as sympathetic statements by Mao Zedong, had suggested that parts of the Chinese business class might survive the revolution intact,[45] such was not to be. The Party attempted to remold the ideology of members of these

43. For example, meetings organized by the All-China Federation of Scientific Soci-eties (ACFSS) allowed scientists to speak out on problems in the scientific community in 1957 during the "Hundred Flowers" campaign. See Suttmeier (1987), pp. 128–129, 130–131. Even so, those who did speak out undoubtedly were criticized during the sub-sequent Anti-Rightist campaign.

44. Anita Chan (1993) implies that Maoist worker federations were state corporatist, and yet the lack of autonomy and inclusion in all cases as part of the Party-state argues against such an interpretation.

45. Mao's (1967) 1940 essay "On New Democracy" discussed the need to protect business in the early stages of transformation, and argued against nationalization of indus-try or the end of capitalist-style production. Mao's (1969) 1949 "On the People's Demo-cratic Dictatorship" declared that the petty and national bourgeoisie (excluding major industrialists) would be treated fairly under the new regime, though it also foreshadowed eventual nationalization.

groups, culminating in the Wufan (literally, "Five-Anti") campaign of 1951–1952.[46] The movement utilized what had by then become the standard campaign methods—of "struggle" and self-criticism sessions led by Party cadres—to harass those who came from "bad" bourgeois classes, including members of what was (incorrectly) labeled the "comprador bourgeoisie." In addition, the first half of the 1950s saw the immediate confiscation of the assets of many of the largest capitalist families. Large businesses were transformed into mixed state-private enterprises that increasingly were controlled by central ministries.[47] Foreign trade was taken over by state organs, while foreign businesses eventually closed or were nationalized.[48] By the time of the completion of the "transformation to socialism," the broader business class was diminished to next to nothing; whereas there had been 8.4 million independent private craftsmen, merchants, and industrialists in Chinese towns and cities in 1953, by 1956 only 160,000 private enterprises remained.[49] Just as significantly, this group now existed and functioned on the state's terms.

Lessons of the Historical Record

As this discussion of merchant-state relations from the late Qing through the Maoist era makes clear, the political role of merchants and their associations has been neither simple nor uniform. Stated in terms of the models set forth in chapter 1, we see in the historical record elements of clientelism, state corporatist strategies, and, though less robust, even civil society. Out of this complexity, several lessons can be

---

46. The five "evil" activities targeted were bribery, tax evasion, theft of government property, cheating on contracts, and use of economic data for private benefit. The campaign's actual targets became broader than merely those engaging in these activities, however. On the Wufan campaign, see Kraus (1991), pp. 52–54; Gardner (1969). Echoing pre-1949 debates, the regime attempted to distinguish between non-exploiting merchants (who were allowed a "legitimate profit" of 10% to 30% annually) and "speculating, illegitimate" businessmen. See Kraus (1991), p. 53; Solinger (1984), p. 136n.

47. The assets of over 2,800 firms were nationalized. See Kraus (1991), pp. 50–58. For a detailed treatment of textile businesses during this period, see Sears (1985).

48. The nationalization of foreign assets was completed by 1954. See Thompson (1979).

49. Owners of remaining private firms were paid an annual fixed interest of 5% of their investment starting in 1955 and continuing for several years. The numbers of private firms apparently rose between 1957 and 1965 to approximately one million, until pressure from the Cultural Revolution again reduced the number. See Kraus (1991), pp. 51–58; Sun (1984), p. 26.

highlighted that will inform our examination of business-state relations in post-Mao China.

First, and most important, although the relationship between merchants and the state was fluid, a Janus-faced pattern emerges that contains elements of both autonomy for a dynamic merchant sector and control and supervision by the central state. Merchant life retained a not insignificant degree of autonomy, and yet with the exception of the "golden age"—the time that came closest to seeing the emergence of civil society—the state maintained a strong hand in the activities of merchants and their associations. This pattern of dualism was evident in the late-Qing reformers' attempts to stimulate industrialization under state supervision and, at the same time, to unleash and yet control merchant energy through the establishment of chambers of commerce. The tradition returned, in a form that had strong overtones of state corporatism, with the Nationalist regime's partly successful effort to co-opt the most powerful of the previously independent merchant associations and, in theory, to focus their energies on modernization.

Second, although this interpretation of the dualism of the Qing and Nationalist eras emphasizes the similarities between these two historical periods, there are of course differences. In the Qing period, the relationship between merchants and the state was comparatively benign. The need to have a vibrant merchant life was reconciled with the desire for some state supervision through efforts of the state to accommodate (in practice and eventually in doctrine) merchant activities. Hence, a good deal of social blending of the literati and merchant classes took place, and some legitimation of merchants and their activities ensued. The Nationalist era, in contrast, was characterized by greater coercion on the part of the state. At the same time, the intent of the Nationalist government to use new state-dominated associations to enforce strong controls and unleash rapid industrialization was not successful in practice. So while state control was a goal in both eras, this goal was met in different ways and produced different results. This difference in "tactics" for reconciling the need for both autonomy and control is instructive as we look forward to the post-Mao era, for it raises the question of whether the post-Mao state will attempt to meet this same goal through the more coercive model of the Nationalists or through the social accommodation and legitimation model of the Qing.

Third, even as merchants became progressively more "modern" and cosmopolitan in their outlook, traditional forms of group organization and behavior remained at the core. An integral theme of each of the eras considered here, even the "golden age," is the predominance of personal ties and (often family- or clan-based) networks. Sometimes such networks of merchants have been at odds with state goals (as when the Nationalists attempted to reorganize businesses) and sometimes they have been in harmony with the state (as in the performance of *gong* activities in the Qing), but at base these elements of clientelism have endured.

Finally, the stage at which the merchant elite came closest to seizing political momentum occurred, not coincidentally, with the central state's period of greatest disarray. Why did this bid by the merchant elite fail? A lack of sufficient organization and coalition building was the most immediate cause. Moreover, it seems likely that the efforts of merchants were actually hindered by the disintegration of the state and the country's slide into warlordism; the merchants' push for economic and political liberalism could not survive in the chaos that surrounded it. But Bergère also suggests that, ironically, the merchant elite's failure was largely a result of the perception that the state was too weak to be worth seizing.[50] It will be interesting to consider henceforth whether the post-Mao business elite is similarly halted from encroaching upon the state by the (unlikely) perception that it is only a marginal prize, or whether other factors interfere—opposition by a state still intact, lack of will on the part of members of the business elite, or even the availability of other channels of influence (such as clientelism).

The preceding discussion points out those elements of modern Chinese business history which may be the most significant lessons for the post-Mao era. But how do we know the history is at all relevant? After all, the immediate context from which China's contemporary economic elite and its business associations emerged in the post-Mao era was that of virtually complete state domination by the Maoist regime. Indeed, the presumption that a pattern similar to the pre-1949 dualism was likely to have reappeared in post-Mao China might be challenged by pointing out that the Maoist era represented a more than two-decade interruption, during which links with the past were decisively severed.

---

50. Bergère (1989). The attempt to establish a "government of merchants" also showed that, in the absence of an alliance with other elites, merchants lacked the power to set up new political structures. See Coble (1986), ch. 2.

Nonetheless, four specific channels through which historical continuity might be seen to flow, despite obvious changes in the type of regime and the organization of society, seem relevant.[51] First, and most important, both the late Qing and the Nationalist regimes, on the one hand, and the post-Mao reformers, on the other, possess and recognize the same *functional* need to harness the resources and skills of the merchant or business elite, something that had long been provided in the functioning of *gong* works. One key way for the state to do this is by forming or by co-opting professional groups of merchants, including merchants with foreign ties, who have enough independence to encourage their expertise but are ultimately supervised by the state. The expectation that co-opted business associations can serve this useful function is therefore likely to have shaped similar policies toward them in different eras. (During the "golden age" the state was not capable of mounting such an effort, while during the Maoist era the strategy of allowing functional groups some independence in exchange for resources was precluded by ideology after the 1956 "transition to socialism.")

Second, there is some continuity between pre- and post-1949 *institutions*. As noted previously, many federations, such as the business federation, the ACFIC, set up in the early 1950s actually were old associations in new socialist clothing. The ACFIC was once again given updated socialist clothing in the 1980s. This is not to say that they have remained the same organizations; they underwent qualitative changes in goals, methods, and links to the state, especially during the 1956 "transition" and the Cultural Revolution. Yet even relatively weak institutional continuity raises the possibility that an institutional memory of past patterns remains, particularly when the functional importance of the associations has carried over as well.[52]

51. These channels are presented with the intention of being suggestive rather than exhaustive. It also can be pointed out that the dual pattern re-emerged under the Nationalists after the fifteen-year hiatus of the "golden age." Of course, no history will be mapped exactly onto the present era. The following discussion attempts to make an initial case for elements of continuity *despite* an obviously changed context. Another effort to draw historical parallels between the state's treatment of merchants during the Qing and post-Mao eras—by emphasizing continuity in strength and functions of the state—is Solinger (1992), pp. 124–125.

52. On institutional continuity before and after 1949 in the science association, see Suttmeier (1987). Historians of Nationalist and early socialist China are increasingly persuaded that the 1949 revolution marked less of a break with the past than often has been assumed.

Third, and more concretely, the post-Mao reforms have sparked a re-examination by contemporary Chinese scholars of late Qing and Republican merchants, including intensive study of the SGCC. Rather than condemning wholesale the role of merchants and their associations, there is now an effort by scholars to search for what might have been useful.[53] This inquiry, in the context of close ties between scholars and the government, suggests the possibility that there may have been a deliberate attempt by the post-Mao state to apply institutional forms from an era of greater business dynamism to current efforts at modernization.

Finally, an enduring cultural and intellectual context in support of a dual role conceivably militates in favor of similar solutions. In other words, the question of state control of the business elite and its associations has never really left the cultural and intellectual agenda, despite the interregnums of the "golden age" and Maoism. The enduring debate is over how much the state should control business, rather than whether control should exist at all.[54]

53. Evidence of consciousness of the past role of guilds is found, for example, in Xinhua (1989). On efforts of Chinese intellectuals to learn from the past, see also Tim Wright (1988), pp. 185–214; Edmond Lee (1991).

54. The fourth hypothesis is suggested in Fewsmith (1991). An attempt to show how Confucian culture shapes business-state relations in Taiwan is found in Zeigler (1988).

CHAPTER 3

The Autonomy of China's
New Business Elite

This chapter describes the employment patterns of foreign-sector managers to show how the new business elite has broken the bonds of dependence on the state that characterized the Maoist era. In doing so, these managers have achieved a striking degree of autonomy compared to their counterparts in state-owned enterprises. Entrepreneurs in the private sector have achieved a similar degree of structural independence. Consistent with their structural autonomy, the ideology of the business elite is strongly reformist.[1] Although this relative structural and ideological independence might at first seem to signal the emergence of an independent civil society, it alone does not tell the whole story. This chapter also begins to show how the informal, vertical variant of clientelism remains important.[2]

The Structural Autonomy
of Foreign-Sector Managers

In the early years of the "open" policy, foreign businesses were tightly regulated by the Chinese government. Recognizing that

1. A discussion of the interviews on which this chapter (and chapters 4 and 5) are based appears in appendix 2. The results of interviews conducted in 1995 on the issues of structural and ideological autonomy were very similar to the results from the 1991 interviews, except to show autonomy had, if anything, deepened. Reference to the specific year of interviews is made only where significant differences were observed. On the interview sample, see appendix 2.

2. The relevance of clientelism is explored more fully in ch. 4.

the strict controls were serving as a disincentive to investment, Chinese reformers over time reduced these controls significantly. This regulatory erosion over the course of the 1980s not only fostered an upsurge in foreign investment (see appendix 1), but it also allowed foreign-sector businesses a greater degree of autonomy than originally had been envisioned by the state. This enterprise autonomy is manifested in managerial discretion such that boards of directors and managers rather than government ministries have been allowed more extensive decision-making authority within the enterprise. They also have greater authority, for instance, to engage directly in international trade without going through foreign trade organizations, and to buy and sell foreign exchange in "swap" markets. Although bureaucratic interference remains a problem in the foreign sector and, at the same time, state-owned enterprises are being granted increased autonomy, foreign-sector businesses nevertheless have gained a remarkable degree of independence from the state compared to those in the state sector.[3] It can even be said that the central government has treated the foreign sector gingerly; foreign businesses were protected from the political crackdown that occurred in 1989, and U.S. businesses operating in China were protected from the vicissitudes in U.S.-China relations in the mid-1990s.[4]

The relative autonomy of the foreign sector has redounded to the benefit of Chinese managers located within it. The term "autonomy" (used here interchangeably with "independence") refers to two specific phenomena: the absence of structural ties to the state, and ideological independence from the predominantly reformist line of the post-Mao era—in other words, autonomy in managers' views of the economy and politics. Both of these types of autonomy are relative; the appropriate measure of judgment is not whether foreign-sector managers are *completely* autonomous from the state (a standard that is difficult to meet in any context) but, rather, whether they have gained significantly *more* autonomy compared to relevant groups in China, particularly to managers in state-owned enterprises.

The concept of structural autonomy is central to the study of change in state-society relations in China. Under socialism, Chinese society has been closely bound to the state by a variety of policies and practices. The work by Andrew Walder on "neo-traditionalism" has shown that employees in state-owned enterprises have been bound to the state

---

3. On autonomy for and bureaucratic interference in JVs, see Pearson (1991). On the same issues in state-owned enterprises, see Chevrier (1990); Boisot and Guo (1991).
    4. See Pearson (1990); Faison (1995).

through the enterprise.[5] Even with the advent of economic reform in the 1980s and the loosening of certain of the structural ties, many of the patterns and institutions that bind managers to the state enterprise have remained pertinent in the state sector in the 1990s.

Three types of structural ties exist. (To use Walder's terms, there are three types of "organized dependence.")[6] First, workers have been made *politically* dependent upon the enterprise by Party cells (led by Party secretaries) and by Party-dominated trade unions. Second, employees in state enterprises have been tied *socially* and *economically* to the firm because it is the vehicle through which the state's welfare system operates. The enterprise provides a huge proportion of life's necessities, including medical care, housing, meals, and care in old age. Third, workers have been *personally* dependent upon their superiors within the enterprise, because shop-floor supervisors and Party cadres have shared wide discretion over the distribution of the benefits and materials controlled by the factory, as well as approval of job transfers. Shop managers and Party branch secretaries in state enterprises have been relatively unrestrained by collective bargaining or bureaucratic regulations in determining how to parcel out goods or incentives (including bonuses and punishments). In response, employees in state enterprises have tried to maintain good relationships and to influence the discretion of higher managers and Party cadres by doing them favors and giving them gifts.

The political, socio-economic, and personal dependencies of state-sector employees have bound state-sector managers tightly to the enterprise and the state. In contrast to the vast majority of state-sector employees, these links have been severed in the foreign sector. We can see a shattering of the state's control over foreign-sector managers in four specific areas: the dominance of the Party cell within the enterprise; the influence of personnel dossiers in the lives of employees; the constraints on labor mobility; and the reliance of employees upon the factory for welfare benefits. These areas of foreign-sector managers' structural autonomy from the state are detailed in the following discussion.

---

5. See Walder (1983, 1986). Walder's main focus is on workers rather than managers. Yet managers are linked into the same structures and networks as workers. Although they are part of the system of control over workers *within* the factory (the side Walder emphasizes), they also are bound by many of the same ties that affect workers, and hence can be analyzed through the neo-traditional prism.

6. Walder (1986), pp. 11–22. Some variations in these patterns have existed across time and type of state worker but the essential pattern remained intact (pp. 40–56). On the continuing importance of "organized dependence," see Walder (1986), ch. 7; Huang (1990).

THE ROLE OF THE PARTY

The CCP built a strong position of authority in state enterprises beginning in the mid-1950s, and it has continued to maintain this position into the reform era. The duty of Party cadres located within the factory has been to provide moral and political leadership in the enterprise, often in the context of political and ideological study sessions. The Party has supervised myriad aspects of employee life, in part through its input into the distribution of benefits and in part through its dominance of personnel matters. The personnel manager in state enterprises is almost uniformly a Party member, perhaps the general secretary of the enterprise Party cell and/or the trade union leader. Party cells have controlled many of the key work- and life-decisions affecting employees. Party cells have maintained substantial (at times nearly unilateral) influence over hiring and promotion. These cells have also maintained political or Party dossiers (*dang'an*) on each employee via the personnel department (as discussed below). At the height of Party influence in factories, employees had no choice but to cultivate relationships with cadres in order to gain promotions or access to scarce benefits. In many periods, the Party also dominated line management and technical matters via its cells on the shop floor and at general management levels, thereby injecting political criteria into day-to-day decision-making.[7]

Urban reforms that were announced in 1984 were intended to reduce the role of the Party in day-to-day management and to increase the authority of production managers and technical experts. Evidence from the late 1980s shows that the role of the Party had declined in state enterprises as a result of broad efforts at decentralization. Political study within factories and the monitoring of factory activities by Party activists, both of which were crucial to maintaining political dependence within state factories, had withered significantly. This withering process halted briefly with the Tiananmen crackdown but accelerated with the return to dominance of the economic reform agenda in the early 1990s, particularly in factories in the south-coastal areas.[8]

But although the Party's role on the shop floor has declined, Party cadres have not relinquished their authority in state enterprises easily.

7. Although there was some fluctuation in the Party's role in the Maoist era, and although the Party's role varied from factory to factory, it always played a central role. See Walder (1986), p. 98 n. 12; Schurmann (1968).

8. See Boisot and Guo (1991); Child and Xu (1991); Walder (1991), pp. 474–475; and O'Brien (1992).

They have often struggled to maintain their power through their continuing influence over personnel and benefits, or by accruing more technical skills themselves in order to legitimate their presence as line managers.[9] Despite evidence of some Party erosion in the late 1980s, it has remained an important institution within enterprises, and Party cadres have continued to hold top posts. Managers have continued to feel pressure to show loyalty to higher-level Party cadres for promotions and to rely on Party contacts in the supervising bureaucracy to carry out their jobs. After the 1989 government crackdown, moreover, Party secretaries in many enterprises were emboldened to reassert their traditional authority as well as some of the previous Maoist norms, suggesting that latent Party authority remains.[10]

The Party's role in the foreign sector is dramatically less than in state enterprises. In joint ventures, the Party presence has not been eliminated completely, but is quite weak. Where three or more Party members work in a JV, they are supposed to organize a Party cell and, as in state enterprises, carry out the work of the Party. Party members are to recruit and promote other cadres, guide political thought of workers and staff to guard against "bourgeois liberalization" (largely through political study), and ensure that the venture complies with Party and state policy. Although Party secretaries are not allowed as such to sit on JV boards of directors, they potentially have a voice there through the trade union, especially since the Party secretary is often simultaneously the trade union leader. As in state enterprises, moreover, managers in JV personnel departments are often Party members, and can inject political criteria into job promotion decisions.[11] Foreign investors and managers are excluded from participation in Party activities within the venture. The Party is therefore a clandestine organization within the JV, excluded

9. The 1984 Enterprise Law, which supposedly had as a central goal the reduction of CCP influence in management, was in fact quite ambiguous about the relative powers of Party cadres and managers in state-owned enterprises. This ambiguity is exemplified by the less-than-clear slogan that Party cadres should be the "core" and managers should be the "center."

10. On the continuing role of the Party, see Walder (1989), pp. 246–249; Chamberlain (1987); He (1990); and Yeung (1991). Information on the continuing Party role in state enterprises during the reform era was also provided in 1991 by a researcher at the China Enterprise Managers Association (CEMA). Walder (1991a) identifies a genuine erosion in Party power, but not the degree of independence found in the foreign sector.

11. Two managers in Beijing JVs felt that the Party remained active in personnel decisions. One felt that Party support of a manager was an absolute prerequisite for promotion, while the second thought that, although the Party did not "control" personnel matters, it "influenced" them.

from organizational charts and outside of the direct control of both (non-Party) Chinese and foreign management.[12]

Yet the Party role in JVs is substantially weaker than it would appear, given its formal role, and its influence has diminished steadily over time. Because the Party is not an open and acknowledged part of the JV organization, it is one step removed from the employees. Its authority is diluted by virtue of the fact that there is a competing, legitimate authority structure. Managers are publicly responsible only to the formal Chinese-foreign management partnership, and therefore can avoid Party sanctions that are inconsistent with the JV's objectives. As JVs have tried increasingly to manage themselves according to international practices, interference by Party members has come to be seen as an illegitimate intrusion. Party secretaries who are not supportive of joint ventures have been replaced. With the exception of a few JVs set up in the early 1980s, most have eschewed a full-time Party secretary. Any Party cadre working in the JV has to maintain a full-time "productive" job. Moreover, relatively little CCP activity is actually carried out in JVs. Some ventures, particularly some of those established in Guangdong Province or other southern coastal areas, have never established Party cells or have only very weak ones.[13] The same can be said of "greenfield" ventures that are created from scratch rather than through a merger with existing factories, since such ventures avoid inheriting extant Party organizations. Party activities in most other ventures tend to be minimal; as early as the mid-1980s, foreign managers in less than one-third of the JVs could identify any Party activity at all. The Party's voice also is not often heard through labor union representatives on boards of directors, since political study and Party cell meetings, when they are held, are generally conducted after working hours.[14]

There was an increase in Party activity following the government crackdown in June of 1989. Political study intensified in some (though

---

12. Internal (*neibu*) regulations from 1987, entitled "Interim Provisions Concerning Ideological and Political Work for Chinese Staff and Workers in Chinese-Foreign Equity and Cooperative Joint Ventures," established guidelines for political and ideological work in JVs. The Party's role is not discussed in public documents, or codified in public laws. Silence about the Party's role is meant to be consistent with the declaration in Chinese law that a JV is an "independent legal person." See Pearson (1991), pp. 186–191.

13. Party cells in JVs in the coastal areas (particularly in small JVs) tend to be even more productivity-oriented than in inland areas, and so are getting very weak.

14. When political study was held in JVs, Party members generally were careful that it did not threaten foreign interests. A smaller proportion of JV employees are Party members compared to state factories. One foreign-sector manager interviewed in 1991 reported that 1.5% of employees in his JV were Party members, whereas the figure may be closer to 5% in state enterprises.

by no means all) JVs, and a few ventures in which no Party cell had existed were directed to form one. The Chinese managers sometimes came under increased pressure from Party cadres to comply with the cadres' wishes, and grew more reluctant to take the initiative in decision-making than they had previously.[15] Yet, although they were wary of the repercussions of the leadership crackdown for foreign-backed business, Chinese managers routinely reported that they did not take the *content* of political study sessions particularly seriously. Some Chinese managers and Party secretaries in JVs even tried to minimize political study in order to avoid the possibility of flight by foreign companies.

Most of this political activity died down by 1991, and the pre-Tiananmen trend to de-politicize joint ventures continued. Chinese managers in JVs, including Party cadres, claimed political activity was minimal. Some political study remained, but it was seen by Chinese managers as a nuisance to be avoided rather than a threat. (Indeed, several managers interviewed in 1991 deliberately scheduled meetings outside the office on Saturday afternoons so that they could avoid political study sessions.) Many Chinese managers described—those from the south with pride, those from the north with envy—how JVs in Guangdong and the Special Economic Zones (SEZs) had succeeded in eliminating Party influence or activity.[16] By 1995, the Party was essentially absent from joint ventures.[17]

Chinese managers in wholly foreign-owned enterprises and representative offices all along have been quite unrestricted by Party reins. Because there is no Chinese state participation in these businesses, they need reserve no role, either open or clandestine, for the Party. Some foreign-sector managers working in WFOEs or ROs are at the same time Party members, of course. But they, as well as the non-Party foreign-sector managers who work with them, argue that Party members do not engage in any Party activities during work and make no effort to influence the business of the ROs or WFOEs. Party members say they have neither time nor reason to engage in political activity at work; Party members in ROs are expected to, and do, attend Party meetings *outside* the workplace. Non-Party managers in ROs, particularly in Beijing, are

15. Pearson (1990). Efforts to increase the Party presence in JVs and WFOEs after June 1989 are reflected in Liang (1990) and "Party to Increase Profile in Joint Ventures" (1990). These articles do not report on the effectiveness of such efforts, however.

16. An exception to this sentiment was voiced by one Shanghai JV manager who was himself a Party member. He felt the role the Party played, albeit small, was appropriate and useful. He did not contend that the CCP role should be enlarged, however.

17. Interviews from 1995.

expected to attend political study sessions at the Foreign Employee Service Corporation (FESCO) each week, usually on Saturday afternoons. If they breach Party rules of discipline they can, in theory, be made to answer to Party authorities in FESCO, though there is no evidence that this has ever happened.[18] FESCO also expects all employees during office hours to "volunteer" for public causes (such as two days of planting trees in the spring), just as state enterprises do. But even these extra-firm activities are minimal. Those who attended FESCO meetings regularly in the early 1990s—as in JVs, many managers tried to avoid them—reported that the content was normally light. There might be lectures or films with political content, but most meetings consisted of films designed more to entertain than to propagandize. FESCO may also organize "dance parties" or sporting events. Even these low levels of political activity are not sustained in the south. As one SEZ-based interviewee explained with regard to the prospect of "voluntary work," "The government is careful with the foreign businesses because if it asks employees in a foreign business to go for one or two days of voluntary work, the foreigners will fire the manager. So it does not issue such demands."

The Party profile is so low that Chinese managers in WFOEs and ROs frequently cannot identify Party members that may be present in their ranks. They further contend that a Party member who chooses to work in a WFOE or RO is unlikely to be a "conservative" who would hinder the business or make negative reports about other managers to an outside Party organization; because working for a foreign enterprise may be viewed as unpatriotic by older, more conservative Party members, cadres who depend upon these older members for their advancement within the Party are unlikely to risk compromising their Party credentials by joining a foreign business in the first place. Where they *can* identify Party members in their ROs and WFOEs, foreign-sector managers claim they are not intimidated by them. As one RO manager noted, "There may be a 'spy' here, but it's no problem. If they asked me why you were here talking to me, I'd just tell them the truth, and tell them that there is nothing wrong with it."

Thus, nearly all foreign-sector managers reported that they feel relatively "free" of Party influence. As one said, "We are not *completely* free. This is China! But foreign companies' offices are much more free.

---

18. Interviewees' reports of the expectation that they attend political study at FESCO are confirmed in Xi (1991).

Besides, I lived in a foreign country for [a few] months, and so I don't care [what the Party says]."

PERSONNEL DOSSIERS

Personnel dossiers have long been kept on every employee in Chinese enterprises. These dossiers have been yet another means by which the Party has secured political ties between employees and the state. Dossiers are usually maintained by the Party-dominated personnel department. In the Maoist era, these dossiers described an employee's occupational status, family background (including the family's designated class background), and any political distinctions (good or bad) of the employee. Any problems, including disciplinary problems, were duly recorded. The files were a source of social control, for to have a "black mark" in the file could have negative short- and long-term consequences. As Walder explains with regard to workers during the Maoist era,

The dossier stays with the worker throughout his or her life. If there is a transfer or job change, the file is transferred also. Workers have no rights to see their files, and there is a high degree of uncertainty over the eventual consequences of detrimental materials. The files are regularly consulted when reviewing candidates for promotions or raises, and they can even influence applications for housing, the severity of punishments for future transgressions or political offenses, or the selection of targets in political campaigns.[19]

Although the dossier system was changed somewhat in 1979, when information on class backgrounds was ordered to be removed from files, dossiers have remained a source of social control. The importance of dossiers was reiterated when, following the Tiananmen crackdown in 1989, the activities of student demonstrators were recorded in the files held at their universities, making it difficult for those who had participated to obtain favorable job assignments or be granted visas.

Chinese managers working in the foreign sector are not exempt from the need to have personnel dossiers. When Chinese managers are transferred to a JV following their companies' forming of a JV, the managers' dossiers remain bound up with and are influenced by the Chinese JV partner. In all JVs, moreover, the dossiers of Party members are kept separately from those of non-Party members. In these cases, managers

19. Walder (1986), p. 91.

therefore face a situation similar to, albeit less onerous than, that of state-sector managers because the Party may maintain a presence in the personnel department or have a special interest in controlling other Party members' dossiers. Yet the increasing numbers of foreign-sector managers hired independently by JVs, as well as all managers in ROs and WFOEs, have been able to distance themselves physically from their dossiers and from those Party officials who maintain them. This distancing is a result of the fact that foreign-sector manager dossiers *may* be, and in the case of ROs and WFOEs *must* be, held in Chinese organizations located outside the foreign company. These managers thus have become remote from the power the Party-state wields through the dossier system.[20]

Foreign-sector manager files not held at a joint venture may be deposited in one of four other types of units: FESCO (for ROs), state-owned companies, government ministries, or new talent exchange centers. In each case, the foreign business "borrows" (*jieyong*) the worker from the unit holding the dossier. Representative offices are required to hire personnel through FESCO. According to its original charter, FESCO provides employees from a pool selected according to certain criteria (primarily language and office management skills). FESCO holds the dossiers of these employees and, in theory, takes ultimate responsibility for the employees if they are fired. The foreign company pays the salary of the employee to FESCO, which in turn pays a portion of those funds to the employee as a basic wage. Increasingly since the mid-1980s, JVs, WFOEs, and FESCO (on behalf of ROs) have "borrowed" employees from state-owned companies or government ministries.[21] Often, these second units are former employers of the manager. One manager, for example, stored his dossier at the branch of the private computer company where he had worked previously, while another kept his dossier with his former state-owned paper company. In these and other cases, the former companies often were located, and hence the dossiers stored, in cities different from where the foreign-backed employer was located.[22] Managers are also able to place their files

---

20. It is illegal for ROs or WFOEs (which are technically "foreign firms," in contrast to JVs' status as "Chinese legal persons") to hold files.

21. By borrowing an employee from another unit, FESCO relieves itself of certain major responsibilities for the employee (e.g., provision of housing or, if they are fired from the foreign business, unemployment benefits). In Shanghai, 70% of those hired by foreign companies via FESCO are borrowed by FESCO from other units, and hence house their dossiers at these second units.

22. The *hukou*, or household registration, may also be in another city.

at companies where they have never worked. One placed his file with a state consulting firm run by his business school classmates, while another placed hers at a department in the agriculture ministry. In a third, rather unusual, case, a WFOE manager's file was held by his street committee; this manager was officially unemployed after having requested a discharge from a good position in the People's Liberation Army to work for a foreign business.

An outside unit can accept the dossier of a foreign-sector manager only if the unit has an unused employee quota. An outside unit is more likely to agree to hold a foreign-sector manager file if that person has personal connections (*guanxi*) with the unit. In the previously noted case of the female manager whose dossier was at the agriculture ministry, the placement was an informal arrangement based upon personal relations with a friend and was not bound by any contract. Or, as a computer company manager said of his arrangement with his former employer, "The man in charge there supports me." These units can benefit from holding the file of a person employed elsewhere. In the case again of the manager with agriculture ministry ties, the foreign employers agreed to pay a one-time "borrowing fee" of three to five times her new monthly salary. This fee, and presumably the funds allocated by quota to the ministry for her salary (but not actually paid to her), could then be put to other uses.

The final place outside the enterprise where foreign-sector managers may deposit personnel files is in talent exchange centers (*rencai jiaoliu zhongxin*), which were first set up in the late 1980s.[23] Managers may store files there indefinitely, or until they move them to another position. Foreign and domestic companies, including FESCO, can then "borrow" managers from the centers, which in the early 1990s charged between 25 and 100 yuan per month (between $4.75 and $19.00) as a basic storage fee.

Foreign-sector managers believe that to keep a file at a talent exchange center carries a degree of risk, largely because the centers are relatively new and because they do not offer the welfare, medical, housing, or retirement benefits that are provided by state enterprises. Some prefer other, more secure options, as in the case of the manager who placed her file with the agriculture ministry because it would "take care of her" if she lost her job at the RO. Still, there is no evidence that

23. University graduates and others who held "cadre" (*ganbu*) status at previous jobs may place their files at the talent exchange centers. "Labor exchange centers" provide similar functions for workers.

foreign-sector managers actually have been harmed by the potential risks of being cut loose from the state enterprise or government-bureau employment system. Because of their belief that the benefits associated with such placement of dossiers are worth any risks, then, many foreign-sector managers are willing to join the talent exchange center system. This attitude is suggested by the comment of a typical manager:

Mostly it is young people who have their files at the center. They are not worried about retirement; they think maybe they can earn enough at their current job [in the foreign sector] that they won't need state retirement benefits, or else they can try to go to a state enterprise [to get retirement benefits] later in life. Because [the centers] are young, there isn't much history to these issues. It is risky to have my file there, but I'm willing to take the risk. I don't see myself as especially brave.

Managers with files at talent exchange centers feel greater freedom from bureaucratic and political constraints than they would at state enterprises. As one put it:

Personnel files have become a lot less important to young people. To be at an exchange center is freeing. The exchange center is really just to help people. You just pay them 25 yuan per month to keep your file. They don't care what you do.

The roles of the organizations at which managers may deposit their dossiers have evolved. When FESCO was first established in the early 1980s, it was responsible for a wide range of control functions concerning employees of foreign firms. Over time, many of those functions have given way to fee-for-service functions. Thus, FESCO has evolved (and the talent exchange centers are set up deliberately) to focus more on providing services for which they can charge fees, such as housing dossiers and securing chops (stamps signifying approval), which are needed, for example, for passport applications. These organizations compete with each other for business. In the Shekou Special Industrial Zone, companies hiring foreign-sector managers who deposit their dossiers with the China Merchants Steam Navigation Company pay a general tax ($130 per year in the early 1990s) to cover a variety of services and insurance for benefits.[24]

---

24. The Shekou zone was founded in 1979 by China Merchants (*Zhongguo lunchuan zhaoshang ju*), a state investment company that administers the Shekou zone from its base in Hong Kong. It has enacted some of the most market-oriented policies in China. China Merchants had its origins in a Republican-era company of the same name.

Thus, foreign-sector managers with files stored at secondary locations are released from an important constraint: their personnel files are kept away from their places of work at locations where the focus is on collecting fees and where the managers spend little or no time. Moreover, their foreign employers have virtually no interest in the contents of these dossiers and are often unaware of the very existence of dossiers.

JOB MOBILITY

The physical distancing of foreign-sector managers from their dossiers has gone hand-in-hand with increased job mobility. The opportunity to job switch in the foreign sector contrasts markedly with the generally poor labor mobility that has existed since the 1950s and continues to prevail in the state sector.[25] Upon leaving high school or university, young people normally are allocated employment by the state. Rather than using a labor market that takes into account employee preferences and talents, job allocation is made according to the priorities of planners, who try to place employees in work units with unfilled employment quotas. Once assigned to the state sector, it is difficult to change jobs within the state sector—the negative side of the job security associated with this system. The relative lack of employee-initiated turnover results from a number of factors. Workers and managers in the state sector have had, historically, the highest level of wages and benefits in urban China, making state-sector jobs highly desirable. With job switching, job seniority is lost, and the state generally will not assign an employee to a second job in the prime state sector. Leaving a prime job therefore usually leads to a lower living standard, since it forces an employee to move to the less generous collective sector. Those lucky enough to be assigned jobs in the state sector are therefore reluctant to leave them. Employees are able in rare cases to transfer (*diaodong*) jobs, but transfers usually occur at the initiative and discretion of the organization, not the employee, and tend to be within the boundaries of one administrative "system" (*xitong*), such as between factories under one ministry. Even if skilled workers or managers can find comparable state enterprises willing to take them, it is often difficult to gain the necessary cooperation of the original factories' directors *and* the supervisory offices for both the old and new employer to transfer their dossiers.

25. On labor allocation and labor mobility in the Mao and post-Mao eras, see Davis (1990, 1992); Lin and Bian (1991); Walder (1986), pp. 71–72; and Alexander Eckstein (1977), pp. 101–104, 139–145.

Recognizing the costs of this system to production and to individual aspirations, reformers took steps to increase job mobility beginning in the early 1980s. It was hoped that a number of the reform policies—decentralization of hiring authority to factories, enhanced authority of line management over Party cadres, sanctioning of the private and foreign sectors, and greater flexibility in wage and bonus scales—would provide incentives for a more flexible allocation of labor. New institutions and procedures were set up to further encourage mobility. Enterprises looking for new staff can now hire through talent exchange centers. Employees are allowed to take temporary unpaid leaves of absence (*tingxin liuzhi*) to move to other factories. Individuals may also apply directly for jobs. The top graduates at the elite universities may be recruited by selected employers, and, in 1995, 90% of college graduates were made responsible for finding jobs on their own. There are plans for easing the household registration system, permitting the freer flow of people between cities.[26]

These reforms have led to some increase in job mobility.[27] However, they have not produced a true labor market. As of 1987, annual turnover of technical and professional staff averaged a mere 3%.[28] As of 1989, annual turnover was less than 2% in the state sector as a whole, and over half of the changes were due to retirements.[29] Higher mobility has remained elusive for a number of reasons. There is reluctance among many central and local officials to move to a full-fledged labor market, in part because of fears of labor unrest caused by rural migration to the cities. Moreover, there are disincentives for factory directors to let go of employees; particularly as enterprises have been pressed to become more efficient, directors are loath to release talented managers, especially if the directors have invested in managers' training. Compounded by the need for multiple permissions to transfer dossiers, the negative incentives for hoarding labor have stifled the ambitions of many of the best

26. On these various policies, see Davis (1990, 1992); Bian (1994); *China Youth Daily* (1995); and "China to Abolish City Hu-Kou (Two-Tier Registration) System" (1994).

27. In addition, for white-collar workers, mobility also often has meant emigrating from China. Rural workers have migrated to cities or emigrated completely from their towns or villages, often without the permission of their *danwei* (unit) authorities. On the other hand, some émigrés have reported that their *danwei* actively encouraged their departure. Brick (1993).

28. There was some increase in job turnover in certain areas in the early 1980s, but this trend reversed itself after 1984. Davis (1990), pp. 86–88.

29. Davis (1992), p. 1066.

employees. Even if college graduates can choose their own first jobs, administrative barriers to job transfers continue to affect them. Talent exchange centers do not completely solve the mobility problem either, again because the need for multiple permissions opens the possibility for vetoes at each stage. The continuing role of state enterprises as providers of key benefits, particularly housing, also creates disincentives for workers and managers to try to take advantage of the new rules.[30] The key to changing jobs within the state sector continues to be the use of *guanxi* with well-placed cadres.[31]

The situation is significantly different in the foreign sector; managers there have shown a surprising, and in some cases extreme, degree of job mobility.[32] It is quite common to find managers who have moved, from the government or state-sector jobs to which they had been assigned, to foreign-backed enterprises where they have been hired independently or via FESCO, and then perhaps to yet another foreign enterprise. In contrast to the state sector, such movement among foreign-sector managers is usually at the initiative of the manager, who is sometimes lured away by the middlemen of executive-level labor markets, "headhunters." Moves outside a given geographical area are not uncommon. This new mobility appears greatest in the coastal areas, particularly in the SEZs, and in Shenzhen. In one extreme case, a Shekou-based foreign-sector manager moved jobs on his own initiative five times in less than three years, after completing a graduate-level business degree. He anticipated that he would continue to move until he landed his ideal job as senior manager of a JV or WFOE. More generally, pools of middle-level managers are beginning to appear in Beijing, Shanghai, and Shenzhen, since those with some formal training are making their way to these areas in

---

30. Davis (1990), pp. 89–106, and Davis (1992), p. 1066. Other odd incentives exist as well. For example, after 1987, factories were allowed to redistribute wages of workers who had transferred among the other employees. As a result, units resisted taking new employees unless they could bring their wage quotas with them—something that old enterprises were highly unlikely to permit. Alternatively, supervisors were known to refuse to give the day off to employees taking exams for further education, or to refuse to release employees who received further training, even if the unit could no longer use them (Davis [1990], pp. 92–93). Davis argued in 1990 (p. 87) that there remained a deep-seated hostility toward the idea of a labor market; labor continued to be seen as an asset to be deployed, as the state would an army. By 1992 (p. 1084), however, she had seen some erosion in this view even though other of the barriers to increased mobility discussed here remained.

31. Davis (1992) and Bian (1994).

32. Increasing mobility for the floating population—another new economic group but a mass-level one—has been documented in Solinger (1991), pp. 15–16.

search of attractive jobs.[33] Foreign-sector managers expect that they will be able to move once again for better jobs, sometimes even to the state sector, if an appropriate job is offered. The direction of mobility for foreign-sector managers is almost always upward.

Job mobility in the foreign sector has been possible because of the relatively greater ability of foreign-backed firms to hire managers independently (rather than having them assigned) and the increasing frequency of job borrowing.[34] As a result, foreign-sector managers often find jobs on their own, and then arrange the transfer of dossiers. Even representative offices, which must hire personnel through FESCO, have been allowed increasingly to identify those managers they would like to hire, and FESCO in turn borrows those managers from their original units.[35] Mobility also has been encouraged by the establishment of the more neutral repositories (i.e., talent exchange centers) for dossiers, which earn fees when job switching occurs. For example, in Shekou, where China Merchants holds all dossiers, foreign-sector managers may change jobs among any of the two hundred companies located in the zone without obtaining permission. Managers there find this feature very attractive, particularly insofar as they believe that the zone administration will not force them to move to another company within the zone against their will.

This is not to say that the mobility of foreign-sector managers is without hindrance. Managers working in state-owned enterprises who wish to take a job in the foreign sector still may face resistance from superiors in their state enterprises. Intra-region or intra-city transfers that require permission from local authorities still can be difficult. In such cases, managers may rely for transfers on the strength of their relationships with their superiors or with local officials.[36] Nonetheless, foreign-sector managers have greatly reduced the obstacles to mobility.

33. Borgonjon and Vanhonacker (1992), p. 18; and 1995 interviews.

34. Laws formally guarantee JVs and WFOEs the ability to hire personnel independently, such as through newspaper advertisements and university recruiting. See, e.g., the 1983 Implementing Act for the Law of the People's Republic of China on Joint Ventures Using Chinese and Foreign Investment (*Zhonghua renmin gongheguo zhong wai hezi jingying qiye fa shishi tiaoli*). Foreign JV partners continue to complain of some pressure to take on staff from the Chinese partner, but the pressure has declined in recent years.

35. After the 1989 crackdown, some foreign managers reported that FESCO temporarily was more resistant to taking such suggestions. This was less likely due to politics than a reaction to the contraction of many ROs, a phenomenon that expanded the rolls of unemployed FESCO personnel and made FESCO more desperate to have ROs hire off of these lists.

36. A 1992 survey of JVs and WFOEs found that 80% were able to transfer some employees (presumably including both workers and managers) without problems, but half

SOCIAL WELFARE BENEFITS

In China, as in the former Soviet Union, employees have relied upon the state-owned enterprise for the distribution of goods, benefits, and services needed for daily living, including housing, ration coupons, subsidized foods, clothing and shoes for work, medical care, child care, and pensions. These benefits have constituted the "iron rice bowl." Alternative means for obtaining these benefits have been few, creating a socio-economic dependence of employees on the state enterprise. Employees also have been personally dependent upon their superiors, who have wide discretion in determining the allocation of many of these benefits. Within state enterprises, a worker's display (*biaoxian*) of correct behavior and thought has been crucial in determining promotions, bonus levels, and the allocation of benefits. Although the criteria by which *biaoxian* is measured have shifted over time—from adherence to broad ideological doctrine during much of the 1960s and 1970s, to loyalty as displayed by devotion to the Party and to the principle of hard work during the 1980s—the need for employees to be concerned about *biaoxian* has been central in state enterprises.[37]

As part of its urban reform program, the government has engaged in initial planning to relieve the burden of social welfare payments for benefits from itself onto the urban population. For example, new entrants to the state and collective sectors in urban areas (who are generally hired under contracts) have been required to contribute to their medical and labor insurance funds, and in some locations officials have required workers to contribute to their own pensions.[38] The government also has begun to allow the market to provide alternative sources of benefits.

Nonetheless, by the mid-1990s the government had not moved very far to break its monopoly on the provision of social services. Indeed, some aspects of the "iron rice bowl," far from being eroded under the reforms, have been strengthened for urban state-sector workers; well into the reform era, employees in state enterprises remained dependent upon the enterprise. For example, price subsidies provided with urban

---

reported that problems had arisen in some cases. One-third reported that they had to compensate the employee's work unit an average of 1,000 yuan ($190) (Frisbie and Brecher [1992], p. 25). Obstacles to transferring from the state sector to foreign businesses became somewhat greater after 1989, as it became necessary to obtain an even stronger endorsement from the original unit in order to change jobs.

37. Walder (1986), pp. 59–67, 137–143, and 228–238.

38. The contributions have generally been small, and the system has not spread to the largest state units. See Davis (1989), p. 588; and China News Agency (1993).

wages rose dramatically after 1978, and especially after 1986. The explosion of enterprise revenues spent for housing (rather than reinvestment) during the 1980s is another example of how much the unit remains the center of employee benefits and—directors hope—employee loyalty. It also illustrates both how workers resist the erosion of these benefits and the pressure they are able to bring to bear on their managers. The potential for enhancing the structural autonomy of state-sector employees through the commodification of social welfare is therefore far from being realized.[39]

Joint ventures share certain similarities with state enterprises in terms of the structure and level of benefit distribution. The Chinese government generally has insisted that the benefits provided by JVs be at least up to the standard found in comparable state enterprises. Consequently, wages paid to workers and managers often contain not only a basic wage but also a hefty package of benefits to be financed through profit contributions to various welfare funds.[40] The level of benefits actually provided to JV managers, particularly housing, varies among ventures. As in the state sector, managers not infrequently are discontented with what is offered them, particularly in terms of housing. One middle-level Chinese JV manager, for example, complained that he and his wife were forced to share a tiny apartment with another couple. Couples with one spouse employed in a JV often try to be sure the other remains in a state enterprise in order to ensure high-level and secure benefits in case the JV should falter. A lack of adequate housing can cause JVs difficulty in recruiting talented managers.[41]

Although Chinese JV managers still rely upon the venture to obtain benefits, there are two crucial differences from state enterprises. First,

39. See Walder (1989), pp. 244, 250–252; Davis (1989). Yanjie Bian has observed that workers who benefited the most from reforms cared much less about the decline in their benefits. Still, the majority of disadvantaged workers oppose the erosion of the "iron rice bowl" (Letter, 8 July 1993).

40. As in state enterprises, the packet of benefits may exceed the amount of the basic wage. There has been some innovation in the channels through which JVs provide benefits, however. Medical care, for example, may be provided under contract with a hospital or insurance company, or arranged through the JV's clinic. See Casati (1991), pp. 18–22. On JV benefits, see also National Council for U.S.-China Trade (1987), p. 162; and Wang, Xu, and Zhou (1984), p. 295.

41. JVs that hire employees from the Chinese partner are generally able to use the partner's existing housing stock for JV employees. But as employees are increasingly hired independently, the provision of housing has become a problem. In response, some JVs have bought, built, or rented housing for at least some of their employees, while others rely upon the employees to arrange their own housing. See Frisbie (1992), pp. 26–27.

the enterprise upon which a foreign-sector manager depends is, by definition, rooted partly in the foreign domain and hence is removed from the Chinese state. Second, foreign businesses, particularly since the mid-1980s, increasingly have incorporated foreign models of personnel management that attempt to standardize benefits systems and eliminate employees' personalistic reliance upon superiors. For example, the general manager of a Shekou JV described with pride his efforts to institute a system that ties wages and bonuses to production-based criteria and ignores employees' attitudes and politics. Even in the sensitive area of housing, foreign-sector companies are increasingly providing housing loans rather than the domains themselves.[42]

Foreign-sector managers who work in WFOEs and, especially, in ROs are even less dependent than JV managers for the provision by the state of social welfare benefits. In contrast to state-owned enterprises, neither talent exchange centers nor FESCO are able to use their authority to distribute benefits in order to discriminate, based on *biaoxian*, between loyal and problematic employees. Talent centers are simply not in the business of deciding bonuses or benefits. FESCO's capacity in this respect is also weak. It is to distribute a "foreign service bonus" to managers it judges to be "good" employees—for example, employees who regularly attend Saturday afternoon political study sessions. In theory, this bonus is to be awarded flexibly, which opens the possibility of discrimination based on *biaoxian*. In practice, however, this bonus amounts to a maximum of only 50 yuan ($9.60 in 1991) per year (distributed quarterly). Foreign-sector managers in ROs, who typically earn at least twenty times this amount each month, consider it to be a trivial portion of their overall salary, rendering the disciplinary function of the FESCO bonus meaningless.

Benefits are provided to RO and WFOE managers through a variety of channels. For many foreign-sector managers, benefits are allocated from outside the enterprise. At one extreme, the Shekou zone administration provides benefits to foreign-sector managers working there, if requested by the manager. (The fee was $22.40 per month in 1991.) Outside of this special area, and hence more commonly, RO managers whose personnel files are held by FESCO obtain some benefits from the

---

42. Bulman (1994). Provision of cash for housing is not universal, however. A very successful manager in Shanghai spent much time and enthusiasm showing plans for the housing he was having built for employees out of company profits. On attempts to incorporate "standardized" benefit distribution systems generally in JVs, see Pearson (1991), pp. 173–176.

practice. FESCO passes on to the manager a portion of the salary channeled to it by the foreign company.[43] It then allocates a portion of the
remainder to cover medical expenses, bonuses and commissions, pen-
sion funds, and, occasionally, housing.[44] If a FESCO-employed manager is fired by a foreign company, FESCO is obliged to continue to provide a base salary, but does not cover the bonus—which can be 5 to 10%
of the annual base salary—that had been paid by the foreign business.[45]
For both Shekou foreign-sector managers, then, and for those under the
direct responsibility of FESCO, while benefits are reasonably certain,
they are provided by government organs outside the workplace.

When FESCO borrows a Chinese manager from a second Chinese
company, benefits are less certain. FESCO is not obliged to provide any
housing or medical care to those managers it borrows. Rather, the second company or the foreign employer is, in theory, to provide these benefits. Foreign-sector managers borrowed in this way sometimes worry
that they cannot rely upon a company they do not work for directly for
the same level of care as it gives full-time, in-house employees. This concern is legitimate. For example, one RO manager who had been borrowed from a second unit by FESCO had to pay for his own medical
care. More generally, while FESCO is to pay a second company a pen-
sion contribution, the firmness of this guarantee has not been tested,
since foreign-sector managers in this situation generally have not
reached pensionable age. Managers with their files in talent exchange
centers are in a still more precarious state when it comes to the provision of benefits, for there is no expectation that the centers will provide
medical care or housing. The manager mentioned previously, whose file
was held by his street committee, also had no benefits provided by the
state. Moreover, managers who are borrowed from talent centers and
are subsequently fired have no chance of gaining unemployment benefits, or a new job, from the center.

43. In the late 1980s and early 1990s, the "return rate" passed back from FESCO to
the manager was only about 10% to 20%. In the mid-1990s, competition among employment services for scarce skilled labor has driven up the percentage to 45%, with some managers regaining as much as 70% of the fee paid FESCO by foreign businesses. See Bulman
(1994).

44. Xi (1991) confirms the reports of interviewees on this subject. FESCO is unable
to provide housing to many of its employees. This payment system and the fact that
FESCO makes some profit off of its employees are two reasons for the nearly universal
disdain in which the agency is held by Chinese employees.

45. The yearly bonus or "commission" in the early 1990s was 10% of the base salary
in Beijing, and in Shanghai was 6% the first year, rising to 9% after the third year.

This system of being provided benefits is clearly a mixed one for Chinese managers in ROs and WFOEs. On the one hand, a secure "iron rice bowl" does not exist for them and most of their benefits must come from sources they perceive as a less reliable (because they believe defaults or layoffs to be more likely) foreign employer. The "safety net" of those with dossiers at talent exchange centers or elsewhere is most fragile. Often, these managers end up relying upon their families for support, especially for housing.[46] Some foreign-sector managers are uncomfortable with this insecurity (though this was the case for even fewer managers interviewed in 1995 than in 1991). On the other hand, the provision of benefits from outside the enterprise has weakened socioeconomic dependence upon the state-dominated firm and personal dependence upon superiors within the firm. Even though many of these managers continue to depend upon the state for benefits, this dependence is qualitatively less than that of their counterparts in state enterprises because the organization that distributes benefits (FESCO or a second company) is located away from their primary place of work. Over time, furthermore, alternative sources of benefits have appeared, making it less risky for foreign-sector managers to turn away from state-supported benefits. The relatively high salaries paid directly to managers in WFOEs often include cash payments to be used to cover social welfare needs. Similarly, ROs may pay their managers huge fees "under the table"—i.e., circumventing FESCO—to cover benefits.[47] Managers can then use such payments to arrange for housing and medical care on what is a very small but growing market for these goods. For example, two managers interviewed in 1991 had purchased apartments, one in Beijing and one in Shekou. Others rented or sublet apartments independent of their workplace (in some cases state apartments, the subletting of which is illegal). Foreign-sector managers who have no state-provided medical care earn enough to pay for medical care. Even as they rely on their foreign employer to subsidize or insure them for medical care, the line of dependence is to an enterprise that is independent from the Chinese Party-state.

46. Solinger (1991, p. 20) documents a parallel reliance upon the family among the floating population. For a discussion of the lower level of benefits provided in many foreign-backed enterprises, see Chen Yulin (1990), pp. 23–24; and Chen Yaoxing (1990), pp. 2–5.

47. The Beijing government made an effort in early 1991 to tax such direct payments. On a monthly salary of 3,500 yuan paid to FESCO, the fee paid directly to the manager might be 2,000 yuan ($385). See McGregor (1991).

Thus, most foreign-sector managers in representative offices and wholly foreign-owned firms, who are relatively young and see alternatives, have chosen a riskier route in exchange for the chance to earn higher salaries, travel abroad, and manage relatively free of Chinese state authority. While they would prefer to have secure benefits, they are willing to break the "iron rice bowl" in exchange for the other advantages they perceive will come from working in the foreign sector.

・　　・　　・　　・

In the foreign sector, economic reform and the foreign business presence have clearly broken "organized dependence." The non-existence or weakness of Party organizations and activity in many foreign businesses eliminates or greatly reduces the political dependence of managers on the Party structure within the enterprise. So, too, does the establishment of institutions and practices (such as talent exchange centers and the legitimacy of job borrowing) that allow managers freedom from their dossiers. The greater job mobility of foreign-sector managers, encouraged by new dossier repositories, reduces their economic and personal dependence on one lifelong, state-sponsored employer. Similarly, the wresting of responsibility for providing social welfare benefits from supervisors who have broad discretion and are located within the enterprise, plus an enhanced ability to exchange the managers' higher salaries for benefits on a growing market, weakens the economic and personal dependence of those managers on the state. Although reforms have begun to affect the state sector in ways that cannot be ignored (such as reducing the role of the Party and providing limited means for job mobility), the degree of structural autonomy offered in the foreign sector clearly has not been met.

Although the greater autonomy of the foreign sector is unambiguous, it is important to emphasize that there is variation between different types of foreign enterprise. The contrasts with state enterprises are even more pronounced for ROs and WFOEs than for JVs. Unsurprisingly, the lack of direct state participation in or ownership of an enterprise has translated into greater autonomy. Regional variation is also apparent. The independence of foreign-sector managers is even more striking in the SEZs and in other coastal areas than in Beijing, particularly as concerns the role of the Party and job mobility. Moreover, despite the breakdown or absence of many of the *formal* institutions of "organized dependence" in the foreign sector, *informal* personal clientelism remains important. When transferring their dossiers from state enterprises or government units or, once they are working at a foreign business, in the course of routine dealings with government officials, managers often feel they need to "grease the wheels" of the approval process by giving, in their words, "small gifts" or doing "small favors" for their superiors or officials. These small signs of clientelism become amplified when examining the political behavior of foreign-sector managers, as is done in chapter 4.

Views of Foreign-Sector Managers toward Economic Reform and Political Change

Does China's new business elite express a degree of ideological autonomy that is on a par with its structural autonomy? The most influential literatures on the national bourgeoisie in developing countries—class-based analyses of dependency and bureaucratic authoritarianism that are based primarily on studies in Latin America—contend that the views of the business elite are likely to be aligned with the interests of an authoritarian state and the "international bourgeoisie." The local bourgeoisie is a "junior partner" to foreign capital, the norms and values of which are introduced by multi-national corporations which enter into direct investment or in other ways have contact with the bourgeoisie.[48]

This depiction of the ideology of the business elite in the developing world has been modified in more recent works. The theory of "post-imperialism" contends that the business elite, more than a mere pawn of international capital, is a modern, technocratic elite that possesses high levels of education and expertise. Although members of the national bourgeoisie are able to distinguish between those ties to foreign state/companies which are useful to their country's development and those which are not, the members of the business elite nevertheless have

---

48. Dependency theories, which are based on Lenin's (1939) theory of imperialism, were until recently the most concerted efforts to analyze the interests and ideology of the Third World business elite. See, e.g., Cardoso and Faletto (1978); Palma (1978). Evans (1979) depicts a "triple alliance" between the state, national bourgeoisie, and international capital, implying that the state is itself controlled by international capital. O'Donnell's (1973) model of bureaucratic authoritarianism carried similar assumptions. Consistent with these views developed for Latin America are arguments that late-Qing and Republican-era compradors were "anti-China," arguments that often were made by communist authorities and intellectuals in China during the early reform period.

been strongly influenced by the norms of international capitalism, and are not unalterably opposed to democratization.[49] Evidence from Brazil also suggests that the ideology of members of the business elite often diverges from that of the authoritarian state, and that, in opposition to the state's dominant ideology, industrialists under certain conditions support democratization.[50]

We shall see in the case of China that the ideology of foreign-sector managers is consistent with the basic expectations set by the more recent literature on business ideology in Latin America. China's foreign-sector managers have been strongly influenced by their contacts with foreigners and often by these managers' experiences abroad. Their views often diverge from and, in terms of both politics and economics, are decidedly more liberal than the dominant views expressed in official policy. A minority, however, are true "democratizers."

VIEWS OF ECONOMIC REFORM

Foreign-sector managers' views about economic reform in important ways are independent from the dominant ideology and policy of the reformist state. Their views are more market-oriented—and they favor change that goes farther—than the policies of the early and mid-1990s. There is some regional variance; managers working in the SEZs of Guangdong Province and in Hong Kong are more reformist than those working in other areas. But managers' views do not range across a wide spectrum. Attitudes toward the need for more extensive economic reform than what had occurred as of the first half of the 1990s ranged from mildly to vehemently in favor of far-reaching marketization of the economy.[51]

Foreign-sector managers see a need for broad changes in the economy, the most crucial of which are the introduction of significantly more

49. See Sklar (1976); Becker (1983). Nationalist sentiments are likely to intensify as this elite develops and defines itself more clearly.

50. Payne (1994), in one of the few studies on the ideology of members of the business elite in developing countries, finds that in Brazil, a large subset of industrialists supported democratization of the regime in the 1980s.

51. See appendix 2 for a description of the interviews on which this analysis is based. Some reformers in the central government, and in certain localities—particularly in Guangdong and Fujian—undoubtedly hold views similar to those of foreign-sector managers. Managers' views are measured against policy that actually was in force in the early 1990s.

market forces into the Chinese economy than existed in the first half of the 1990s. They desire much greater competition—competition among enterprises, among people, and with other countries.[52] While acknowledging that some competition has been fostered by the reforms, they believe it should be much more extensive. They favor vastly greater enterprise autonomy in the state sector. Significantly, in light of what we will see is their extensive reliance upon clientelism, they claim they would prefer less dependence upon personal "relationships" in doing business. The pace of these changes should be orderly, but swift. Some managers also emphasize the need to change the way people think, saying that updating "software" (ideology, behavior, etc.) is more crucial for producing lasting change than updating hardware (technology and equipment).

Foreign-sector managers interviewed in 1991 made few direct calls for private ownership; they tended to frame their views about the need for change in terms of increased marketization rather than the private ownership of capitalism. Even these opinions, however, were somewhat vague. For example, one JV manager in Beijing specified that socialist ownership should remain dominant in China, but when asked to identify a model for change suggested what he termed the "market socialism" of (capitalist) West Germany! By 1995, foreign-sector managers had become more committed to privatization, but were also more sophisticated about its dangers. Many argued strongly that privatization of enterprises was not only good but necessary for China if economic development were to continue. They worried about the drag placed on the economy by inefficient state-owned enterprises. At the same time, they believed that privatization should occur slowly and—in a fashion typical of post-1949 policy-making in China—should be allowed to happen in practice before being announced as national policy. To announce such a change would raise the opposition of conservatives in the Party and of local officials who would bear the brunt of the impact of increased

---

52. Foreign-sector managers hold this belief in extensive competition, as well as in the value of foreign ties, in common with Shanghai's economic intellectuals writing in the 1980s. (Many of these writers had links to the reformers in the Party-state or were themselves "state intellectuals," and yet most of their ideas were more radical than those adopted by Party reformers.) See Edmond Lee (1991). Foreign-sector managers, in some respects, were more radical than the Shanghai intellectuals in that they cited as models for change the countries of Western Europe or the U.S., whereas the intellectuals often cited the hybrid market socialist systems of Hungary and Yugoslavia. (Both groups also sometimes looked to Taiwan and the other "dragons" of East Asia for models.)

unemployment. More importantly, to move too rapidly toward privatization would provoke social unrest. On this point the 1995 interviewees
were nearly unanimous: a "Soviet-style" program of rapid privatization
would prove disastrous. A safety net of social security would need to be
in place before such a change should be contemplated.[53]

Foreign-sector managers are more specific about reforms they wish
to see applied to the foreign sector itself. They feel that the "open" policy in general should be expanded as much as possible. When speculating about changes that should be made at a high level of policy, many—
especially those working in JVs—think foreign businesses should be
allowed to sell more of what they produce in the domestic Chinese market rather than being forced to export. They often link this view to their
more general advocacy of competition. The suggestion for increased
domestic sales is also consistent with the desire of many foreign
investors.[54] Managers in 1991 also complained about the related difficulty in gaining access to foreign exchange; they believed that the Chinese yuan should be freely convertible. Those interviewed in 1995
approved of the rapid (if controlled) steps the government had taken in
recent years toward convertibility, not only because these steps were
introducing another market element to China, but also because they
ended the need for foreign-backed enterprises to balance their foreign
exchange accounts, thus freeing them from the need to export.[55] Managers further desire liberalized import- and export-licensing requirements and the ability to make direct contacts with suppliers/end-users
rather than being forced to go through foreign trade corporations at the
ministerial level.[56]

Although foreign-sector managers believe that broad reforms such as
domestic sales and currency convertibility are important, their most pas-
sionate complaints concern narrow problems they face when conduct-

53. It was striking how frequently fears of social unrest by workers and immigrants to
cities were expressed by members of the business elite.

54. Most foreign investors prefer domestic sales rather than exports so that they can
crack the untapped market in China, and can avoid undercutting their exports from other
bases in Asia. See Pearson (1991), pp. 31–34.

55. During the first half of the 1990s the government devalued the yuan to close to
the point where most economists believed it would fall under a freely convertible regime.
Nonetheless, foreign exchange balancing requirements for foreign enterprises were not
lifted.

56. Although there were some moves to reduce the role of foreign trade corporations
in the mid-1980s, their role was revived in the late 1980s and early 1990s. Interviewees
were reacting to this revival in 1991.

ing day-to-day business. Many managers want the Chinese government to issue exit visas more easily so they can travel freely on business; they miss important business opportunities abroad because it routinely takes several months for a visa to be issued. Other widespread complaints, particularly among RO managers, concern personnel issues. Foreign-sector managers in ROs resent that they must hire employees—and be hired themselves—through FESCO, and they resent administrative barriers to free hiring (even though these barriers are much lower than in the state sector).

The most radically reformist attitude toward economic reform concerns what foreign-sector managers see in the international economy that they do *not* want China to adopt. For the most part, managers see virtually *nothing* in the operation of the world market that they would reject as inappropriate for China. One mentioned that not all Western management methods are appropriate to China at this time; she pointed out that economic forecasting is not much use, for example, because Chinese managers cannot obtain the data necessary to carry it out. Only a small minority of managers believe that certain behaviors, goods, and values they perceive as "foreign" to China (such as drugs, lax sexual norms, and prostitution) should not be allowed in China. Interestingly, this view was voiced with greatest frequency among managers working in Guangzhou and the SEZs, where such behaviors are apparently more widespread. But these characteristics are not central to, or even necessarily related to, the operation of market economies. In general, then, foreign-sector managers place virtually no limits on foreign participation in the Chinese economy.

Two further points about foreign-sector managers' views of economic reform should be noted. First, two managers, both of whom do substantial business through the government, recognized that greater reliance on markets could hurt their businesses, for it would force them to find new marketing and supply channels and would prevent them from drawing on established connections in the planned economy. Yet these managers nonetheless were highly supportive of further marketization. This suggests that more than narrow self-interest can underlie the desire for reforms. Second, when asked whether their views are shared by other managers in the foreign sector, most interviewees responded positively. Many believe, moreover, that their views are common among young people. But they also believe that state enterprise managers are less reformist than they themselves are, citing the fact that foreign-sector managers usually rely more on a well-functioning market than do state enterprise managers, who still can depend on quotas for inputs and sales. For the same reason, foreign-sector managers believe state enterprise managers are likely to be more protectionist in their views of international trade.[57]

Thus, the predominant views of foreign-sector managers toward economic reform mark them as a group that favors change beyond what is embodied in extant policies, and beyond what is desired by their counterparts in the much less autonomous state sector. Although their greatest passion is reserved for narrow problems, such as personnel and visa issues, they also would like to see broad-based reforms that will take China much farther down the road to a market economy.

VIEWS OF THE PARTY-STATE AND POLITICAL REFORM

As with their views of economic reform, foreign-sector managers hold strong opinions about political life in China and exhibit independence from state policy in their views about the Party-state. Most favor greater change than what was being mentioned in the official agenda in the first half of the 1990s.

A small minority of interviewees took the opportunity to express positive views of the Party and the government, although they uniformly agreed that Party influence should be absent from operations (if not all personnel matters) in foreign-backed enterprises. Unsurprisingly, those in this minority were themselves Party members. In contrast, most foreign-sector managers, particularly those who work in representative offices and in wholly foreign-owned businesses, are hostile to what they call "politics," a label that for them includes political study and interference in business by political campaigns and hostile officials. High-level managers in ROs and WFOEs claim routinely and with pride that they do not allow politics to enter into business. A Shekou general manager, for example, boasted of how he ignored telephone calls from government officials inquiring into his activities. Some (non-Party) foreign-sector managers, especially those interviewed in 1995, expressed direct hostility toward the Party itself, with several saying, simply, "I don't like

57. The opinions of foreign-sector managers about their state-sector counterparts are consistent with survey data showing that, despite support among state-owned enterprise managers for some degree of enterprise autonomy, many directors wish to maintain their protected relationships with supervising bureaus, and are reluctant to support radical reforms that might increase enterprise autonomy. See O'Brien (1992).

the Party."[58] Many foreign-sector managers choose jobs in foreign businesses precisely in order to escape "politics," with several citing this as the primary reason for their job choice.

Anti-Party sentiment among foreign-sector managers is unsurprising, for a number of them had been affected adversely by the Cultural Revolution. Those who are children of intellectuals or managers often suffered discrimination along with their families, while others were themselves old enough to have been sent to the countryside or to have their educations interrupted during the Cultural Revolution. One manager, who had been active in the 1980–81 district elections while a student in Beijing and whose political behavior had caused him difficulty in finding employment upon graduation, reported that he no longer wished to talk about politics. Younger managers in their late twenties and thirties often were similarly hostile to politics. Many who had been in China's top- and middle-tier universities during the 1989 student protests expressed strong disillusionment with the government as a result of that experience.

At the same time as they expressed intense dislike of politics, foreign-sector managers were reluctant to talk about their views on the desirability of political *change*. However, even those who are not openly critical of the government and who are concerned that dramatic change could bring dislocation and chaos believe that far-reaching reform should come about. Many 1995 interviewees who favored some liberalization (but not democratization) believed that change could occur with a generational shift in the government. They expected such a change to occur when younger people, with more experience in the West or with Western ideas, gain access to political positions, and as the interests of those managers with experience in the private and foreign sector come to be channeled into the government.[59]

A minority of foreign-sector managers said explicitly that they favor greater "democratization" of the political system in China. Those who most freely discussed political change, and had the most radical views about what is needed (including "democratization"), tended to be from

58. Other informants who were not themselves foreign-sector managers but have extensive contacts with them claimed that virtually all foreign-sector managers are fundamentally "anti-Party."

59. This view that change would come about as a result of the growing influence of business interests was ironic given the fact, explored further in ch. 4, that these people themselves were uninterested in and pessimistic about presenting their views to the government.

the south. Two interviewees from Shekou in particular noted with enthusiasm that local candidates for office have at times held open forums at which they had to respond to questions, such as how they would handle unemployment, or why they appeared to live better lives than what their official salary alone could provide. One interviewee noted that when he first arrived in Shekou in the mid-1980s there were often open discussions and quarrels about political change, adding that "in one year, this changed my ideas [about politics]." He also stressed his belief in the rule of law rather than dependence on the goodness of the leader. Several foreign-sector managers, including some outside the south, spoke of the desirability of a multi-party system, with one man suggesting that China should look to Taiwan for a model of how to evolve from a single-party to a multi-party system.

In many cases, foreign-sector managers who expressed opinions about the desirability for extensive change were those who had spent time as students or interns abroad. These managers claimed that the experience changed them fundamentally. As one said in a particularly emotional comment:

Before I went to Germany, I had no idea of the West. I was just told that it is "capitalist," which was bad. But when I found out the real meaning of "capitalism," and found it to be good, my views really changed. . . . My friends and I were impressed first by the standard of living, but then also by the democratic system. My friends and I thought, "Freedom and a democratic regime are really what we want." . . . My German friends say that there are bad things about capitalism. But I just ask them, "Tell me one thing that is good about socialism?" . . . *Nothing* in China is beautiful!

Not everyone with strong views on the desirability of democratization adopted these views while overseas, however. Some formed their basic views of political and, indeed, economic reform on Chinese campuses, or prior to entering the foreign sector or Western-style training programs.

The ideas of foreign-sector managers about political change often were not concrete. As was the case with the student protesters in 1989, foreign-sector managers were generally vague about defining precisely what kind of change they desired. The specific change most commonly mentioned in both 1991 and 1995 was the ability to travel freely abroad—certainly a narrower goal than what is commonly implied in the West by the term "democratization." Despite this narrowness, the attitudes of foreign-sector managers clearly have been influenced by liberal ideas coming to them from the outside world. Just as significant is that they are clearly not advocates of "neo-authoritarianism," a view that has gained popularity among many urbanites in recent years. In other words, they are not advocates of the view that China needs a strong, authoritarian leadership to guide it, at least in the near term, through economic modernization.[60] The anti-authoritarian political views of the foreign-sector elite, taken in tandem with their pro-market views, establish them as firm ideological liberals.

The Replication of Foreign-Sector Patterns in the Private Sector

Many of the policies and institutions that have allowed foreign-sector managers to break ties to the state—particularly freedom from state-controlled job assignments, welfare benefits, job mobility, and work units—have been replicated in the private entrepreneurial segment of China's new business elite. As with the foreign sector, the very growth of the private sector has expanded the opportunities for young people, particularly in urban areas, to work outside the state or collective sectors, in other locations, or in trades different from those of their parents. Indeed, the percentage of new entrants to the labor force who went into the private sector rose from zero in 1978 to 10.6% in 1987. Perhaps the most dramatic exit from the state and collective sectors has occurred in the private-enterprise mecca of Wenzhou, where "about 80 per cent of the workers in both local state and collective enterprises have either asked for leave or taken second jobs in the private sector."[61] Although potential entrants into the private sector continue to face administrative barriers (such as the need to gain permission from a state employer to leave the unit), urban job mobility has been expanded by virtue of a wealth of new opportunities. Once in the private sector, moreover, individuals have a tremendous opportunity for job mobility. This has led one analyst to comment that those in the non-state sector "now move in an essentially private labour market."[62] Talent exchange

---

60. On neo-authoritarianism, see Sautman (1992). There is some evidence that another segment of the business elite, high-level-officials-turned-entrepreneurs, are more favorable toward neo-authoritarianism. Drew Liu (1995, p. 2) asserts that "government-based entrepreneurs . . . became immensely rich by plundering public property. . . . They have a high stake in the current anti-democratic regime and are fearful of any social change that might undermine their power."

61. Ya-Ling Liu (1992), p. 297. See also Davis (1990), p. 94.

62. Sabin (1994), p. 945. On administrative barriers, see Sabin, p. 958.

centers help entrepreneurs and skilled employees in the private sector to switch jobs or set out on a new venture in much the way such centers have for foreign-sector managers. Private entrepreneurs also have been able to place their files in residential committee offices and to travel at will for their businesses.[63]

As with many foreign-sector managers (particularly those in WFOEs and ROs), these new opportunities deprive entrants to the private sector of the regular benefits that are provided by the state. Housing is a particular problem. It is, however, true that some entrepreneurs running larger private enterprises may have the benefit of company-sponsored health insurance and retirement pensions or of company-subsidized housing. The higher salary that the wealthiest of the private-sector entrepreneurs can earn allows them to purchase benefits such as housing and medical care on the small but growing market. Even where these benefits are not provided, young entrepreneurs increasingly are willing to forgo job security and social welfare benefits to engage in free-lance, non-mainstream work.[64]

The most obvious form of state control, the Party presence, is also minimal. Although in 1989 Party cells were set up for the first time within private enterprises, and although 15% of private-enterprise owners have been reported to be Party members,[65] in general the Party presence in this sector is on a par with or even less than in the foreign sector, where after all a small Party presence can be maintained through labor union branches. The absence of labor unions and state-controlled personnel departments eliminates in private enterprises the venue in which much Party control is institutionalized in the state sector.

Existing data on the economic and political ideology of private entrepreneurs are quite sketchy, and more research could usefully be done. Nonetheless, it appears that entrepreneurs in larger *siying* enterprises are broadly similar in their views of economic reform to foreign-sector managers.[66] This contrasts with smaller *geti* entrepreneurs in the service

63. Gold (1989), p. 199.

64. As in the foreign sector, often a spouse will remain in the state sector in order to ensure benefits. On benefits, see Sabin (1994), p. 958; Wank (1992), p. 13.

65. Solinger (1992), p. 131. The report of a Party branch being established (in Shenyang) was in January 1989, and hence before the general crackdown of that year. The Party also has made an attempt to co-opt private-enterprise owners by encouraging them to join the Party.

66. Information on the political views of private entrepreneurs comes primarily from Bruun (1995); Gold (1990a); and Wank (1995). The desire of the largest, most successful entrepreneurs to keep a low profile, reported in 1995 interviews, will make sustained field research on this elite group particularly difficult.

industries, who tend to support economic reform but focus mainly on the narrow individual benefits they receive from it and do not appear to have a very distinctive outlook compared to the population at large.[67] More distinctive pro-reform views among *siying* entrepreneurs were evident in results of a survey of 117 successful private entrepreneurs, who complain that reforms have not progressed enough; these entrepreneurs believe that "their competitiveness is still confined by an immature market mechanism and willful suppression."[68]

The evidence available on the political views of *siying* entrepreneurs is that they tend to be less liberal than foreign-sector managers, who favor extensive—albeit evolutionary rather than revolutionary—political change. This greater conservatism is suggested in David Wank's finding with regard to Xiamen entrepreneurs' views of the 1989 student movements:

[T]he general attitude of the entrepreneurs can be described as unease. One of their commonly voiced complaints was that the students were demanding too much, too quickly. Political change should be gradual and initiated by state policies "from above" in an orderly reform (*gaige*) rather than forced by popular pressure "from below" in a potentially chaotic transformation (*gaizao*). As one entrepreneur said, "We must go slowly generation by generation. A country's stability is connected with its order." . . . In the eyes of many entrepreneurs, student demands for change through concessions from national leaders, while based on pure and noble sentiments, were politically naive. As one entrepreneur put it: "The students don't understand reality. . . . The more you tell the Communist Party to do something the less it is willing to do so."[69]

This belief that change should be state-initiated was clearly lacking among foreign-sector managers. As noted previously, foreign-sector

67. Evidence for a distinction in ideology between *geti* and *siying* entrepreneurs, which supports my exclusion of the former from the business elite, is found in Bruun (1995) and Wank (1995). (To Wank, this cleavage between smaller and larger entrepreneurs means private entrepreneurs are not a cohesive "interest.") It is also to be expected that foreign-sector managers and *siying* entrepreneurs may share a number of traits insofar as they often come from the same educational backgrounds, and insofar as there is "intra-elite" circulation between them, primarily in situations where foreign-sector managers leave to start or join private businesses.

68. Tan (1992). Respondents had an average registered capital of above one million yuan (181,000 dollars in 1992). Those with a college education were reportedly most suspicious that reforms would proceed smoothly because they were more likely to be involved in technology-intensive enterprises that were more sensitive to changes in availability of capital and to the long lead times in bringing their products to market.

69. Wank (1995), pp. 63–64. Wank finds this attitude common to both small and large entrepreneurs.

managers tended to be considerably more sympathetic to the student protesters. One attitude found by Wank

was that the students' goal of democracy is incompatible with Chinese political culture. As one entrepreneur put it: "The people want a good emperor, not a democratic environment." To some [entrepreneurs], "anarchy" and "democracy" were the same thing.[70]

Furthermore, large entrepreneurs were particularly impatient with student demands to end corruption.[71]

Some entrepreneurs, however, are quite radical in their political views. One entrepreneur interviewed in 1995, who had been jailed following the 1989 protests because of his connection with the very pro-reform *World Economic Herald*, held an extremely negative attitude toward, and expressed extreme disappointment (*shiwang*) about, the government. News reports are common of former student protest leaders becoming private entrepreneurs, and yet retaining their liberal political views.[72]

Siying entrepreneurs on the whole tend to be reasonably cautious about their public image, a trait consistent with their political moderation. In part this is a reaction to the reputation for conspicuous consumption among *geti* entrepreneurs, an image that they too have been saddled with. (Gold reported in the mid-1980s that *geti* entrepreneurs "can easily be spotted in garish and tight-fitting clothes, riding motorcycles, going to discotheques, and hanging out in expensive restaurants.")[73] Several 1995 interviewees emphasized that the most successful *siying* entrepreneurs keep a low profile, such that they cannot be recognized on the street. They report that they conceal their personal

---

70. Wank (1995), p. 64. Wank (p. 64) quotes one entrepreneur who favors democracy in the long term but believes it is not suited for "China's current level of development because it requires a literate, well-informed population to debate issues, a condition not yet met."

71. This contrasted with the views of smaller shopkeepers, who felt corruption was a problem (though there was little to do about it). See Wank (1995), pp. 64–65.

72. See, e.g., *Business Week* Editorial (1994). The location of the entrepreneurs—in cosmopolitan Shanghai or Guangzhou as opposed to the only recently developed Xiamen of Wank's study—may also affect ideology.

73. Gold (1990a), pp. 172–174. See also Xinhua (1992a). Young (1991, pp. 128–129) suggests that the entrepreneurs' conspicuous consumption is an effort to gain prestige that is on a par with their income but is denied by cultural taboos against merchants.

assets and their companies' profit figures out of a fear of being known as rich.[74]

．　　●　　●　　●

Summarizing, we see that the foreign sector's stronger market orientation and alternative source of authority have been translated into a significant degree of structural autonomy for the Chinese foreign-sector managers. We also see a strong independence among foreign-sector managers in terms of their ideology. That this structural independence and, though to a lesser degree, ideological independence also appear to exist among members of the private-sector elite suggests that these types of autonomy are broadening phenomena in China. Although there are important variations from sector to sector, the leading sectors of the economy in important ways have broken bonds with the state.

Despite these dramatic indications of autonomy, however, it is necessary to be mindful of the signs that autonomy is total in neither of these sectors and, particularly, that vertical clientelism and ties to officials remain salient. It is this question of ties to the state that the next chapters consider.

---

74. Tan's (1992, p. 49) report of a survey of 117 large private enterprises says these are "universal precautions."

CHAPTER 4

The Political Behavior
of China's New Business Elite

The structural autonomy and independent opinions that
are generally widespread among the members of China's new business
elite are remarkable. But autonomy is not the only issue that must be
examined in order to understand whether and how state-society relations have evolved as a result of post-Mao economic reforms. It needs
to be considered whether the members of this elite actually have converted their relative autonomy into new behaviors, such as formal and
regularized attempts to bring pressure to bear on the government. We
also need to inquire into whether they have formed strong horizontal
ties among themselves that might facilitate collective action. This chapter's examination of the behavior of foreign-sector managers and entrepreneurs shows that these elites in fact have not drawn on their autonomy to find new ways to press the state for change.

At first glance this pattern appears not to be out of the ordinary. Business elites in other developing countries as well as in China's own history tend not to be "revolutionary" in the classic sense. While students
and intellectuals may "take to the streets," members of the business elite
tend to maintain, first and foremost, a pragmatic commitment to putting
business first.[1] Nevertheless, even if their behavior is not revolutionary,
business elites elsewhere, including East Asia, attempt to influence government through direct lobbying or through peak associations.[2] Yet in

1. Becker (1983), p. 331. See also Brus (1983), pp. 125–127.
2. See Anek (1992); Becker (1990); Bennett and Sharpe (1985), p. 235; Cleaves and
Stephens (1991); Doner (1992); and Levy and Szekely (1987), p. 61.

China, as we shall see, members of the business elite are politically inactive even in these channels of influence. They rely instead upon the use of personal ties to gain influence. The pervasiveness of clientelism suggests strongly that the new business elite does not represent an emerging civil society.

The Absence of Horizontal Ties and Political Activism

Some foreign-sector managers in their pasts have engaged in political activism. As mentioned previously, one manager had been involved in political activities at a Beijing university in the early 1980s. Another acknowledged participating in the demonstrations in Tiananmen Square in the spring of 1989. Still another had contacts with dissidents while working abroad, though he was not a participant himself.[3] But most foreign-sector managers are not politically inclined, and wish to be left alone to do business; consistent with their desire to enter the foreign sector to escape politics, the majority are studiedly apolitical. This is not to say they are ignorant of politics. Many express quite eloquent views on the desirability of political change, as can be seen in the previous chapter. And most follow politics to the degree that can be expected of intellectual elites anywhere. But in their actual behavior, they sit back. This apolitical posture was especially strong among managers interviewed in 1991 but, despite some exceptions (see below), continued to be the norm in 1995. The comment of the former university activist was typical: "I'm just a businessman. I don't engage in politics." Or, as a Shekou JV manager claimed, "I pay little attention to politics. The company should just pay attention to profits."

Even though they are not political activists, do foreign-sector managers attempt in less radical ways to bring about changes in policies

---

3. A different type of activism also needs to be noted: activism on behalf of the Party. A Party member who manages a large Beijing JV played a role in the Tiananmen protests by trying to discourage his workers from participating in demonstrations, insisting that if they chose to march they must not interfere with work or display the banner of the JV.

related to their work, engaging in a Chinese version of organized lobbying?[4] The answer is decidedly negative. They do not seek out opportunities to engage in regular contacts with the state for broader political or policy-related purposes. Even though they are located in a crucial economic sector, and hold potent opinions about the need for political and economic reform, they do not attempt to organize independently to press for broad changes at either the local or national level. In part this is because their ideology supports avoidance of even routine activism. Not only do foreign-sector managers not wish to take to the streets, but also the way they perceive "freedom" means they prefer to keep their distance from politics of any sort.

Further, they do not feel that they *can* express suggestions for change upward to political officials; they believe themselves to be relatively powerless. This sense of powerlessness was expressed especially strongly in 1991 interviews, regardless of the type of foreign business in which the managers worked. When asked, broadly, whether they can and do express to the government their suggestions for changing or improving the "open" policy, foreign-sector managers almost uniformly give negative answers. As one typical respondent said, "There is no way to express the need for change to the government. I don't know what channel a person could use." Or, as another put it, "Chinese managers could complain to the Foreign Investment Bureau [of MOFTEC], but this is no use at all. They would just try to explain the [existing] policy to you" rather than try to change it.

As these responses indicate, many feel that there are no formal channels through which to complain. RO managers in particular feel they have no routine contacts with the government outside of FESCO, and so have nobody to whom they could complain if they so wished. Chinese managers in all types of foreign enterprises also lack the resources of state-enterprise managers, who can voice complaints at annual meetings with their superior ministries and through their representatives in the National People's Congress (NPC). Even private entrepreneurs have representation in the national and local-level people's congresses. In contrast, members of the foreign-sector's new business elite believe they are not—and, because of mistrust of Chinese who work in foreign busi-

---

4. Foreign-sector managers were first asked to describe their companies' relationship with relevant government bureaus, the degree of government interference, and any problems they have that result from current policies. If interviewees believed a government policy could be changed to help their company, they were asked whether they might try to get it changed and, if so, through what channels. On ways in which state-sector managers attempted to influence the state in the past, see Lynn T. White (1987).

nesses, will never be—represented in formal bodies such as the NPC.[5] Generally, they do not also seek to join the Chinese People's Political Consultative Conference (CPPCC, or Zhengxie). Nor are independent interest groups permitted to form.

Managers believe it would be ineffective, moreover, to express the need for change to central or local officials who are formally in charge of an issue, either because those officials do not care enough to help, or because the officials mistrust or wish to thwart the wishes of foreign-sector managers. In the words of some managers:

It is hard for Chinese managers to express complaints, because people in government don't have the same feelings as you, and are only thinking their way. Maybe they will listen, but it goes in one ear and out the other.

An official may be jealous about the higher salaries in joint ventures, and so he won't want to help with problems.

The government doesn't trust Chinese people who work in foreign companies. This is partly because of the traditional Chinese mistrust of foreigners. Also, if you work in a foreign company others cannot understand it. You are viewed as being not patriotic enough. . . . Foreigners have power to influence the government, but Chinese people don't. But if I were general manager of this company, the government wouldn't consider what I say. This is discrimination against the Chinese by the Chinese government itself.

Although some managers concede that they might find a sympathetic ear at low levels of officialdom, they argue that, on important issues, these low-level officials themselves have very little authority over policy. Although lower officials could perhaps pass a suggestion up the hierarchy, this still would be unlikely to lead to a change. As one manager said: "You can suggest changes to upper levels, and they may agree with you, but it is very hard for them to change things. Because policy is not just due to one person, even if the person you talk to is sympathetic, there can be no change"[6] Moreover, it might be risky for a manager to suggest changes. This view was implied by one interviewee:

To suggest changes, you can give a report to your leaders in the company, or an oral suggestion, and then ask them to transfer these ideas to their leaders. This does not happen often. It is too complex to say why not. I have ideas

5. Some large JVs have Chinese members who are representatives in local people's congresses, but they tend to be "old-line" managers who are influential because of their past stature within the state-owned enterprises or the Party, rather than as part of the "new elite" as defined in the introduction.

6. This is not, of course, very different from the situation in systems characterized by greater pluralism; one person's complaint does not automatically move a bureaucracy.

[for change], but as a *young* man, I should just try to do my work well. I should remember that point all the time. Some things are out of my control.

One manager even placed the burden for suggesting policy changes on *foreign* managers, and sharply criticized expatriates for not pressing for change in China:

Foreigners haven't tried their best to change China to a more favorable free-market economy or a more free-market view, or to make China more humanitarian. Instead, they have adapted themselves to do things the Chinese way. For example, the Chinese authorities want to tax Chinese employees in representative offices. . . . Foreigners should do something to protect Chinese employees' interests, and should argue with the government.

Rather than trying to fight on behalf of their own interests in China by voicing their problems, some managers preferred to consider escaping their problems by going abroad. This possibility was suggested by two managers from the SEZs, both of whom claimed that if things got too bad they could leave China fairly easily. As one said, "If I don't like it here, I can go to Europe."

A minority of managers interviewed in 1991 felt there *are* ways to express to officials their feelings about the need for change. The deputy general manager of a large Beijing JV described the process:

Can I suggest changes in policy to the government? Sure! To suggest changes I usually arrange a meeting with government officials—such as from the State Planning Commission, the industrial bureau [the department in charge of the Chinese JV partner], MOFTEC, the customs bureau, or the tax bureau. In most cases I invite the officials one by one on a yearly basis, sometimes twice a year, to the company to hear a report on what we've achieved and the problems we face. Sometimes I present issues on which the JV and the government differ.[7]

The deputy general managers of two other prominent JVs, one in Shanghai and one in Shenzhen, reported that it is possible to make suggestions to the local branches of MOFTEC, as well as to local development bureaus, the local branch of the business association of foreign enterprises (discussed in chapter 5), or foreign chambers of commerce. These two interviewees manage high-profile JVs that are viewed favorably by the local or national government either because they are "showcase" projects or because of their excellent production records. Man-

---

7. The suggestions for change made by this manager have concerned the company's difficulty in complying with the pace of localization of production materials set by the government.

agers from such enterprises undoubtedly carry some weight in their contacts with officials. Moreover, Chinese managers who attain these prestigious positions are often those with good ties to officials in the first place. (Although these managers felt more influential, none had actually engaged in the types of activities noted above.) A few RO managers felt they could try to effect influence by writing letters to newspapers or complaining to FESCO. Again, they had not actually engaged in these activities.

The lack of interest in politics and the sense of futility about organizing change that were expressed in 1991 held generally in 1995. But some interesting exceptions appeared. Several foreign-sector managers were active in political bodies or considered becoming so. One was a member of the CPPCC branch in a northern city. He felt his delegation, made up of overseas Chinese or PRC nationals working in Hong Kong (he was in the latter category), was the only delegation to have any influence as indicated by media coverage and attention from the city's mayor. Another RO manager in Shanghai was a member of both a "democratic party" and the China Council for the Promotion of International Trade, a government-sponsored trade promotion organization. The most extreme exception was one manager in Guangzhou who, despite his disdain for the Communist Party, was considering joining it in order to help bring about political changes:

Do not think that blond people [foreigners] can change Chinese people's intrinsic characteristics. . . . Substantial change can only be made by [Chinese people] and that is the reason why I am thinking to join the Chinese Communist Party. It sounds ludicrous for a potato-like individual person to say this, and I also admit I am not powerful enough to make this change. But I am ONE. If a big number of ONEs join together they will become MANY. And these ONEs are slowly, gradually looming up in China.[8]

Perhaps more striking than these individual cases of political activity (or inclination toward it) was the opinion of most interviewees in 1995 that the new business elite (including private entrepreneurs) will have more influence as a group in the future. This was usually expressed as a vague belief that the holders of economic power in the system will somehow gain political power. A few argued more concretely that, although their own group's current influence in formal organizations is limited by the small numbers of this group and the suspicion of their ties to foreign companies, they will gain influence as their size grows and the

8. This manager communicated this opinion by facsimile transmission (in English) after our interview.

foreign sector becomes even more respectable and entrenched.[9] This may happen first in cities where foreign businesses are concentrated, particularly Beijing, Shanghai, and Guangzhou. Indeed, a number of Shanghai-based managers pointed to their new mayor, Xu Kuangdi—who in the past worked for a Swedish trading company and was a professor—as an example of where such influence may already be in place.[10] Another manager noted that people with ties to the international community through their education or overseas experiences are already becoming entrenched in some portions of the Chinese bureaucracy, for example, in the State Commission on Reforming the Economic System (Tigaiwei) and the Chinese Securities Regulatory Commission. Such officials, he argued, will naturally be sympathetic to the views of foreign-sector managers, and they may even be part of the same circle of acquaintances. One 1995 interviewee argued that he already was quite influential—as an advisor to municipal financial institutions—*because* of his foreign ties; he has influence because his views are seen as less threatening than those of someone inside the system who might hold the same views. More generally, these foreign-sector managers also have faith that future influence will be extremely positive, since the group will be able to put to good use both its members' high level of education (both Chinese and Western) and their experience with foreign practices.

As tantalizing as these views of current and future influence are, it is difficult to take them as a dominant or inexorable trend. Most foreign-sector managers see their current influence as negligible, and their faith in their own future influence is quite ill-defined. More importantly, the majority remain quite uninterested in political participation under the current regime. Those who are uninvolved in political organizations, but even those few who are members of the democratic parties and CPPCC, say they do not take those organizations very seriously because the groups are not truly independent. Besides, the managers claim they themselves have no time to devote to such organizations.

---

9. Interviewees distinguished between society, which tends to respect them as a group, and conservatives in politics, who tend to be suspicious. Societally based hostility toward foreign-sector managers is not unknown, however. Protesters in Lanzhou (Gansu) hung a banner reading "Chinese who work for foreigners are traitors" outside a JV department store under construction which, ultimately, did not open (*Beijing Youth News* [1993]). The idea of the importance of large numbers was widespread, even though this group clearly understands its elite—and hence small—nature.

10. Xu is also an alternate member of the Central Committee, and a protégé of Zhu Rongji. See Zeng (1995); Kyodo News Service (1995).

Reliance of Foreign-Sector Managers on Personal Relations

Although individual foreign-sector managers do not, for the most part, feel willing or able to convert their structural autonomy into an effective force for policy change, they do try to influence the government on issues that are immediately related to their specific businesses, not through dramatic new patterns of state-society interaction but, rather, by fostering informal personal relationships (*guanxi*) with central and, most often, local officials. They may try to work through official channels, such as a MOFTEC bureau or a JV parent ministry, yet the basis of their ability to proceed through these channels is their careful cultivation of ties with selected offices and officials, rather than a regularized and impersonal adventure into the bureaucracy.

Many managers acknowledge that they find it necessary to oil these relationships with gifts, favors, and monetary bribes. These illegal methods of attempting to influence the government are, of course, found in capitalist economies as well. What distinguishes China is that these means appear to be the *foremost* mode of influence (and, it appears, the only viable mode) that managers attempt to use. Often, foreign-backed businesses try to embed relationships with officials into their organizational structure by placing a key official (such as someone from the supervisory bureau) on a board of directors or high in the management structure so the firm can use that person's connections and influence to its own advantage. In most cases, however, relationships are less institutionalized. Relationships may be sought for one-time benefits, as was the case when the deputy general manager of a Beijing JV searched for and found a "contact" in the city government who helped break an impasse with a ministry over payments to the JV during the 1988–1990 recession.[11] Managers cannot be certain, however, that these one-time efforts at influence will be effective. More effective use of ties involves the active cultivation of relationships that last over time. The top manager of a small Beijing WFOE described how he developed and used such relations:

---

11. In the recession, the government recentralized power over many decisions, making it difficult for foreign enterprises to deal directly with upstream and downstream contacts and forcing managers in these enterprises to go, once again, through the ministry system.

I am responsible for maintaining contacts with officials. So I will invite officials to dinner, and give them gifts such as calendars. I will also send them brochures, and let them know that my company will *help* China and will raise the level of technology. We have a pretty good relationship. There has to be a good relationship, because the ministry is influential in my industry. If they don't like us, they may tell potential customers that we are a bad company, and this would be bad. So even though the ministry doesn't directly regulate us, I just want to keep them happy.

Having cultivated relationships, managers call on them to achieve narrow types of influence, ranging from evading an existing rule, to gaining a favorable interpretation of a rule, to assuaging the anger of an official about past deeds, to moving a procedure along faster. Good relationships can be especially important when the government provides approvals, or when the government is a customer or supplier. For example, one WFOE manager cultivated favorable ties with an office in the Ministry of Metallurgy in a successful effort to convince the officials to approve a new JV despite an ongoing dispute with the same office on a different matter. During the late 1980s recession, a Shanghai JV used its managers' long-standing contacts with then-mayor Zhu Rongji to obtain a loan. Managers with good relations in the Shanghai Public Security Bureau were able to get visas processed more quickly.

Foreign-sector managers therefore believe that, although their businesses may be obstructed by government laws or the actions of officials, the problem can often be gotten around by using the "Chinese way" of getting things done. The goal of using contacts is usually to avoid formal rules set down by the government rather than to change the existing regulatory regime.[12] This strategy, which is ultimately an individualist strategy rather than a collectivist scheme, works *because of* tight vertical links between managers and officials, not because of a separation between them. Despite their desire for a new economic system, then, foreign-sector managers do not reject—and indeed see as highly functional in the current environment—traditional clientelist means available to them to get the compliance of officials.

Consistent with the belief of foreign-sector managers that they are unable to influence the government outside of informal vertical clientelist strategies is the fact that they have only weak horizontal ties to each other. Interviews revealed virtually no evidence that foreign-sector man-

---

12. This is a common strategy for expatriate managers in foreign-backed businesses as well.

agers have established *formal* organizations of any sort on their own. (This lack of cohesiveness contrasts with the behavior of expatriate managers in China, many of whom have established nationally based groups to share experiences and lobby the government.) Senior Chinese managers may attend conferences together, but these meetings tend to be sponsored by MOFTEC or other government organizations, and so are not free of state supervision. In any case, such meetings do not seem to have produced lasting ties.[13] Foreign-sector managers working in different foreign businesses do have contact with each other in the context of business dealings, but claim that lack of time (the main reason), lack of inclination, and/or business competition preclude them from building stronger horizontal networks. Business meetings, they say, stick close to the issue at hand.

This group of managers exhibits only a marginal degree of *informally* organized cohesiveness. Foreign-sector managers who work in buildings with many foreign offices may gather informally for lunch ("if you want to"). Foreign hotels occasionally sponsor events for foreign-sector employees, such as dances for FESCO employees. Some traditional horizontal links do exist, though they fall short of the strong clan-based ties of the "golden age" of the bourgeoisie. In particular, managers who were trained at the same elite schools often have formed close friendships. Classmates also have the chance to meet and revive links at alumni events, but discussion at such gatherings focuses mainly on social matters, such as family news and stories of friends. Occasionally managers use these ties in order to help them find new jobs or gain other information, such as about foreign-sector salaries. They may speak with some of their classmates about broader issues of reform, although several indicated that this required a high degree of trust. Close friendships and opportunities to gather together could potentially form the basis for greater group identification in the future. Even with the growth of these sorts of linkages, however, foreign-sector managers are a long way from becoming a cohesive stratum. They themselves do not find in such ties or events the seeds of greater group cohesion. It is notable, moreover,

13. I was invited in December 1991 to participate in a conference to discuss issues in China's foreign investment policy sponsored by the Tigaiwei. The conference was attended primarily by a mixture of Chinese officials from central, provincial, and municipal levels and high-level foreign-sector managers from prominent JVs. At neither the formal meetings nor group meals could I detect much contact between the invited foreign-sector managers. Indeed, competition along with posturing among them during the formal sessions was the more characteristic attitude.

that reliance on more traditional sorts of ties, those of classmates and friends, is exceedingly commonplace in China, but has failed to produce much group action in the post-revolutionary past.

Not only are foreign-sector managers a loose-knit group, but many managers reported that their circle of acquaintances is limited mainly to school friends or those they met within their foreign company. Most did not socialize with people from different walks of life, such as workers. This is perhaps to be expected, given that these managers are part of an elite. But this behavior does not bode well for the possibility of ties to other potentially revolutionary societal groups.[14]

Vertical Clientelism and Horizontal Ties in the Private Sector

Political dissidents such as Hu Jiwei, a former chief editor of *People's Daily* and official of the National People's Congress, have placed faith in the potential of private entrepreneurs to spur democracy. Some commentators have pointed to banners of support hung by *geti* entrepreneurs and to monetary and material donations made by entrepreneurs, such as managers of the Stone Corporation to demonstrators in 1989, as evidence for growing activism and political consciousness among entrepreneurs.[15] But as a rule, and like foreign-sector managers, members of the business elite in the private sector have shown strong inclinations toward neither political activism nor the formation of strong horizontal ties. Stone's actions and supportive banners cannot be used to proclaim the existence of a politicized, much less democratizing, class. Donations by the Stone Corporation were not exceptional and, as noted previously, most entrepreneurs—as exemplified by those in Xiamen—did not actively support the student demonstrators.[16] More generally, entrepreneurs' participation in politics outside of state-sponsored organizations has been unusual, and has not been sustained.

14. Such cross-class ties were seen as crucial to the emergence of civil society in Hungary according to Szelenyi (1988), p. 218.

15. Hu urged entrepreneurs to "become the main army of establishing China's theory of democracy and promoting the building of democracy." See "Debate on Political Rights Reopened in China" (1993). Similar hopes by dissident Chinese writers are noted in Strand (1990), p. 14. On *geti* activism in 1989, see Perry (1992), p. 154. Stone Corporation officials also lobbied NPC members to rescind martial law. See Nathan (1989), p. 16.

16. On the apolitical norm, see Wank (1995) and Halpern (1989).

In the private sector, one potential channel for formal, organized influence is representation in existing political organs, notably the CCP, NPC, CPPCC, and their local counterparts. Indeed, entrepreneurs had significantly more representatives in the people's congresses as of the mid-1990s than did foreign-sector managers. Moreover, twenty-one entrepreneurs were chosen to be delegates to the March 1993 meeting of the CPPCC.[17] The CCP set up its first Party branch for private entrepreneurs in Shenzhen in 1994.[18] Delegates to these bodies have not been especially vocal, however, presumably because of the desire to keep a low political profile.[19] None of these bodies, of course, are forums in which members freely seek representation and then freely press for group interests. Indeed, in contrast to the growing and vocal representation of private businesses in Russia's new Federal Assembly, it is likely that China's private entrepreneurs have been included in these political bodies as loyal tokens, or in order to co-opt them.[20]

More typically, like foreign-sector managers, private entrepreneurs feel vulnerable to the existing power of officials. Entrepreneurs' attempts at influence are similarly individualistic and lead them to form dense clientelist alliances with the cadres, especially at the local level. Their success depends on extensive involvement with local cadres, both government officials and managers of state and collective enterprises. Ties may be built on existing family relations or, among the well-educated, on bonds developed in school, as in the case of one entrepreneur who had connections with schoolmates who were now in the *Tigaiwei* and in securities regulatory agencies. For those in their forties, ties may be based on shared Cultural Revolution experiences. *Siying* entrepreneurs build new connections in several ways, including through bribery and the giving of small gifts to lower-level cadres, by employing

17. This followed an attempt by the government to bolster the image of the private sector at the 14th Party Congress in 1992, and the subsequent lifting of many restrictions on private businesses. See Sabin (1994), p. 962. In 1991, four "self-employed" people from Shenzhen were members of national and local PPCCs, and two were delegates to the local people's congress. See Xinhua (1991).

18. The Yuanling Market Party branch had seven party members. Shenzhen had 230,000 entrepreneurs (both *geti* and *siying*) at the time. See Zhongguo Xinwen She [China News Agency] (1994).

19. One 1995 interviewee argued that even those delegates from other (i.e., non-private-sector) functional interests who do try to influence policy on behalf of their group tend to do so only on an ad hoc and temporary basis. He gave as an example of a highly vocal member who proposed innovative ideas to the governor of the Shanghai branch of the Bank of China.

20. In 1993 elections to the two chambers of the new Federal Assembly, 20% of the candidates were from private companies, according to one report. See Bohlen (1993).

middle-level officials in their businesses or by cultivating high-level officials as patrons.[21]

Connections with cadres are important for both the registration and the operation of private-sector businesses. To navigate the highly bureaucratic registration procedure, avoid the risks associated with identification as a private enterprise, or benefit financially from state contacts, entrepreneurs often register falsely. They may claim to be attached to a collective enterprise—becoming what is known as a *guakao* ("hang on") enterprise—and pay the collective a "management" fee. An entrepreneur may pay a local bureau or neighborhood committee to set up a real or even a dummy collective (a practice called *dai hong maozi*, or "wearing a red hat"). Or an entrepreneur may contract to manage the business of a state or collective enterprise in return for part of the profits. The most prosperous private enterprises, in fact, appear to be those with "official" covers.[22] Official ties also can help solve myriad problems once an enterprise is operating, even if it is classified "private." As one *siying* entrepreneur stated: "If you have some contradiction with an official, you deal with the matter personally. You can't solve business problems by asking the government for more policies."[23] Thus, entrepreneurs have relied upon local cadres to look the other way at illegal economic practices, such as land transfers and the supplying of private business with "underground" private capital from organizations such as money clubs and specialized financial households. Entrepreneurs may collude with local officials to evade central taxes in exchange for investments from the locality.

To some degree local cadre involvement is forced upon entrepreneurs out of the avarice of cadres, who find plenty of opportunity to exploit this new sector. Cadres gain from their connections with the private sector in a number of ways. In return for their support for private business, they can enrich themselves through "management fees," as noted above, or through "voluntary donations" and authorized and unauthorized fees and taxes levied on private businesses.[24] They may take "power shares" in private enterprises in return for protection and favors. Cadres

21. See Wank (1991, pp. 11–15; 1992, pp. 8–16; 1995); and Young (1991), pp. 129–130.

22. Tan (1992), p. 49. On ties to officials see also Ya-ling Liu (1992), pp. 293–316; McEwen (1994); Shi (1993); Solinger (1992), pp. 126–128; and Sabin (1994).

23. Quoted in Wank (1995), p. 65.

24. These fees may be a crucial source of revenue. Shi (1993, p. 161) reports that in Beijing's Xicheng district, tax revenues from open markets (with private vendors) and self-employed entrepreneurs have become street committees' main source of funds.

also rely on private businesses to be channels for re-selling at higher market prices goods bought at low state-set prices, or to gain inside channels for exports. They may benefit personally from access to these market outlets, but they also benefit enterprises or regions under their jurisdiction. Indeed, local cadres sometimes have become the embodiment of the private-official linkage by running private enterprises themselves (with spouses or family members as "fronts"), using their political connections to advantage.[25]

It is in the interest of entrepreneurs to cooperate with local cadres. Cooperation allows private-sector businesses to operate more smoothly, and sometimes just to get started in the first place. As Wank argues, "Capitalist entrepreneurs see capitalist growth as possible because of, not in spite of, the involvement of officials."[26] Rather than the larger *siying* enterprises being most autonomous, moreover, ties to officials matter tremendously for the development of the largest and most profitable enterprises.[27] Even a large and innovative private enterprise like the Stone Corporation had to depend upon strong bureaucratic connections to succeed.[28] Odgaard reports that managers in some of the larger *siying* enterprises in some localities have gained enough power to thwart the controls that local officials, sometimes illegally, have attempted to impose.[29]

As many of these reports suggest, the efforts of private entrepreneurs to build connections are often illegal. But to paint the use of *guanxi* as corrupt oversimplifies the matter. The complexity of the issue was suggested by one interviewee, who had spent considerable time overseas:

To be generous, we can say that elites have their own ways to influence the government. In what they do, if they do it well, officials will support it either

25. On the benefits for cadres, see Wank (1995a); Ya-ling Liu (1992), pp. 304–305. Liu argues that Wenzhou cadres have been more supportive of private enterprises than cadres elsewhere, in part because of a history, dating back to the 1940s, of such support and of independence from higher Party authorities. Solinger (1992) also emphasizes the mutually dependent nature of the relationship. On this phenomenon in township and village enterprises (TVEs), see Oi (1992).

26. Wank (1991), p. 3. See also Nee (1989).

27. On the ties to officials of *siying* enterprises, see Odgaard (1992), p. 102; Wank (1995), pp. 67–68. Older entrepreneurs and former cadres are more likely to possess these ties, while *geti* entrepreneurs sometimes shy away from close ties to officials (though they will offer gifts and bribes) and from business activities that involve the state sector.

28. Stone required government ties to gain import licenses. The company reportedly relied on its patron, Zhao Ziyang, prior to Zhao's ouster. See Solinger (1992), pp. 133–134.

29. Odgaard (1992), pp. 107–108.

publicly or privately. If they succeed, they have government officials on their side; in part this is due to ideology—China wants reforms. But business professionals also reach private understandings with officials. It is illegal to take a cash bonus if you are an official. But in the U.S. if you give money to your congressman's favorite charity, the congressman will like it—and he then has an interest in what you're doing. There are always ways to befriend officials, and the law on this is not clear. If you think hard enough about it there is always something you can do to meet the interests of an official.

Although the use of personal connections is important for foreign-sector managers, a greater degree of cooperation with the state distinguishes the private sector from the foreign. The explanation for this difference between these two leading-edge sectors lies in both political and market conditions. Entrepreneurs have faced harassment and extortion from officials, have been subjected to periodic campaigns against "spiritual pollution" and, as noted previously, have seen the low prestige accorded by society to small entrepreneurs spill over to them. In contrast, foreign businesses have been protected from such harassment by the central government.[30] Lacking the independent basis of authority in foreign corporations and subject to harassment, it makes sense that entrepreneurs would build protective alliances with amenable and supportive (or even venal) local cadres. Moreover, because of the absence of well-developed capital markets from which private economic enterprises can obtain funds, they must continue to rely on connections with the state for some resources which foreign-sector enterprises may obtain from their foreign backers. Similarly, the still-fledgling markets for inputs and products also encourage private enterprises to sell their products to government bureaus with existing sales channels; foreign-sector businesses can more often use their knowledge of export markets instead of depending on the state as a customer.

Like foreign-sector managers, entrepreneurs have failed to form extensive horizontal ties among themselves. There is a division between *siying* and *geti* entrepreneurs based on different backgrounds, interests, and behaviors.[31] But there is also little cohesiveness within the *siying* elite itself. As one survey concluded, "Contact among private entrepreneurs is rare. They are likely to make friends with government func-

---

30. On private-sector harassment, see Gold (1989), p. 197; Gold (1990a), p. 172; and Young (1991), p. 124. Some harassment of foreign businesses occurred during the "anti-spiritual pollution" campaigns of the 1980s, but was put to a halt by the center. See Pearson (1991), ch. 4.

31. See ch. 3; Wank (1995), p. 69.

tionaries, enterprise managers, and technicians."[32] By the mid-1990s new social clubs that often were frequented by private entrepreneurs had sprung up, particularly in south China. These members-only clubs are extremely expensive, with membership fees commonly of 100,000 yuan ($12,350) or more in 1995. Some of these clubs sponsor illicit activities, most commonly prostitution. But many are reportedly intended as social gathering places where China's new wealthy (as well as foreign executives) can gather for social purposes or to conduct business, and also can display their wealth. Despite the seeming potential of these clubs to create ties among the business elite, interviewees did not take them seriously as such. The price of membership and entrepreneurs' wariness of exhibiting conspicuous consumption act to keep many *siying* entrepreneurs away. But when they do join, they are reported sometimes to give free memberships to local officials in order to be able to have opportunities to speak with them—yet another sign of the importance placed on personal connections with officials.[33]

•   •   •   •

Although China's new business elite is distanced structurally and ideologically from state authority, there is no compelling evidence that it has tried to influence government policy as an independent class, or that there is even sufficient cohesiveness for it to do so. Rather, its members collude extensively, and for well-defined purposes, with officials, especially at the local level, in order to create better chances of success. In other words, clientelism is the major currency of interaction. For private entrepreneurs, ties with local cadres are absolutely necessary to their success. This clientelist strategy is often effective, but only to accomplish what are ultimately narrow ends. Contrary to predictions that economic reform would lead to strong pressures from below for change, then, China's new business elite has not evolved into a strong, independent, politically active, democratizing stratum. Indeed, there is evidence that the state has initiated its own strategy for organizing the business elite, with the aim of pre-empting any independent societal pressures. Such efforts at corporatist co-optation on the part of the state are the subject of the next chapter.

32. Cai (1994).
33. Interviews from 1995. Hong Kong and Taiwan businesspeople also are sometimes members. One club in Guangzhou reportedly has Rolls Royces and Mercedes 600s in the lobby, available for rent.

CHAPTER 5

The Socialist Corporatism
of Business Associations

Post-Mao China has witnessed a revitalization of "associations" (*xiehui*). Partial political liberalization, combined with extensive if incomplete decentralization of the economy and the concomitant strengthening of economic actors, has allowed a limited, Chinese-style associational life to emerge. The foreign and private sectors have not been excluded from these developments. New associations for the post-Mao business elite differ markedly from their "mass organization" (*qunzhong tuanti*) counterparts of the Maoist era, which were "transmission belts" for state policy and hence rather completely dominated by state interests. Do associations truly promote the interests of their members from a position of autonomy, and reflect, as some have suggested, the emergence of pluralism or civil society?[1] Alternatively, are associations tightly controlled by state actors, having undergone face-lifts but remaining in their essence mass organizations? Or do they simultaneously exhibit elements of *both* state domination and autonomy?

The historical record of Chinese merchant associations, discussed in chapter 2, offers initial insight into the role of these new institutions. Merchant organizations in Qing China were neither wholly autonomous nor state-dominated; rather, guilds were situated between state and society, often performing, on behalf of the state, *gong* ("public") acts that reached well beyond guilds' commercial activities. Guilds and other associations were, on the one hand, self-regulating bodies that

1. The view that civil society can be found in associations in post-Mao China is found in Ostergaard (1989); Gordon White (1993); and Whyte (1992a).

had much freedom to supervise their own business activities. But, on the other hand, these organizations lacked authority to oppose the state on behalf of their private interests. The tradition of dualism was adapted to the modernizing nation-state in the twentieth century when the court created chambers of commerce designed to both unleash commercial power on behalf of China and to control a growing dynamic group. The court's attempts were in vain, for the dynasty disintegrated after 1911 and merchant organizations subsequently entered the "golden age" of merchant autonomy and political influence. The Nationalists tried once again to re-establish control over business by draining the existing organizations of their independence, co-opting many of the business elite, and re-orienting the associations toward serving state functions.

This historical dualism has been reshaped in the post-Mao context into a socialist version of state corporatism.[2] The concept of socialist corporatism introduced in chapter 1 begins with the classic state-corporatist situation. Institutionally, the state sanctions a limited number of associations, centralizes the organization, controls leadership selection and interest articulation, and retains ultimate authority. In terms of function, the state recognizes the legitimacy and limited autonomy of certain societal interests, but—with overtones of the *gong* realm of the Qing— coordinates them with its own interests in rapid development and regime maintenance. The concept of socialist corporatism builds on state corporatism to accommodate features of a transition from Leninism, namely, the socialist regime's efforts to pre-empt the emergence of more autonomous business groups, the devolution of limited power to groups (some of them outside the Party-state), and the context of a huge existing bureaucracy and weak societal institutions. This chapter examines the socialist-corporatist associations that link business to the state in post-Mao China.

The Growth of Economic Associations in the Post-Mao Era

In tandem with economic reforms, greater intellectual and organizational diversity have emerged in post-Mao China. Over the

2. Although the history of merchant associations in China is not generally viewed as state corporatist (Fewsmith [1985] is an exception), the historical dualism presages and complements the pattern of socialist corporatism found in post-Mao associations.

past decade, and in contrast to the Maoist era, reformist officials and many intellectuals have come to argue that Chinese society is made up of different yet manageable interests, and that societally based groups should be permitted, within limits, to pursue these interests.[3] In reasoning that echoes the views of late Qing reformers, contemporary reformers have advocated granting authority to intermediate organizations in order to harness their members' expertise. While it is not claimed that merchant energies will "save China" (*jiuguo*), business associations are seen as facilitators of the state's economic work. Market reforms and the growing complexity of the economy dictate that the state devolve many functions to social groups which, "free from the restrictions of departments and regions . . . are highly responsive to changes and able to meet the requirements of socialized management."[4]

Based on this rationale, professionals and intellectuals in urban China have been allowed and even encouraged to organize into "social organizations" (*shetuan*) including associations, chambers of commerce, federations, societies, research units, foundations, cooperatives, and "privately run" (*minban*) research institutes. By early 1988, nearly one thousand national-level groups had been formed officially across a range of fields, with eleven hundred more reportedly established between 1988 and 1989. Local-level associations also have flourished; over 100,000 had been formed by the late 1980s. The number of registered groups in Shanghai reportedly grew more than 300% between 1981 and 1984. Economic associations formed throughout the 1980s, particularly after what one report called "a nationwide campaign for horizontal association" in the mid-1980s.[5] Associations specific to the economy include those for rural marketers, specialized households, trade, export, and industrial organizations, managers in the state and collective sectors, individual entrepreneurs (*getihu*), and private businesses (*siying*).[6] Part of this process was the strengthening at the local levels of Mao-era

3. See Zhao (1987, 1987a); Luo et al. (1987).

4. Chen Jinluo and She Dehu (1988). Similar views are expressed in Wang Lingling (1985). See also Burns (1989), pp. 499, 503; Whyte (1992a), p. 92.

5. See Chen Jinluo and She Dehu (1988), p. 26; "Regulations Issued on Social Organizations" (1989); Whiting (1991), p. 17; Xinhua (1987). These numbers likely exclude groups—such as discussion "salons" (*shalong*) that sprang up in urban areas in the mid- to late 1980s—that did not form publicly or register (through the procedures described below).

6. Over 3,000 trade associations were reportedly set up in the few years prior to 1992. See Lam (1992). On economic social organizations, see Gold (1989), p. 199; Gold (1990a), p. 170; Kraus (1991); Panagariya (1991), pp. 17–18; Wang Lingling (1985); Gordon White (1987), pp. 432–433; Gordon White (1993); and Whiting (1991).

mass organizations, including the formation of 150 voluntary branch "guilds" under the All-China Federation of Industry and Commerce (ACFIC, or Gongshanglian) between 1987 and 1989, which reached a total of nearly 2,300 by early 1994.[7]

Beginning in the mid-1980s, it became de rigueur in China for these associations to describe themselves as *minjian* ("non-governmental"). The term *minjian* implies a distance from the state; on a hypothetical spectrum of state-society relations ranging from state domination to autonomous society, *minjian* suggests that an organization is located toward the pole of autonomy. The term distinguishes them from the mass (*qunzhong*) organizations—"transmission belts"—of the Maoist era.[8] As we shall see, *minjian* groups have made attempts to influence the government. For example, managerial associations at times have voiced complaints about bureaucratic abuses, stimulating debate in local representative assemblies.[9] There also has been some pressure for autonomy. A *Beijing ribao* article argued, for example, that the state and associations should not have the relationship of "leader and led," and that state administrative organs should refrain from intervening in the internal activities of associations or transmitting administrative directives.[10]

But *minjian* groups are decidedly *not* the equivalent of autonomous Western-style interest groups, and the term does not suggest they are free from government ties. Rather, consistent with the broader rationale for pluralization of society, their "intermediary status determines that they are a bridge of relations linking the party and government with the broad masses of the people."[11] They are, moreover, to serve as "the aide of the party and government" in the economic reform effort—in other words, to take on functions with which the government itself no longer wants to be burdened. The state, accordingly, plays a central role in the establishment and management of such groups, even when such groups are not formally part of a government organization. Some organizations that have been labeled *minjian* in the reform era are actually revamped

7. These figures are from Xinhua (1989, 1994a). The ACFIC's full Chinese name is Zhonghua Quanguo Gongshangye Lianhehui.

8. The term *shetuan*, or social organization, also conveys the idea of "non-governmental." See also Bonnin and Chevrier (1991), pp. 573–575, 580.

9. Chevrier (1990), p. 127, p. 344 n. 86.

10. Wang Lingling (1985). Similar views are found in Chen Jinluo and She Dehu (1988), p. 28.

11. Chen Jinluo and She Dehu (1988), p. 27. Note that such language linking *minjian* institutions with the state was common even prior to the 1989 government crackdown. See also Xinhua (1989); Chevrier (1990), p. 127, p. 344 n. 86.

mass organizations from the pre-reform era. A prime example is the ACFIC, a mass organization under the Party's United Front Department (which itself had origins in the Nationalist period). Despite their history, mass organizations have been granted significantly greater autonomy in the post-Mao era, though they are subject to the same constraints as other *minjian* groups.

The enthusiasm that reformers were expressing in the mid-1980s for the growth of "interest groups" and "social pluralism" was accompanied by the growth, immediately prior to and during the Tiananmen demonstrations, of what appeared to be an autonomous Chinese associational life. Examples of new organizations included the Beijing Autonomous Students' Union and the Capital Independent Workers' Union, which were founded during the 1989 protests. Similarly, the Beijing Institute for Research in the Social and Economic Sciences was founded in 1984 by Chen Ziming and Wang Juntao, both of whom had been active in the 1979 Democracy Wall movement and, later, the publication of *Beijing Spring*. These organizations were perceived by some to be harbingers of a second "golden age" or even of civil society.[12] Yet these liberalizing trends of the mid-1980s, along with many others, were reined in by the 1989 Tiananmen protests. The autonomous organizations proved to be highly vulnerable and failed to become enduring features of post-Mao state-society relations. The unions were crushed by the government, while the Institute saw much of its autonomy undermined subsequent to the arrests of Chen and Wang for their role in the 1989 events. Dualism—expressed in the post-Mao era as the idea that societal interests can exist legitimately but have only "relative independence" and must "adhere to the principle that the interests of the part must be subject to the interests of the whole situation and immediate interests must be subject to long-term interests"—resurfaced, and the state-linked aspect of *minjian* was reinforced.[13]

12. On the unions, see Whyte (1992a), p. 92. On the Institute, see Whiting (1991), pp. 30–33. Even though Whiting offers the Institute as an example of the most autonomous kind of non-governmental organization, she (p. 31) acknowledges that "the autonomy of the organisation was somewhat limited because only a fraction of the researchers associated with the institute were full-time and actually received their salaries from the institute itself. Most researchers worked only part-time [at the Institute] and held full-time posts in government-run institutes and universities." While Whiting does not assume that these organizations presaged civil society, Whyte does. Still, Whyte (p. 101 n. 32) concedes, "The degree of autonomy from the state of such organizations, in terms of both funds and administrative control, varied widely, and perhaps few could be regarded as entirely independent."

13. This argument was made with regard to enterprises and enterprise groups in Li Zheng (1990). Even stronger statements against pluralization than this appeared, related

The official criticisms of "pluralism" signaled a concerted effort by the state to prevent the further emergence of autonomous social groups. With the drafting of laws on associations, *minjian* groups were required after the autumn of 1989 to register with the Social Organizations Department (Shetuansi) of the Ministry of Civil Affairs and to adhere to the department's regulations.[14] (This department actually had been formed in mid-1988 as part of broader administrative reforms, suggesting that plans to maintain a grip on social groups existed even during these groups' apparent heyday.) By law, an approved "social organization" is to be granted a monopoly in its functional area. But to register in the first place, an organization must show that no other similar organization has been approved. Perhaps the most important part of the regulations was the requirement that such organizations be affiliated with an official unit (*guakao danwei*), most often a government office (to whom the organization might pay a fee and from whom it might receive some funding and staff). Affiliation with a government organization was already a fact for many of the larger *minjian* associations that existed prior to the promulgation of the regulations. This was the case, for example, for former mass organizations such as the ACFIC, that had long been under the jurisdiction of the State Industrial and Commercial Administration (Gongshangju). The regulations thus were designed to ensure similar restrictions on *minjian* organizations, regardless of their origins in either state or society.

The unstated intention of these new regulations to co-opt social groups was bolstered in the early 1990s by evidence of the government's public consideration of state corporatist arrangements in the economy. The State Commission on Reforming the Economic System (Tigaiwei) proposed in 1992 that the regulatory functions of industrial ministries be shifted to the *minjian* peak association in each industry.[15] The ministries would be abolished, and a new "super agency"—called the Economic and Trade Office and modeled on Japan's Ministry of International Trade and Industry (MITI)—would be left to give indirect "guidance plans." A similar proposal was made by Deputy Premier Zhu

---

to fears over the emergence of spontaneous "workers' associations" during the 1989 protests. See Walder (1991), pp. 487–488.

14. On the 1989 "Regulations on the Registration and Management of Social Organizations" (*Shehui tuanti dengji guanli tiaoli*), see "Regulations Issued on Social Organizations" (1989), pp. 19–20. Whiting (1991, pp. 22–27) offers an excellent analysis of the regulations and the department.

15. The Tigaiwei is located under the State Council and has played a major role in designing the economic reforms.

Rongji at the 14th Party Congress later that year. While Zhu's proposal was deferred at the national level, a local version was tried out in Shanghai, where the fourteen municipal industrial bureaus were abolished and fourteen industry associations set up in their stead.[16]

These moves did not completely squelch pressure by associations for greater autonomy, and group interests sometimes have been voiced. For example, the association for entrepreneurs has called for more autonomous management of state-owned enterprises.[17] Yet with the regulations on social organizations and the active consideration of replacing ministries with corporatist economic bodies, the reform government made important steps toward initiating not civil society but socialist corporatism. We see the results of these trends carried out specifically in the foreign- and private-sector business associations.

China's Foreign-Sector
Business Association (CAEFI)

The China Association for Enterprises with Foreign Investment (Zhongguo waishang touzi qiye xiehui, or CAEFI) was established in 1987.[18] After making a strong initial push for membership, the national organization claimed 15,000 enterprises as members by late 1992.[19] It has sub-associations in each province, municipality, and autonomous region, as well as local associations in provincial or municipal jurisdictions containing large numbers of foreign-funded enterprises. (In the early 1990s, these branch associations numbered forty.) Membership in the association is usually held by the enterprise itself, though individuals may join. Foreign managers may become members, but the vast majority of members are Chinese, and the association is geared heavily toward their participation. Membership appears voluntary, since there have been no signs of coercion to join. Even so, the association's leaders claim to have a fairly broad membership. For example, the Shanghai branch (which was founded in 1988) claims that

---

16. Unger and Chan (1995), pp. 42–43; Lam (1992).

17. Jiang Shaogao and Li Jie (1992).

18. Where not otherwise noted, information for this section was gathered in 1991 through interviews with representatives of the national CAEFI office and the Shanghai, Guangzhou, and Beijing branches, and with Chinese and expatriate managers, some of whom were members of the association.

19. Xinhua (1992).

71% of the seven hundred foreign-funded enterprises that had begun operations in Shanghai as of late 1991 were members. Nationally in that year, the figure was said to be about 40% of the eligible businesses.

Like other social organizations, CAEFI treads the familiar path between state and society: it is dominated by the state in key respects, and yet manifests certain types of autonomy. In three dimensions, establishment, leadership, and functions, CAEFI and its branches are closely tied to the Chinese state, and particularly to MOFTEC. The association was formally organized and approved—"licensed," in the language of corporatism—by MOFTEC, with the support of the State Council's Leading Group on Foreign Investment, the State Planning Commission, and the (now-defunct) State Economic Commission (SEC). Local officials have been influential in founding branch associations. Government offices also have provided financial backing. Although the national association and its branches are primarily self-funding, MOFTEC allocated 300,000 yuan (approximately $58,000) to CAEFI to meet its initial costs.[20]

State personnel pervade the organizational structure. Most top leaders of the association are former high-level officials who are retired from MOFTEC or the SEC.[21] (This led one interviewee to joke that CAEFI is a "retirement home for old cadres.") The two heads were previously vice-ministers of MOFTEC and, as of 1990, ten of the fourteen standing councilors of the national association were officials (both active and retired) from bureaucracies concerned with foreign economic affairs.[22] A similar situation exists at the branch level; for example, the acting head of the Shanghai branch in the early 1990s was the retired leader of MOFTEC's Shanghai office. Prominent officials also serve as national-level advisors, as exemplified by State Councilor Gu Mu's position as "Honorary Chairman." This interlocking directorate between MOFTEC and CAEFI has the potential to institutionalize ministerial influence within the association. An interlocking structure also exists among associations. For example, a CAEFI vice-chair, Ma Yi, is also a

20. See Wei (1991); "Guanyu caiwu qingkuang de baogao" (1991).

21. These positions seem to represent full-time, second careers for fully retired (*lixiu*) officials. Melanie Manion, in personal correspondence, provided useful clarification on this issue. See also Manion (1992). This personnel linkage is not as close as for mass organizations, in which the top positions appear on the *nomenklatura* of the party Central Committee. See Burns (1987).

22. This "double posting" (*jianzhi*) of government cadres in leading positions in associations in a wide variety of realms is reported by Gordon White to be widespread (1993, p. 78).

vice-chair of the ACFIC, as well as a former SEC advisor. The state's influence in personnel reaches into the middle ranges as well. Both central and local governments are obliged to "support and assist the associations by providing the necessary personnel," though the association should also recruit its own personnel.[23] The middle-level staff is not always professionally qualified, however, as officers frequently have been assigned from related or even unrelated government bureaus (as in the case of one deputy director transferred from an office that oversees prisons), based on *guanxi* or as a reward for past work.

There is a hierarchical relationship between the national association, located in Beijing, and the branches. The position of the national organization was in fact strengthened when the original 1987 constitution was revised in 1990 to state that the sub-associations would be "directed by" the national association.[24] Echoing tensions that are rife in central-local fiscal relations, the effort to strengthen the national bureau may have been precipitated by difficulties in collecting what it argues is its share of membership dues from branches.[25]

The functional ties between CAEFI and the government are extremely close, and continue the pattern of state domination. The association's original constitution specifies that two of its main functions are "to implement the government policies, laws and provisions" relating to the open policy, and "to publicize the governmental policies" on foreign enterprises (Article 4). The goal of transmitting information from the government is reflected in the publications of local branches. The Shanghai and Guangzhou branch journals, for example, devote much space to reprinting laws concerning the operations of foreign-invested enterprises. CAEFI's leaders also have endorsed traditional methods of social control, including ideological and political work.[26] Suggesting close links, too, are the familiar ways in which association officials depict CAEFI's relationship with the government. While calling CAEFI *minjian*, its leaders (often in the same breath) described the association as a "bridge between enterprises and government," a "braid" in which the government and foreign-invested enterprises are intertwined, or the joining together of state and people (*guan min hejie*).[27] At times, though, the state's strand of the "braid" is depicted negatively as dom-

23. Wei (1991), p. 42.
24. See SAEFI (1991); CAEFI (1987), Article 13.
25. "Guanyu caiwu qingkuang de baogao," (1991), p. 51.
26. Wei (1991), p. 42.
27. This view was confirmed in interviews, and in Wei (1991), p. 34; Xinhua (1990).

inating association activities. Even the former MOFTEC official who heads the national office complained that, while the association receives virtually no funding from the government, the government nonetheless tries to control it (*"zhengfu bu yang women danshi yao guan women"*).

Toward what common end are CAEFI and the government supposed to cooperate, then? They are to work together to create an environment favorable to foreign investment. This can be achieved if the association passes information from the government to member enterprises, and transmits data, suggestions, and complaints from the member firms up to MOFTEC and other relevant ministries. As Wei Yuming suggested, "The association should cooperate with the relevant departments of the government to make thorough investigation and study of the causes, and put forward solutions and proposals, to help those enterprises that have troubles."[28] The association also is charged with carrying out activities that the government feels it should or can no longer perform as a result of economic reforms. Reflecting the rationale voiced for all post-Mao associations, an official of the Shanghai branch explained that foreign-funded enterprises "have met problems [but] it is inconvenient for government organizations to coordinate these things." So the association is to step in to do so, in effect allowing the state to capture the benefits of the efforts of a semi-autonomous group.[29] In addition to helping solve problems between foreign-invested enterprises and the government, the association has assumed the post-1949 government's tradition of giving citations to model enterprises; it annually commends enterprises that meet the state's goals for foreign investment, i.e., those that have high export earnings and profits.[30] CAEFI and the government are also to coordinate their actions and share expenses in defending themselves against foreign governments' accusations of dumping and of protectionism by member firms and, by extension, by China, though such activities were not well organized as of the early 1990s.[31] As this latter example suggests, the formal functional line between the association and MOFTEC is not always clear, a fact acknowledged by the Shanghai branch head. In short, CAEFI and its branches—established, officially sanctioned, and licensed by the government, run with the involvement of former or active foreign trade officials, and charged

28. Wei (1991), p. 38. See also CAEFI (1991). On how export associations work with government bureaus in similar ways, see Panagariya (1991), p. 17.
29. See also Whiting (1991), p. 21.
30. Xinhua (1993).
31. Interviews and Shen (1991).

with helping the state implement, promote, and improve China's investment policies—have strong ties to, and in some respects are controlled
by, the state.[32]

Reflecting these ties with the state, CAEFI is identified with government offices in the minds of many foreign-sector managers. Although
some have never heard of it, and others confuse it with FESCO
or MOFTEC's Foreign Investment Association (both of which are
unambiguously government offices), those who have heard of CAEFI
and know its status as an association perceive it to be primarily a
government-linked organization. At the same time, consistent with the
belief (discussed in chapter 4) that formal means for influencing the
government do not exist, most do not consider CAEFI to be a serious
channel in which to put forth suggestions or have complaints redressed.
Although they have not done so, a few interviewees reported that they
would consider trying to use the association to solve problems because
CAEFI leaders often are former officials or have close ties to the government. They see such ties as the crucial means by which CAEFI can
influence officials on behalf of its members. Also consistent and expected are their reports that they would use CAEFI to redress only narrow
business problems.

The association is not wholly state-dominated in the tradition of mass
organizations. In contrast to the views of most of those whom the association is to represent, its leaders often emphasize the autonomy
implied in the term *minjian* and reinforce the claim that CAEFI is "non-
governmental" by pointing out that the members join voluntarily and
that the organization supports itself primarily through membership fees.
(Annual dues amounted to about 1,000 yuan [$200] in the early
1990s.) The government leaves the association a fair amount of discretion in its area of functional expertise. Many of its activities are geared
toward helping foreign-invested enterprises, individually or as a group,
solve problems or meet business goals. For example, CAEFI promotes
business activities by organizing exhibitions in China and abroad, much
as chambers of commerce do elsewhere. CAEFI also sets up permanent
marketing points for member companies, and trains Chinese managers
and staff; in late 1992 it set up a service center to provide information
to foreign investors.[33] Its leaders also hope to engage in more fee-based
consulting to investors. Taking seriously its charge to improve the envi-

32. The association does not carry out *gong* works similar to those in the Qing. It lacks
the money and its officials do not view such activities as within their charter.

33. Xinhua (1992).

ronment for foreign investors, it tries to help member businesses solve problems involving the government bureaucracy. Such assistance often involves minor problems, such as coordinating the installation of telephone lines.

CAEFI is involved in the resolution of more important issues as well. For example, it has facilitated arbitration over disputes among member enterprises. A branch may also arrange for the local MOFERT bureau to help members coordinate with other government offices, such as customs and foreign exchange bureaus. It serves further as a representative to officials on behalf of joint ventures and wholly foreign-owned enterprises. As the Shanghai branch leader said, "Foreign-funded enterprises may have a conflict with the government enterprises themselves, and so we need non-governmental organizations to speak on their behalf." Toward this end, CAEFI claims to pass complaints of members upward to relevant governmental authorities, and holds seminars or retreats at which managers may question officials directly about policies. The Guangzhou branch, for example, holds three or four meetings a year with government officials to try to solve the problems of its members.

In the course of helping foreign-invested enterprises solve their problems, CAEFI is, of course, helping the government achieve one of the government's goals; it is wholly consistent that a state which wishes to promote foreign investment—and recognizes that bureaucratism is a major disincentive—allows a semi-autonomous organization to help sort out investors' problems. But CAEFI's actions have gone beyond helping firms troubleshoot. It has occasionally criticized government policy through the business press. For example, the secretary-general of CAEFI in 1994 called for the government to cede its monopoly on exporting agricultural products and to allow participation by foreign investors. He further lent support to the government's efforts to allow foreign banks to engage in currency transactions and open more branches in Chinese cities.[34] Moreover, on issues involving disputes between foreign-sector enterprises and government officials or regulations, CAEFI has on occasion taken up positions *against* existing policy or the decisions of government officials. Such opposition, even if gentle, clearly distinguishes this post-Mao association from mass organizations of the Maoist era.

Directors from the national office and local branches offered illustrations of how the association has intervened on behalf of enterprises.

34. The official was quoted in the English-language *China Daily*. See Agence France Presse English Wire (1994).

The Beijing branch pressed the Beijing municipal government to standardize the issuance of visas, for Chinese managers working in foreign enterprises, to travel overseas on business. This was a response to complaints of members that they lose precious business opportunities overseas while waiting for a business visa to be issued. The Shenzhen branch complained to local authorities that an anti-pornography campaign, which aimed to shut down all sauna houses, was too sweeping, for it closed legitimate businesses as well as those linked with prostitution. The national association also intervened when the parent (local ministerial) office of the Chinese partner to a Hubei Province joint venture tried to fire the Chinese general manager by going over the head of the supposedly autonomous board of directors. The manager was reinstated. The Shanghai branch strongly lobbied on behalf of its members against a new rule, promulgated by the State Administration for Exchange Control (SAEC), requiring foreign-invested businesses to report to it any transaction that earned foreign exchange soon after it transpired. The branch successfully lobbied the central SAEC office to require only quarterly reports of transactions, and only transactions over a minimum amount. CAEFI reported to the Jiangxi provincial government that components produced by a member business in Guangdong Province were not being allowed to be shipped through Jiangxi to Shanghai; a joint investigation between the association and the Jiangxi government ensued. The Guangzhou municipal branch also coordinated the settlement of a dispute between the local public security bureau and a Hong Kong businessman whom the bureau had illegally detained and arrested.

There is no guarantee that government officials will respond to complaints articulated by CAEFI, and it is not clear if the association was successful in the cases of the Shenzhen sauna houses or the Jiangxi shipments. Yet the success of the lobbying effort in cases involving the business visas, the change of the SAEC rule, the jailing of the Hong Kong businessman, and the reinstatement of the general manager—all of which involved sensitive issues—demonstrates that CAEFI has been able to effect *some* influence on officials on behalf of its members. Although it is by no means impossible that the state organs would have made changes at their own initiative, it is unlikely that they would have suppressed their own rules absent the outside pressure. It also should be noted that, in most of the examples, the association (particularly the branches) was pressing for rule changes by local rather than central officials. The focus on action at the local level reflects in part the fact that much of the interference in foreign enterprises is made by local governments. It also suggests that attempts at influence are made more often, or are more successful, at the local level.

CAEFI intended in 1991 to press for further autonomy. The revisions made to its charter in 1990 attempted to institutionalize further the concept that the organization is "non-governmental," and to downplay (though by no means eliminate) its work on behalf of the state. New articles replaced a commitment "to explain requirements and objectives of the national development plans" to members, a role which was felt to be too onerous, with a commitment merely to "introduce" the investment environment and to "provide information" for foreign businesses. Other new language explicitly guaranteed the right of members to withdraw from the association.[35] These and other constitutional changes were made at the prompting of branches, again suggesting that the strongest impetus for further autonomy may come from the local level. Some association leaders also seemed anxious to redefine their organizations' tasks on a more Western model, as indicated by one branch leader's comment that "we intend to change this association toward a kind of chamber of commerce as you have in foreign countries." Both he and a key figure in the national association requested that they be sent materials on American chambers of commerce and business associations.

In these ways CAEFI's experience reflects the elements of limited autonomy that are accommodated in the concept of socialist corporatism. CAEFI enjoys some autonomy in its realm of expertise. Its efforts to change certain government regulations show in particular that it has been able to exercise a degree of independence on the basis of its claim to protect the legitimate interests of the foreign sector. Its very establishment outside of the state structure signifies an effort by the government to devolve power away from its own organs to more functionally specific and competent organs with some basis in a societal constituency.

Yet these promising signs of autonomy and dynamism from the early 1990s, while real, are only part of the story. The limits on CAEFI's autonomy are brought into relief by the recognition that it does *not* engage in a number of the types of activities that its guild predecessors in the "golden age" did, notably the overt political activism that challenged the government and led to boycotts of foreign goods. Nor does CAEFI's role as an independent advocacy group appear to be deepening over time. Although foreign-sector managers interviewed in 1995

---

35. CAEFI (1991), pp. 43–50. There is no evidence that, prior to this, members had been prevented from withdrawing.

identified the association correctly more often, they continued to feel that it was state-dominated and at the same time unimportant as a channel for helping them resolve problems. They stated regularly that they had no time to participate in such an association, an attitude further suggesting the irrelevance of CAEFI to their lives, i.e., its weak institutionalization. Personal ties to officials remain the most important channel for solving problems involving government rules.

Thus, it is clear that, although the state does not wholly dominate CAEFI, the state's intention is to remain heavily involved. It fits the criteria central to the concept of socialist corporatism, to wit: (1) the state has sanctioned and established this functionally based association and its branches; (2) the state has granted CAEFI a near-monopoly such that it approximates a singular "peak" association—there is only one national association in the foreign sector, and each locality has only one branch;[36] (3) a clear hierarchy exists between the national association and local branches, with the predominance of the former being even further strengthened in 1990; (4) officials, often from high levels, constitute the leadership and have a role in setting the agenda; (5) many members believe they may only raise narrow complaints, and the officials are elected to leadership positions unanimously, suggesting an implicit agreement that members will observe certain controls on the articulation of demands.[37]

All these controls play a regime-maintenance function, moreover, for they help to stabilize the role of the socialist state at a time of rapid economic and social transition. Corporatist controls are further designed to foster cooperation by the foreign sector in meeting the regime's goals of economic development without threatening systemic change. The state's formation and oversight of CAEFI is an effort to pre-empt the rise of independent organizations representing new social forces. The fact that many of the association's branches (such as in Tianjin and Henan) were established after the 1989 Tiananmen events also suggests an effort to co-opt potentially disruptive social forces at the local level. In many ways these moves are reminiscent of the imperial court's 1904

36. While there is only one association exclusively for the foreign sector, foreign-sector managers may join other associations. For example, there is an association especially designated for Hong Kong–backed businesses—the *Wugang* association in Shanghai. (Managers from Hong Kong–backed businesses can join CAEFI as well.) Moreover, foreign-sector managers were allowed to join the ACFIC after revisions to its constitution in 1988. On the latter, see Xinhua (1988).

37. Compulsory membership is the one criterion of Schmitter's state corporatism that does not apply to CAEFI. Nor does it apply to membership in China's so-called "democratic parties" and groups. See Seymour (1987), p. 89.

call for the formation of chambers of commerce. Also reminiscent of that earlier period is the fact that these institutions are as of yet not taken very seriously by foreign-sector managers; the state-corporatist intentions of the central government appear to be only weakly realized.

The Business Associations for Private Entrepreneurs: ACFIC and SELA

Support for the existence of a socialist corporatism framework outside the foreign sector is found in studies of the association for large *siying* entrepreneurs, the All-China Federation of Industry and Commerce (ACFIC). As noted in chapter 2, the ACFIC was formed as a mass organization for former capitalists under the Party's United Front Department. In the reform era, it is intended to represent the private sector's business elite. Significant steps have been taken to remake the ACFIC into a *minjian* organization along lines similar to CAEFI. Its revised constitution makes no formal acknowledgment of any ties to the Party, and instead the ubiquitous "bridge" metaphor appears.[38] It has been given a second, less ominous sounding name, the National Non-Governmental Chamber of Commerce.[39] Although, historically, state-owned enterprises could be members, none have been permitted to join since the mid-1980s, and the membership has focused primarily on private enterprises. As with CAEFI, among its main tasks are protecting the interests of members, helping members improve quality and standards, providing education, and the like.[40] It also runs its own enterprises in many regions of the country, including technology and glass companies.[41] During the 1980s, moreover, the ACFIC became vocal on behalf of private enterprises. For example, in a report to the State Council the federation called for protection of private enterprises, and for freedom from harassment by local officials in the wake of the 1988 austerity program and Tiananmen. It has also called on the government to

---

38. The most recent constitution—*Zhongguo gongshangye lianhehui zhangcheng* (hereafter *GSLXZ*)—was promulgated 16 November 1993. (Text of the constitution was provided by Christopher Earle Nevitt.) Although Article 11 lists democratic centralism (*minzhu jizhongzhi*) as its organizational principle, Article 13 says its highest authority at each level is to be the federation's representative congress, which is governed by its constitution.

39. Xinhua (1994a).

40. *GSLXZ.*

41. Li Zongbo (1992).

establish private banks to provide capital to individual businesses. The federation's local branches also have lobbied on behalf of its members. In Tianjin, for example, the district branch reported that it has tried to locate sources of credit for its members and to negotiate lower rates for municipal services.[42]

But as expected, there remain important elements of state control. Beyond its historical links to the Party, the top leaders of the federation continue to be former or active government officials. China's most famous reformed capitalist, Rong Yiren, served as chair of the federation at the same time that he was vice-chair of the NPC Standing Committee in the early 1990s. Wang Guangying, the brother-in-law of Liu Shaoqi, followed Rong in both those positions in 1993.[43] The federation receives a substantial amount of funding from government sources.[44] It takes as a main task the education of members about relevant policies, including tax laws and corruption, both serious concerns of the government with respect to private business. Indeed, these and other tasks designed to coordinate the work of the private sector with the state's goals are reported to have been designated by the Party Central Committee, and to have been communicated through its old controlling body, the United Front Work Department.[45]

The actual influence of ACFIC appears to be similar to that of CAEFI. Although the Tianjin branch has apparently been successful at helping private businesses gain access to municipal services and credit, the federation often does so based on personal and former institutional connections of its officials.[46] At the same time, members of the business elite who had reason to be involved with the federation claimed that its work was not particularly important or influential, either for them or for the private sector as a whole.

The finding of dualism in the activity of the business associations of the foreign and private business elite sets an outer limit on the extent to which we might expect to find autonomous associations more general-

---

42. On protection from harassment, see Tan Hongkai and Zhang Xiaogang (1991). On the call for banks, see Agence France Presse (1994). On the Tianjin branch, see Nevitt (1994).

43. Xinhua (1992b); Liu Donghua and Niu Changzheng (1993).

44. The precise amount of government funding is unclear. Nevitt (1994) claims that it is fully funded by the government, whereas Oi (1992a) argues that it receives substantial funds from the branch associations.

45. The tasks for the ACFIC were suggested in speeches made to the executive committee of the ACFIC by Politburo member Tian Jiyun and United Front Work Department director Ding Guangen. Xinhua (1992c). See also Xinhua (1994b).

46. Nevitt (1994).

ly in post-Mao China. Given the corporatist constraints on the foreign- and private-sector associations, it is unlikely that associations in other, less independent, sectors will be able to build an independent associational realm. Consistent with this expectation, studies of associations in other areas of the economy suggest that certain aspects of socialist corporatism are being replicated for other groups, and yet these associations have even stronger ties to the state.

A key example is the association for the non-elite members of the private business class, *geti* entrepreneurs. Like the constitutions of the ACFIC and CAEFI, the 1986 constitution of the Self-Employed Laborers Association (SELA) stresses dual control and advocacy functions. Much like its counterparts, SELA is supposed to perform minor advocacy functions, to protect the "legitimate" (i.e., state-sanctioned) rights and interests of entrepreneurs against arbitrary officials, to help solve problems of individual businesses, and to represent their opinions and demands to higher levels.[47] SELA draws on personal connections of its officers to do so.[48] On the other hand, it too was set up and licensed by the government and is under fairly strict control of and co-optation by its superior organ, the Industry and Commerce Bureau (Gongshangju). Government organs provide many of the association's top personnel.

SELA has some significant differences from the other two associations discussed here, differences that push the association in the direction of much greater state control. The SELA constitution fails to use the term *minjian*. It states directly that it is a mass organization under the "leadership" (*lingdao*) of the Party and government and receives the guidance (*zhidao*) of the Industry and Commerce Bureau.[49] In at least one location, Beijing, it has worked in conjunction with the local Communist Youth League branch to coordinate CYL work among *geti* entrepreneurs.[50] Three-quarters of its funding comes from its supervising

---

47. *Zhongguo geti laodongzhe xiehui zhangcheng* (Constitution of the China Individual Laborers Association, hereafter *GLXZ*), 5 December 1986, ch. 2. (Copy of text was provided by Christopher Earle Nevitt.) The role of SELA (the Geti Laodongzhe Xiehui) is discussed in Bruun (1995); Gold (1989), p. 199; Nevitt (1994); Odgaard (1992); Solinger (1992). On the state-corporatist nature of another former mass organization, the All-China Federation of Trade Unions, see Anita Chan (1993) and Unger and Chan (1995), who argue that the ACFTU increasingly has injected itself into the administrative and legislative process on behalf of worker interests.

48. Wank (1991, pp. 14, 21) reports this for Xiamen's SELA branch as well as the Xiamen Chamber of Commerce and the Young Factory Director and Manager Association (Qingnian Changzhang Jingli Xiehui). Odgaard (1992) also found personal relations to be key in his study of associations in rural Sichuan.

49. *GLXZ*, ch. 1.

50. Xinhua (1994).

bureau—a much higher figure than for CAEFI.[51] Membership appears to be compulsory, since entrepreneurs are forced to join at the point of registering their businesses with the local government.[52] To the degree that there is activism it is found within the local branches; yet it appears that the SELA is in fact much less vigorous about promoting its members' interests than are the ACFIC branches (particularly at the district level). For example, one study finds that rather than addressing the genuine problems of its members (problems such as competition from unlicensed vendors) the Tianjin branch organized several trips abroad for members to develop business contacts, even though "the vast majority of small-scale entrepreneurs . . . are far too parochial for foreign contacts to be of any use."[53] This irrelevance is surely one of the reasons its members "hold the organization in very low regard. Further, if faced with any kind of business problem, . . . [they indicated that it] would be the last place they would go for help."[54]

The fact that SELA is in the jurisdiction of the Industry and Commerce Bureau and does not consider itself *minjian* seems to place it at the outer edge of China's socialist corporatism. This higher degree of state control when compared to CAEFI and the ACFIC makes policy sense from the perspective of the central and municipal governments. Although the *geti* entrepreneurs who make up the SELA membership provide a useful economic function of providing consumer services, the *geti* sector arguably serves an even more important function of alleviating unemployment among those who might otherwise generate social unrest. SELA's effort to control this potentially dangerous group (through compulsory membership, for example) is a logical extension of the social control function of the sector itself. SELA's unique character also suggests an effort by the state to tailor its new institutions according to different needs.

•   •   •   •

The comparison of these three associations, CAEFI, ACFIC, and SELA, highlights an important point: socialist corporatism does not exist uniformly in all business sectors. One key difference between these associations concerns how close the formal ties of the organization to the state are, as illustrated at one extreme by CAEFI's relatively greater

51. *GLXZ*, ch. 7; Nevitt (1994), p. 7.

52. See Odgaard (1992), p. 99; Bruun (1995).

53. Nevitt (1994), p. 9. Some degree of activism is noted by Odgaard (1992), pp. 99–100; Solinger (1992), pp. 130–131; and Bruun (1995).

54. Nevitt (1994), p. 8.

(but incomplete) organizational autonomy, and at the other extreme by SELA's explicit subordination to the Gongshangju. A related difference is the degree of activism—ranging from non-existent to moderate—by local branches on behalf of its members. Indeed, the state likely considers greater autonomy necessary for CAEFI and ACFIC if they are to fulfill a primary goal for foreign and larger private enterprises, namely, to be an important force for modernization. Greater activism on behalf of their constituencies makes sense in light of this goal. In contrast, the control function associated with small entrepreneurs (SELA) limits the need and desirability for them to have even the limited independence of CAEFI and ACFIC.

Despite the lack of uniformity, there are sufficiently similar characteristics to consider them all part of a new socialist corporatist strategy. Reflecting the core features of socialist corporatism, they each have the dual task of serving both control and co-optation functions, on the one hand, and advocacy for newly legitimized interests, on the other. Proposals to expand corporatist institutions to cover ministries, in conjunction with the transformation of existing mass organizations and the establishment of functional associations, also suggest that the state intends corporatism to be a part of the evolving picture of state-society relations in post-Mao China.

Yet evidence from the foreign and private sectors suggests that the socialist corporatist institutions are not especially effective, at least as of yet. Despite some evidence of determined activism by association officials at the local levels, neither foreign-sector managers nor private entrepreneurs feel that, on balance, these associations are very effective advocates. Rather, what *is* useful to these members of the business elite is the vertical, informal clientelism embedded in these associations. Local associations may press through formal channels against the state, but entrepreneurs are right to perceive them as channels through which entrepreneurs can develop or draw on existing *guanxi*. Thus, although socialist corporatism is a crucial element of a rather complex picture of state-society relations in post-Mao China, the whole of state-society relations cannot be understood through the corporatist prism alone. Socialist corporatism operates in tandem with clientelism. The hybrid quality of post-Mao relations between state and society is explored further in the concluding chapter.

CHAPTER 6

The Emergence
of Hybrid State-Society
Relations in Post-Mao China

Among the myriad changes brought about by the post-Mao economic reforms, one of the most profound has been the birth of a new business elite in the non-state sectors. The preceding chapters have elucidated the specific characteristics of two segments of this elite, foreign-sector managers and private entrepreneurs. Beyond merely describing the origin and characteristic of this new elite, this book has addressed the broader problem of the impact of economic reforms on state-society relations. Will a stratum born of the economic reforms generate direct pressures for political reform, and even be the carriers of civil society? If not, in what ways *do* new economic elites in fact interact with the state and what political outcomes have resulted from economic reform?

This book's examination of China's new business elite has revealed a pattern of state-society relations that diverges substantially from Maoist neo-traditionalism and the "transmission belt" mode of mass organizations. But, instead of democratization, we see in the leading-edge sectors of both foreign and private business a pattern of state-society relations that combines informal clientelism and socialist corporatism. This final chapter elaborates on this conclusion, and then proceeds to address two additional issues: the question of whether the new patterns of state-society relations that we see in China are compatible with the broader statist patterns found elsewhere in East Asia, and the implications of this study's findings for the likelihood of a future evolution toward liberal democracy or the emergence of civil society in China.

New Groups Arise from Economic Reform, But to What Political End?

The managerial elite that has emerged from the post-Mao reforms differs significantly from the predecessor elite that managed the state-owned economy during and after the "transition to socialism" of the mid-1950s. That earlier generation of managers lived almost totally under the purview of the Party-state. But the growth in the reform era of markets and the concomitant devolution of authority away from the state sector, plus the opening of the country to foreign businesses, have allowed people in some sectors to structure their lives largely outside the state-owned, neo-traditional unit (*danwei*). Hence, in the foreign sector, managers are provided an alternative to the pattern of "organized dependence" that has dominated state industries.[1] They have escaped from close supervision and from control by means of Party dossiers and are much less dependent upon the state for the provision of medical care, housing, and other social welfare benefits. They have significantly greater job mobility. In the private sector, too, entrepreneurs have become quite mobile and are more free of Party surveillance, and increasingly provide for their own welfare through the market.

Autonomy can also be seen in the ideology of foreign-sector managers. Although many of them were drawn to the foreign sector in the first place because of their more independent spirit, they have, through their overseas experiences and their contacts with international managers, developed further ideas about the desirability of changing the status quo. Compared to the reforms actually being implemented in the early 1990s, members of the business elite hold quite strong views about the need not only for further economic change but also for further political change. They favor not only full marketization and unfettered participation by China in the world economy, but also a greatly reduced role for the state and Party in the economy. They clearly have been influenced by foreign ideologies.

These signs of autonomy are not insignificant, and yet they do not tell the whole story. Despite their structural independence and their

---

1. Walder (1991a, p. 337) emphasizes the lack of alternatives as central to "organized dependence."

views about the need for change, most foreign-sector managers wish to avoid politics, wanting simply to "check out" of the domain of state control. They are not, and do not perceive themselves to be, at the forefront of political change. Private entrepreneurs also are apolitical in their behavior. Neither group has taken to the streets in protest of policies with which they disagree, nor have they extensively or regularly lobbied the government for policy change. It is true that their associations in some instances have represented business interests against those of the state, but for the most part members of the business elite rely on personal relations with officials to gain highly individualistic benefits for their businesses.

There are several reasons for the lack of activism by members of this elite. Foreign-sector managers view their anti-Party stance as based on ideology, but they often come to their belief for very practical reasons based on personal experiences. Having been forced into activism, particularly during the Cultural Revolution era when they came of age, they tend to have a strong distaste for "politics."[2] They do not readily distinguish between activism forced by the state on behalf of the state (which constitutes the bulk of their political experience) and more spontaneous organization in their own interests; both are to be avoided. This is consistent with their "business first" orientation. In fact, their interest in avoiding politics is supported by the current business environment; they *can* immerse themselves in business. Brus made the point over a decade ago with regard to business elites in Eastern Europe:

[T]he very extension of the role of the market and enterprise autonomy (depoliticization of the economy) may be enough to satisfy managerial interests without generating pressures for pluralization of the polity. . . . It is true that people must feel personally less constrained when the command system gives way to the market-oriented one, but whether this fact in itself becomes a spur to political action is another matter; greater economic independence from the state may well have the opposite consequence of promoting both non-political attitudes and the pursuit of strictly private interests.[3]

The business elite's lack of activism derives not only from the ideology and experiences of its members, but also from their belief that they are powerless to pressure the state and are unimportant as a group. They

2. Their lack of activity therefore cannot be said to render their reformist political views mere window-dressing. Rather, to be apolitical does not mean that managers have no political views, but that they do not wish to engage in political activity.

3. Brus (1983), pp. 125–127.

still perceive themselves as too vulnerable to forge a new relationship. And they are correct in perceiving that they possess an alternative strategy for influencing officials—namely, personalistic ties—that is more acceptable to the state and does not require activism of the sort members of the economic elite wish to avoid.

Many characteristics of the foreign-sector business elite have a familiar ring. They are characteristics of the broader international managerial bourgeoisie. Like their overseas counterparts, China's foreign-sector managers have in particular a cosmopolitan, even internationalist, outlook when it comes to economics. They are imbued with "modern" technocratic values of efficiency and rational management. Their lifestyle, too, is cosmopolitan when judged by Chinese standards. Their apolitical nature and lack of revolutionary zeal are typical of comprador elites, as is the tendency to rely on clientelist strategies. Their subordination to the state through state corporatist structures also is relatively common.[4] Yet China's elite appears weaker vis-à-vis the state than comparable groups in most developing capitalist countries—particularly Latin America and, as we shall see below, East Asia—that have a longer, uninterrupted history of a private sector and international business ties.[5] It is weaker than China's own bourgeoisie of the "golden age." It is even weaker than the very new business elite that has emerged at the pinnacle of Russia's new power structure, a group that has gained considerable control over the executive and legislative arenas of that postsocialist state.[6] In other words, although China's business elite is a clearly defined group, it lacks horizontal ties that bind the members of the group together and facilitate collective consciousness and collective action. The weakness of this group's associations and its members' sense of powerlessness to effect changes that would help foster policies they favor reflect the absence of such horizontal ties.[7] Thus, China's new

4. On the pragmatism, subjection to corporatist structures, and reliance on clientelism among members of the Latin American business elite, see Payne (1994).

5. Even so, the business elite in developing capitalist countries often is portrayed as relatively weak; it is seen as internally fragmented and dependent on the state to protect its interests. (This is the picture drawn in the literatures on bureaucratic authoritarianism and dependency. See O'Donnell [1973] and Evans [1979].) Payne (1994) argues that, although it faces great challenges in engaging in collective action, the business elite in Latin America has at times overcome these challenges to mobilize to support military coups as well as to support moves toward democratization.

6. Journalistic accounts of this group in Russia include Erlanger (1995) and Stanley (1995).

7. The ability to formulate its strategy on a national level is a hallmark of the "new bourgeoisie." See Becker (1987), p. 97 n. 15.

business elite cannot, at least yet, be conceived of as a "class for itself."
In part this circumstance occurs because China's managerial elite is new.
It also has few direct and personal ties to others who previously had
played a similar role in China. The nationalization of property that was
completed in 1956 and the elimination of managerial and private interests as legitimate interests cut the links of such a group with the past.[8]
The disadvantage posed by the group's relative youth has been magni-
fied by the state's efforts to pre-empt the process of class formation.[9]

New (Old) State-Society Relations
in the Leading-Edge Economic Sectors

Returning to the question of the link between economic
and political change, it is clear that the economic reform's creation of a
new elite with structural and ideological autonomy is insufficient to produce democratization or civil society in the short term, or in a direct
manner. Yet while the outcome of the link between economic reform
and change in state-society relations is neither simple nor foreordained,
change nevertheless can occur. Economic reform does indeed loosen old
(in this case, Leninist) structures, but this loosening process interacts
with other variables which exert a powerful and often decisive influence
over what shape political change actually takes. In post-Mao China,
three intervening factors have shaped the manner in which state-society
relations have evolved in the leading-edge sectors of the economy. The
first factor, discussed previously, is the concrete interests and ideology
of foreign-sector managers; the practical ideology of managers translates
into a freedom *not* to be involved in politics and, concretely, an interest
in avoiding politics so that they can focus on business. The second element is the continuing use of personal ties to effect influence. The final
intervening factor, and arguably the most important, is the effort of the
state to create channels of interaction between state and society, specif-

---

8. An exception is Rong Yiren, who comes from what was arguably Shanghai's most
prominent capitalist family of the 1930s and who has risen to prominence under the Deng
regime. Most former capitalists fled during the revolution.

9. Another way to think about the class situation of China's new business elite is to
see them as holding what Erik Olin Wright (1985, esp. pp. 25, 43–44, and 89) has called
a "contradictory location" in socialist society—it simultaneously is subordinate to the state
and dominant over local employees and "the masses." I thank an anonymous reader for
this insight.

ically to attempt to co-opt members of the business elite before they have a chance to engage in independent action on their own behalf. Thus, in contrast to the "golden age" of the 1920s, when the bourgeoisie failed to seize state power because the state was too weak to be worth seizing, China's post-Mao business elite has failed to transform its economic position into political power because it is uninterested in doing so, because there is a viable clientelist option, and because the socialist corporatist strategy of the state is designed to prevent it.

These three factors together have created a new form of state-society relations in China's leading economic sectors. This new pattern is far from pristine. There are inklings of civil society. But while these inklings are clearly part of the picture of post-Mao state-society relations, to report them alone or exaggerate their importance would render the picture woefully incomplete. The structural and ideological autonomy of these elites has failed thus far to provide a decisive basis for coordinated behavior independent of the state. Seeds of civil society represent the weakest part of the emerging pattern of state-society relations.

Instead of civil society, the dominant pattern consists of a combination of socialist corporatism and clientelism. In their actual behavior (as opposed to their ideology), China's new business elites choose safe, well-established, and effective clientelist strategies to maneuver their way vis-à-vis the state bureaucracy. For even though the formal institutions of neo-traditionalism have been seriously eroded in the foreign and private sectors, no equivalent, highly effective formal channels have emerged. The absence of thoroughgoing marketization, moreover, has meant that incentives for using personal ties remain; foreign-sector managers recognize the tremendous importance of cultivating good relations with officials in order to achieve their business goals. Clientelist strategies are most important in the private sector, since entrepreneurs are still quite dependent upon the discretionary favoritism of local officials for protection and resources. The entrepreneurs use a variety of strategies to cultivate good relations with officials, such as paying local officials to establish a collective. (One distinguishing feature of the foreign sector is that foreign businesses have pressed the government to regularize the business environment and codify regulations, reducing by comparison the need for informal relations with officials.)[10] Clientelism is also a central feature of the interactions between business associations

---

10. In other words, although bribes for the provision of services also are demanded in the foreign sector, the effort to regularize and formalize foreign business's access to public goods is much more extensive than in the private sector.

and the state, for members and association leaders alike know that their personal ties are paramount in making the organization effective in pursuing members' goals.

The foreign and private sectors also provide substantial evidence for the other major component of this new pattern of state-society relations: socialist corporatism. We have seen that the associations of the foreign and private sectors, particularly their branch organizations, at times press the interests of their members on the state. But their dominant mode of interaction with officials is state corporatist. As with the formation of chambers of commerce at the turn of the century, the post-Mao government has legitimated interests outside the Party-state in an attempt to unleash the power of societal groups, but in a way that directs that power toward the government's own goal (national economic development) and prevents the newly created forces from acting contrary to state interests. For such reasons, the associations have been organized and sanctioned by the state, and their leadership has been dominated by cadres dispatched from related ministries. The legitimacy of associations derives solely from having received state sanction. In their major tasks, including helping to promote a favorable business environment by working with both businesses and the Chinese bureaucracy, they have served the goals of the state.

As the perceptions of these associations' constituents make clear, however, at this stage of development socialist corporatism is more of a government strategy and a set of institutions than an effective channel linking state and society. The continuing perception of members that these associations are fully governmental and can be only weak advocates of members' legitimate interests reflects the weight of China's Leninist past.[11] The lack of importance that business elites assign to associations means that, for business elites, clientelism is the most salient part of the hybrid pattern.

Socialist corporatism, which dominates the state's efforts in the associational realm, and clientelism, which characterizes the behavior of both individuals and associations, are consistent and complementary. Far from seeming out of place in post-Mao China, this hybrid seems quite natural there. One reason is that each half of the clientelism-corporatism marriage has a deeply rooted legacy in China. The use of informal personal ties existed not only prior to 1949, but has also pervaded the post-1949 context in conjunction with the formal authority

11. The weakness of these associations also becomes apparent in the comparison (drawn below) with business associations in Taiwan and South Korea.

relations of neo-traditionalism. The Janus-like pattern that underlies socialist corporatism is rooted in a long history of merchant-government ties. Indeed, the post-Mao government's corporatist strategy can be conceived of as an attempt to have business serve the same function—aiding economic development while controlling the political role of merchants—as it did in the Qing period, and as the state-sponsored guilds did in the Nationalist era.

Each half of the hybrid pattern, clientelism and socialist corporatism, is rational in the post-Mao environment. Though perhaps not optimal (for either normative or efficiency reasons), this hybrid nevertheless works—and in some ways works *well*—for both state and society. The proof that this pattern is not wholly dysfunctional is that the business elite has thrived financially without significant political change. Hence, clientelism works well for members of the business elite because it allows them access to officials in an environment where formal channels of interaction are poorly developed. Where they do have a formal channel, through their business association, it is useful in significant part because of its leaders' *guanxi*. Although some members of the business elite complain about the need to rely heavily upon *guanxi*, most are comfortable with the central role it plays in their business activities.

Clientelism also serves the interests of the central state and of individual officials.[12] It provides the government with a relatively costless means (measured in terms of state power) of quelling unhappiness within the crucial foreign and private sectors. Such piecemeal distribution of public goods by the state undermines the ability of societal actors to pressure the state in an organized way. Although use of *guanxi* creates pressure on officials to meet the needs of business, it is too individualized and fragmented to be a regular channel to promote lasting policy change. Distributing public goods in response to personal requests diffuses societal energy rather than concentrating it; it allows the state to buy off discontent short of a point where such discontent might foster organized lobbying or opposition.[13] In other words, informal vertical

12. Thus, the norm of reciprocity central to the idea of clientelism (the idea that both sides benefit) is present in post-Mao patterns of clientelism, as it was in Maoist neo-traditionalism.

13. This is not to say that there are no costs associated with the state's need to respond to demands made through clientelist channels. The distribution of material state resources may be much less efficient than what could be achieved through a more collectivist bargaining pattern with business elites. In other words, clientelism can undermine bureaucratic capability. Calculation of costs to the state would have to net out the benefits the state—or individual officials—may gain through both legitimate (access to privately developed resources) and illegal (bribes) channels.

clientelism helps prevent the strengthening of horizontal ties within or between economic groups and hinders class formation. Moreover, benefits of clientelism also accrue to individual officials. Because officials benefit financially, and often illegally, from their ties to business, particularly in the private sector, they are at least as eager for such ties as are the members of the business elite themselves. Still, corruption is not always the motive of entrepreneurial local officials; many officials find it rational, for political and economic reasons, to use informal ties to aid the development of businesses within their jurisdiction.[14]

The other half of the hybrid, socialist corporatism, benefits foreign-sector managers and entrepreneurs insofar as it sanctions significantly more freedom within their functional realm than they had previously had under Leninist patterns of government control. Moreover, although corporatist business associations co-opt business elites, these organizations in theory provide a formal channel of access to the state. Corporatism obviously is beneficial for the state because it gives the state access to the resources of society to put toward economic development, while at the same time divesting it from the burden of directly carrying out all economic tasks. Socialist corporatism therefore complements clientelism's tendency to prevent the emergence of a stronger, more organized society. Nevertheless, these benefits of socialist corporatism to the state could be given fuller play if the system were more effectively implemented.

The hybrid nature of emerging state-society relations in the leading economic sectors is not surprising insofar as pure typologies are more often a convenience of analysts than a reflection of reality. If pure typologies cannot be expected in stable times, they can be expected even less during a time of transition as dramatic as that of the post-Mao era. Nor is the way in which this pattern manifests itself uniform across sectors, as seen in the different strengths of clientelism in the foreign and private sectors and in the somewhat different roles played by associations. China has long been recognized as having great diversity in its regions and sectors, and so to find differences even within the most advanced portions of the economy is not especially surprising.

Given that the two segments of China's new business elite in which we are most likely to find greater independence from the state (the elite in the foreign and private sectors) exhibit patterns not primarily of civil society but of a clientelist-corporatist hybrid, it is highly unlikely that

14. See Oi (1992).

other segments of the business elite that start out more closely tied to the state—particularly officials-turned-entrepreneurs and *taizidang*—will be at the forefront of even more liberal patterns of state-society relations. Rather, these other segments of the business elite are more likely to fit easily into the corporatist-clientelist hybrid identified here. By the same logic, it is unlikely that the other key sectors of the economy, the state-owned and collective sectors, will establish patterns of interaction with the state that are more independent than those found in the foreign and private sectors.[15] And there are no signs in practice that greater independence or pressures for political liberalization have occurred in other sectors of the economy. As the economic reforms deepen and organized dependence breaks down, individuals within these other sectors must increasingly rely upon the market for jobs and the provision of other necessities of life. But these changes have not occurred at the pace or to the degree found in the leading-edge sectors. As in the foreign and private sectors, moreover, we see that the central government has considered extending corporatist controls to industrial associations. Clientelism remains a prominent feature in these sectors as well.

China in the East Asian Context

A more nuanced perspective on the patterns of state-society relations that have emerged in China's leading business sectors can be gained through a comparison of the institutions of China's business-government relations with those found in other East Asian nations, particularly South Korea, Taiwan and, to a lesser extent, Japan.[16] The picture of business-government relations painted in the core literature on statism in Taiwan and Korea shows these countries to possess autonomous states that have, through talented and uncorrupted bureaucracies, intervened intelligently in the economy (often by promoting exports and screening foreign investment) in order to mold market forces to the state's goals of rapid industrial development. Strong, authoritarian states are insulated from and dominate relatively

15. This conclusion follows the logic of the critical case study discussed in the introduction.

16. The small size and non-national character of Singapore and Hong Kong (and the colonial status of the latter until 1997) make comparisons between them and China less useful. The East Asian "statism" literature is summarized in ch. 1.

weaker and more malleable business communities, often through intermediate corporatist associations. Recent additions to the founding
works in this literature modify this picture to show that a range of institutional structures, and particularly of mechanisms to coordinate business and government, is possible under the "statist" guise. In addition,
over time business has grown into a more influential partner. It has also
become clear that the competent bureaucracies of these regimes coexist with deeply rooted personal networks. These networks often engage
in corrupt and rent-seeking activities, and modify earlier works' claims
of state autonomy.[17] Despite these variations and imperfections, however, the works in this second wave of the statism literature continue to
validate the importance of strong, competent states working effectively
with business elites.

To the extent that China's business-government relations have
evolved in a corporatist direction, that country has grown more similar
to Taiwan and Korea. At a very broad level, similarities exist in these
countries' formal institutions of business-government relations and in
the goals of the regimes. Yet China's marriage of clientelism to socialist
corporatism contains key *dis*similarities, particularly a relatively weaker
set of government and corporatist institutions, that cast in relief key features of China's hybrid pattern of clientelism and socialist corporatism.

Business-government relations in contemporary China exhibit three
core similarities with other East Asian countries. The first similarity centers around the goals of the regime. China's reformers have adopted the
same broad goal as did their East Asian counterparts: rapid, stable economic growth, based in large part on exports.[18] Similarly, the Deng
regime has been committed to stability, particularly after the chaos of
the Cultural Revolution.

Second, the Taiwanese and Korean governments have established
cooperation-promoting institutions that link the state with business.
These institutional linkages reflect governmental strategies quite similar
to the Chinese regime's effort to marshall the resources of non-state sectors and at the same time retain ultimate authority over them. Business
historically has been a subordinate partner in the relationship, moreover;
the major task of business elites and their associations has been to facil-

17. On these modifications, see Cheng, Haggard, and Kang (1995); Kang (1995).
18. China has not relied as heavily on exports as did its East Asian neighbors; it has
not needed to, given the size of the domestic economy. Still, exports from China have
been an important engine of growth since the mid-1980s. See Lardy (1992).

itate implementation of government policy. Thus, in Korea the government has sanctioned and granted monopoly representation to a host of business associations, including peak associations such as the Korean Chamber of Commerce and Industry and the Federation of Korean Industry (FKI). The Korean government has also cooperated closely with the *chaebol* (business conglomerates, such as Hyundai), organizations which it had a strong hand in promoting but which have grown into dynamic business concerns with significant influence.[19] Taiwan has also seen the growth of bodies to coordinate between business and the state, although these have taken a somewhat different form from, and became influential later on than, their counterparts in Korea. In Taiwan, the industrial and commercial associations that represent businesses were established along classic state corporatist lines. They have been subject to government approval in exchange for a functional monopoly. Any business sector with more than five firms is required to form an association, which is approved and controlled by the Guomindang's Committee on Social Affairs. The committee influences the appointment of top staff members, the most important of whom are usually loyal former military, security, or government officers. Indeed, the leader of the two national business federations during much of the 1980s was the same man, C. F. Koo, who not only owned the enormous Taiwan Cement Corporation but also was a member of the Guomindang Standing Committee for many years.[20] However, these state corporatist associations, much like their PRC counterparts, were without much influence as they were established by the Guomindang in order to prevent the emergence of an independent power base among native Taiwanese businesses.

The third broad similarity between China and its East Asian neighbors is clientelism's place at the core of the system. As we have seen,

<hr />

19. On peak associations and *chaebol*, see Cheng, Haggard, and Kang (1995); Johnson (1987); Jones and Sakong (1980); Koo (1987); Onis (1991), pp. 115–116; Park (1987, pp. 905–908); and Woo (1991). Park (pp. 915–916) finds corporatist institutions in other sectors of South Korean society (professions, workers, and peasants), but offers the caveat that corporatism works quite differently in each sector; business associations in Korea, he argues, are the most influential even though they are susceptible to government manipulation.

20. On Taiwan's state corporatist business associations, see Chu (1994); Tien (1989), esp. pp. 43–63; Winckler (1992), pp. 241–242; Wade (1990), pp. 271–272; and Zeigler (1988), pp. 182–183. The Taiwanese government did not corporatize the small and medium-size firms that have been the basis for Taiwan's phenomenal export-driven growth over the past two decades, however. See Unger and Chan (1995).

clientelism in China pervades the business elite's encounters with government officials. Despite the arguments of the earliest works in the statism literature that East Asian states are autonomous and insulated from social pressures, and despite the picture of a pure Weberian bureaucracy,[21] clientelism is far from absent there; personal ties undergird the formal organizations that coordinate business and government, and are central to business-government relations. Such networks were first noticed to be important in Japan's industrial policy. There, state bureaucrats from the Ministry of International Trade and Industry (MITI) retire early to key positions in corporations or industry associations, where they provide crucial coordination between industry and the bureaucracy. This carefully institutionalized process is known as *amakudari*, or "the descent from heaven."[22] Similarly, in Korea "many big businessmen have other channels [than business associations] through which business elites can influence the government: personal relationships, power brokering, outright corruption, and political contributions to the ruling party or politicians."[23] *Chaebol* relations with the government are based heavily on personal ties of top business leaders with the office of the president and key bureaucrats. These ties, and their corrupt nature, were dramatically illustrated by the scandals that erupted in the mid-1990s at the highest levels of Korea's political system. The institutional links between Taiwan's business associations and the state are also underlain by a web of complex clientelist relationships. At the top of this network, for example, business leaders are married to members of the Guomindang's central leadership.[24]

Comparisons of goals and broad institutional structures suggest that business-government relations in China have come to look on the surface quite a bit like what exists in Taiwan and Korea. Nevertheless, there

---

21. The argument that relatively great autonomy, particularly early in the process of development, shielded East Asian states from societal pressures that could seriously undermine their goals was made by, for example, Haggard, Kim, and Moon (1991, pp. 859, 869); Onis (1991, p. 124); and Wade (1990). The early works in this literature played down "traditional" rent-seeking behaviors, perhaps because the authors were attempting to argue (against the neoclassical development school) that the state could be efficient, honest, and rational.

22. See Okimoto (1989); Gerlach (1992).

23. Park (1987), p. 907; see also p. 915. The use of personal ties in South Korea is facilitated by the fact that Korean elites in both business and government are from the same schools and types of family, and often know each other personally.

24. Chu (1994), p. 119. See also Evans (1995), pp. 56–57.

are important differences in the pattern that is emerging in China, of which three features are most significant. Each of these differences reflects, at least in part, the socialist context from which post-Mao state-society relations have emerged.

The first difference is the relative strength in Taiwan and Korea of the institutions linking the business sector to government and the effective coordination these institutions foster between business and government. The institutions of business-government relations in Taiwan and Korea in some ways look quite different from each other, and yet in both countries these institutions help provide *effective* coordination between business elites and the state. The peak associations of business in Korea were relatively weak when formed in the 1950s and 1960s. Yet they have grown in organizational capacity and in influence. Such growth is especially evident in the FKI; at the same time as the government manipulates the FKI's support and plays a strong role in choosing its leaders (many of whom have been retired government officials), the federation has been influential in the policy process and in the 1980s has even grown more oppositional in some of its policy stances. Business federations also have close links with the industries they represent, as measured in terms of how satisfied the business community is with their activity. In one survey, three-quarters of the business representatives reported they were basically satisfied with the activities of their associations.[25] Business federations are very closely tied to leaders of Korean industry, moreover. Because corporatist associations in Korea are legitimate and authoritative in the eyes of their constituents, they are better positioned for genuine, value-producing coordination with the government, even if they tend to be state-dominated. The *chaebol* conglomerates are even more important than the federations for linking business with government. Indeed, business power has been so concentrated in the *chaebol* conglomerates that their direct firm-level ties with the country's president and relevant portions of the bureaucracy have tended to eclipse the role of peak associations. Through the strong institutions it has created, the Korean state has fostered a highly effective division of labor between government and business based on complementary roles.

Taiwan's institutions for government-business coordination, although they started out quite similar in form to those in China, have also been strengthened over the past decade. As Taiwan embarked on a

25. Park (1987), p. 908.

strategy to shift its productive capacity to more sophisticated industries, the government allowed what were relatively contentless corporatist shells to grow into much more significant actors on the political scene, both by providing input on policy and by participating (through financial contributions) in the electoral process. Just as important has been the appearance of a deliberation council, the Industrial Development Consultative Committee, modeled on Japan's *shingikai*, to bring together private-sector, bureaucratic, and academic voices in policy consideration. An Industrial Policy Advisory Board, established in 1982 under the Ministry of Economic Affairs, also sought private-sector input. Though still generally dominated by government and academics, such organizations have given further authoritative voice to business.[26]

In contrast to both Taiwan and Korea, China's business associations do not have strong links with industry. Weak links are evident, for example, in foreign-sector managers' lack of understanding of CAEFI's role, and the feeling among both foreign-sector managers and entrepreneurs that their associations are not particularly effective (see chapter 5). China's associations are poorly institutionalized and possess little clout—that is, have little authority and legitimacy with their intended constituents, or with the state.

The comparative weakness of corporatist institutions in China is due in part to the fact that they are relatively young; because they have existed only since the mid-1980s, and are several decades younger than the Korean and Taiwanese associations founded in the 1950s and 1960s, they cannot be expected to have developed their capacities fully. But the fact that the Chinese association with the greatest autonomy, CAEFI, does not appear to have strengthened much since its founding suggests that the comparative weakness of such institutions has other causes. In addition to youth, the weak organizational foundation of business itself appears to bear part of the responsibility for the weakness of associations. The business elite is not, as we have seen, a cohesive or secure group with a collective consciousness of its role. The role the state has assigned to these business organizations is further responsible for their weakness. The Chinese government has tried to use corporatist arrangements to *preclude* the growth of counterparts to Korea's FKI or *chaebol*; it has not

---

26. Cheng, Haggard, and Kang (1995); Chu (1994); and Tien (1989). The growing voice of business in Taiwan has been in large part a result of the ongoing democratization of the regime.

fostered strong businesses or business associations. Rather, China's industrial policy thus far has been aimed more at protecting old state-owned industries.[27] One must question how effective the coordination function that corporatist institutions *should* play can in fact be when the societal stratum with which government wishes to coordinate is poorly developed, and when the agent of coordination has no real authority.

The second feature of China's business-government relations that differentiates it from Taiwan and Korea is the quality of the bureaucracy. China's central economic bureaucracy since the 1949 revolution has not focused on the cultivation of excellence in its officials, and policy is made in what continues to be a politicized context that promotes caution. The situation differs markedly in Korea and Taiwan, both of which in the 1960s and 1970s undertook reforms to strengthen the capacity of the state to make economic policy.[28] Economic bureaucracies were reorganized and were granted strong coordinating authority over the economy (though Korea's were more centralized and interventionist than were Taiwan's). Personnel reforms were perhaps even more important than reorganization. Under these reforms, meritocracy was made the key to entrance into the economic bureaucracies. The result was to create a small group of highly trained, if not wholly uncorrupted, bureaucrats with the talent to make intelligent economic policy. As Onis argues,

The system was designed in such a way as to attract the best managerial talent available to the ranks of the bureaucratic elite, which in numerical terms was quite small by international standards. Rigorous standards of entry not only ensured a high degree of bureaucratic capability, but also generated a sense of unity and common identity on the part of the bureaucratic elite. Hence the bureaucrats were imbued with a sense of mission and identified themselves with national goals which derived from a position of leadership in society. . . . The common educational backgrounds plus the high degree of intra-elite circulation were instrumental in generating an unusual degree

27. In the late 1980s the Chinese government tried to promote the formation of business "groups," essentially agglomerations of several existing state industries. While some have succeeded, the intention in forming them was primarily to use strong factories to bail out weaker ones, not to strengthen them into internationally dynamic industries along the lines of *keiretsu* (Japanese conglomerates) or *chaebol*. The protectionist focus of policy may be changing, however. Industrial policy (of which only small bits are made public due to the fact that evidence of such policy would harm China's entry into the World Trade Organization) appears slowly to be gaining in sophistication.

28. See Cheng, Haggard, and Kang (1995).

of cooperation among the bureaucrats, the executive, and the entrepreneurial elites.[29]

Together, business and the bureaucracy were able to promote industrialization through well-designed policies of export-led growth.[30] In other words, a talented bureaucracy has allowed these countries to take advantage of the potential for cooperation with business that was embodied in their corporatist structures.

The PRC government has carried out some organizational and personnel reforms of the economic bureaucracy along lines similar to those made earlier in Korea and Taiwan. As mentioned previously, the Economic and Trade Office was created as a new "superministry" in the early 1990s under the leadership of Zhu Rongji. A central goal of this agency has been to coordinate economic policy. Personnel reforms also have been carried out to compensate for problems arising from personnel policies of earlier years. Whereas during the Maoist era, recruitment into the bureaucracy was based less on ability than on seniority and (increasingly over time) "virtue" or political loyalty, since the early 1980s reformers have tried to create a technocracy by emphasizing ability in recruitment. New bureaucrats have been selected from among the best-educated college graduates, and from among those who have had training relevant to their work. The ministries responsible for the foreign business sector and for many parts of the domestic economy appear to have been major beneficiaries of these efforts. The quality of the economic bureaucracy is therefore improving.[31]

---

29. Onis (1991), p. 114. Onis (p. 125) criticizes the public choice literature for assuming that bureaucrats will necessarily seek rents; in East Asia, he argues, bureaucrats have been extremely effective at producing socio-economic outcomes that are broadly beneficial.

30. Amsden (1989) argues that the Korean bureaucracy's talent at disciplining enterprises (through selective incentives and subsidies) has been key in producing that country's economic successes. Kang (1995) argues that the motivation for effective economic policy was not primarily economic, it was driven by the desire of leaders to meet the external security threat.

31. On the Maoist-era bureaucracy, see Hong Yung Lee (1991), pp. 47–74. In the early 1950s the relative lack of expertise in the bureaucracy was due to the fact that the pool of educated people (particularly those who were politically reliable) from which to draw was tiny. (The government in fact kept on some functionaries from the Nationalist government to combat this problem.) By the late 1950s, the emphasis on "red" over "expert" was a matter of revolutionary policy. On post-Mao bureaucratic reforms, some of which improve policy coordination, see Halpern (1992); Hong Yung Lee (1991), pp. 387–388; and Zhang (1993). Intra-elite circulation of the sort praised in the above quote by Onis is also on the rise.

Still, China's economic bureaucracy stands in stark contrast to that of its neighbors in several respects. The most obvious difference is its huge size, which hides a redundant and overlapping structure. Fragmentation of authority and difficulty in coordination, at least in part a reflection of the bureaucracy's size, appear to have increased with the decentralization of resources during the reforms. Such fragmentation has necessitated extensive bargaining between offices, bargaining that enhances coordination but more toward the end of satisfying all parties than generating the most effective policy. Decentralization and fragmentation have not been accompanied by an increase in central coordination, at least in the areas of fiscal and monetary policy. Yet in Taiwan and Korea, these were arenas in which reforms enhanced state capacity.[32] Just as important is that flaws remain in the strategy of meritocratic recruiting. Economic policy-makers in the PRC often are well educated and extremely bright, but their training tends to be in engineering or in other production-related fields that are not best suited to policy-making. Although the importance of "virtue" has declined, use of personal connections as a means of entering and advancing in the bureaucracy is still a major constraint on meritocracy. The most flagrant examples are the *taizidang*, the sons and daughters of high-level officials who hold top ranks in the policy structure.[33] Finally, policy-making is still subject to incentives and uncertainties dictated by politics. In the mid-1990s, for example, the jockeying of top officials to position themselves for the post-Deng era, and the general uncertainty introduced by Deng's ill health, dictated a conservatism among bureaucrats that prevented the construction of an overall policy to guide the reforms.[34]

---

32. On "fragmented authoritarianism," see Lampton and Lieberthal (1992). On fiscal and monetary controls in China, see Huang (1996), and in Korea, see Amsden (1989).

33. On these problems with meritocratic recruitment into the Chinese bureaucracy, see Hong Yung Lee (1991), p. 403. As has been acknowledged in the government's myriad anti-corruption campaigns of the reform era, many of these high-level officials typify the "rent-seeking" bureaucrats criticized by Onis. Chen Yuan, the son of Chen Yun who has been a vice-governor of the People's Bank of China, is one of the more talented of these *taizidang* ("princes"), and therefore is an exception.

34. This is not to say, of course, that the reforms cannot be judged successful on many dimensions. As is discussed below, however, the successes came about largely because of initiatives released from below by a gradual policy that was not well planned in advance. The reform leadership did have a key insight, then, that "feeling the stones to cross the river" could lead to success. But this insight—almost an intuition, it would seem—was not the output of a "crack" bureaucracy.

The third characteristic that differentiates China's situation from the "statism" of other East Asian countries concerns the role played by clientelism. We have seen that, as in China, clientelism is important elsewhere in East Asia, and that corruption has not been eliminated. But in Korea and Taiwan, as well as in Japan, the negative effects of clientelism appear to have been reduced. In part the less problematic role of clientelism in Taiwan and Korea can be assumed to reflect the fact that the wider expansion of markets throughout East Asia makes personal ties less crucial, whereas in China personal connections are important for even the most basic of business operations. Bureaucratic reforms also have reduced the role of clientelism in economic policy-making, at least in Korea. There, the bureaucracy was bifurcated in the 1960s so as to concentrate patronage, which was still a valuable source of support for the regime, into non-economic bureaucracies such as Construction and Home Affairs, while keeping the financial ministries, which had the strongest role in economic policy-making, relatively clean.[35]

The most important factor distinguishing clientelism in China goes beyond the suggestion that there is simply *less* clientelism in Taiwan and Korea. Rather, the clientelism that exists in those countries appears to be more *functional* for producing competent policy.[36] This point can be explained most easily with reference to the literature on networks in East Asia. Peter Evans has developed the concept of "embedded autonomy" as a way to integrate the reality of East Asian networks into the "statism" literature's vision of a strong "developmental state," and in doing so has helped capture the notion of functionality. "Embedded autonomy" means that the state is connected to (embedded in) those segments of society with whom it shares the goal of economic development, and yet the state maintains its own robust internal structure, often bound by its own corporate norms, that allows the state to formulate policy that transcends individual or parochial interests (autonomy).[37] In Evans's con-

---

35. Kang (1995).

36. These comments comparing the functionality of networks are somewhat speculative, and are intended to be hypothesis-generating.

37. See Evans (1995, esp. pp. 49–50, 59). Embedded autonomy is characteristic of "developmental states" and is lacking in "predatory states" such as Zaire. China would not be considered by Evans to be a predatory state, however, as it does have the capacity to formulate policy that is separate from the individual interests of its bureaucrats. China bears more resemblance to Evans's "intermediate" states, which lack a high level of corporate coherence and competence, and have less well-organized external ties. (The idea of the "developmental state," or a state that positively fosters rapid economic development, was first suggested in Johnson [1982].)

cept, state competence remains central to the explanation of the success of Korea and Taiwan. But a less obvious point concerning the functionality of informal networks also emerges: policy coordination may not only be unharmed by, but actually may be *enhanced* by, informal personal ties between government leaders and business elites.

Thus, networks in Japan and Korea have been shown to tie together relatively strong, cohesive, and effective business organizations (both businesses themselves and their federations) with relatively talented government bureaucracies. In Japan, the personal networks within the bureaucracy exist in a setting where entrance into the bureaucracy is itself based on merit. In this situation, the network provides internal coherence to the bureaucracy. As Evans notes, these "nonbureaucratic elements of bureaucracy reinforce the formal organizational structure."[38] Much the same can be said about the networks that bind the state to business, networks fostered in part through the practice of *amakudari*. In Korea, even though corruption emanating from personal networks has not been eliminated from the economic bureaucracies, the government channeled the role corruption was to play. As one study notes, "The government exercised control over the *uses* to which rents were put by limiting the opportunity for speculative activity and capital flight and insisting on productive investment as the *quid pro quo* for government support."[39] Taiwan's situation is different still from that of either Korea or Japan. It lacks the extremely close interpersonal networks seen in the other two countries, in part because the business-government divide echoes the Taiwanese-mainland ethnic divide. Yet, though poorly understood, such networks do exist. They appear crucial to Taiwan's business-government relations, and have only increased with the Taiwanization of the state.[40]

If the kinds of clientelist networks that exist in Korea, Japan, and Taiwan can be said to create competence, the same does not appear to be true of China's informal business-government ties. We have already seen how clientelism is extremely useful for individual members of the Chinese business elite. Yet China's clientelism appears much less functional from a developmental point of view. It is a connectedness that fails to

---

38. Evans (1995), p. 49.
39. Cheng, Haggard, and Kang (1995), p. 76. See also Kang (1995), p. 21. Corruption also was reduced because the external security threat provided a major incentive for the regime to seek genuine developmental policies rather than "rents."
40. Evans (1995), p. 56.

increase competence.[41] It is uncoordinated, in the sense that it does not increase the collaboration between business as a whole and economic bureaucracies but, rather, provides for a one-time satisfaction of demands by each side in the interaction. Unlike in Japan, networks are not considered a legitimate part of bureaucratic life. Even what might be considered the Chinese version of *amakudari* fails to be very useful in the Chinese environment; rather than providing a means for the trans-feral of competent bureaucrats to the private sector, we hear jokes from members of China's business elite that business associations are "retire-ment homes for old cadres," and we are presented evidence that people with inappropriate skills are assigned to at least some staff associations.

Thus, China can be said to fit only very loosely into the category of "East Asian statism." Although the Chinese government is beginning to set up institutions that facilitate government cooperation with busi-ness, business associations have neither close enough links to, nor suffi-cient authority with, either industry or government to make them effec-tive tools to stimulate business or coordinate it with government. Chinese corporatist institutions are unable to nurture business as effec-tively as they might if they were more institutionalized and legitimate, and perhaps if they had well-functioning personal networks underlying them. The result in China is poorer coordination between government and business—exactly the advantage that corporatism is supposed to afford.[42]

This relatively unfavorable comparison with Korea and Taiwan of China's institutions of business and government, and the comparison of the role of clientelism, raise a question that this book can neither fully address nor fully ignore. If China's institutions are so much weaker than the institutions that are said to have produced growth elsewhere in East

41. The link between connectedness and competence is made by Evans (1995), p. 50. It is interesting that the situation of non-functional clientelism in the PRC appears simi-lar to what existed in Taiwan prior to the 1970s. See Chu (1994), pp. 120–121. While not studied directly, anecdotal evidence suggests that the personal networks that exist at the very top of the Chinese economy between top government leaders, on the one hand, and the *taizidang* and high officials-turned-entrepreneurs, on the other hand, also fail to be highly functional.

42. For example, in the foreign sector there has been much criticism by central state officials of the duplication of investment projects such as in real estate. Similarly, local offi-cials have been criticized for setting up numerous "special investment zones" that need-lessly compete with each other for investment. Better coordination could have allowed the state to avoid these problems.

Asia, then what explains the comparable growth in China?[43] Indeed, the real growth in gross domestic product that occurred in the first decade of China's takeoff (9.7% growth between 1980 and 1990) was on a par with parallel periods in Korea (8.6% between 1960 and 1970; 9.5% between 1970 and 1980) and Taiwan (9.2% between 1960 and 1970; 9.7% between 1970 and 1980).[44]

Three possible explanations for this conundrum present themselves. First, it is possible that the differences identified here with regard to China are too insignificant to produce differences in levels of growth. While this possibility should be examined more systematically, the evidence of differences in the quality of the bureaucracy and the strength of institutions appears on the face of it great enough that, if these are relevant factors for explaining growth, then the different levels at which they exist should produce different outcomes in growth.

Second, it is possible that, contrary to the suppositions of the statism literature, the institutions of a competent state and the practice of effective coordination with business are not in fact the causes of growth in East Asia. This argument has support from several sources. Some economists have argued that East Asian growth has resulted from "an astonishing mobilization of resources. Once one accounts for the role of rapidly growing inputs in these countries' growth, one finds little left to explain. Asian growth . . . seems to be driven by extraordinary growth in inputs like labor and capital."[45] In both China and Korea, for example, industrial growth was fueled by a massive input of labor that was released from agriculture as a result of rural reforms. Partial support for this second possibility also can be found in the fact that formal corporatist institutions have not always guaranteed strong economic results; plenty of well-institutionalized state corporatist regimes (notably in

43. This discussion of China's "fit" into the East Asian statism literature can only with difficulty ignore the question of how to explain growth because, as noted in ch. 1, explaining growth is the whole point of that literature. This discussion cannot fully address the question of growth, though, as it is a subject that requires a much more detailed analysis of the sources of economic growth. The comments in this section are therefore intended to be suggestive and provocative rather than decisive.

44. Dixon and Drakakis-Smith (1993), p. 2.

45. Krugman (1994), p. 70. Although in this article Krugman is directing his comments against the view that increases in efficiency created growth, his argument could also be directed against institutional explanations for growth. He demurs in the case of China, however, saying the causes of growth are very difficult to identify because of poor information and difficulties in identifying a benchmark for growth.

Latin America) have demonstrated poor economic performance.[46] Moreover, it can be noted that growth in China and East Asia alike might be attributable in part to a propitious international economic context: world trade, a key stimulus to growth, was expanding at an unprecedented rate. China in particular had favorable access to huge amounts of foreign direct investment and foreign loans. Investments based on these sources have fueled the country's phenomenal export growth.[47]

Third, it is possible that growth in China has occurred *despite* the lacuna of corporatist institutions which have produced growth elsewhere in East Asia. Some of the factors mentioned above are also relevant here, notably the role of massive inputs of labor and foreign investment. But other factors that many analysts credit with a leading role in explaining China's growth are absent from other East Asian countries. An important factor may be the *strategy* of economic reform. Reform in China did not occur according to some grand scheme created by central policy-makers, and yet it created incentives for that country's innovative local officials, enterprises, and individuals to engage in growth-generating behavior from below. By allowing some competition within non-state sectors, the reforms stimulated tremendous growth in those sectors and, to a lesser degree, pulled state enterprises into the arena of market competition. Moreover, local officials played a crucial role by acting as innovative "corporate directors" on behalf of their localities.[48] The crucial possibility to be raised here is that the central Chinese state, even though it lacks the capacity and the robust institutions to coordinate with business, may not have gotten in the way of innovation from neophyte business entities in business, agriculture, or local government.

That China's stunning growth during the reform period appears to have been achieved with institutional features other than those found in

46. Haggard (1990).

47. On expansions in world trade, see Wade (1992), pp. 315–316. On investment and export growth in China, see Lardy (1995). Lardy further argues, however, that these foreign investments have not created backward linkages to the state sector of the economy, leading him to be skeptical that levels of growth achieved up to the mid-1990s can be sustained.

48. "Gradualism" is the label that has been put on the economic reform process. See Jefferson (1992); McMillan and Naughton (1992); and Naughton (1994). Goldstein (1995) argues that the base for this local innovation was laid during the Maoist era, as economic policy was significantly decentralized compared with the Soviet Union. On innovation by local governments, see Oi (1992).

its East Asian neighbors suggests that the government-business relations in China, and patterns of state-society relations more broadly, may also carve their own channel in the future. It is to the question of the future that the next section turns.

The Leading Sectors and the Future of State-Society Relations in China

The hybrid pattern of state-society relations that has emerged in the post-Mao era is a comfortable pattern for China as it undergoes economic transformation. But will this pattern remain comfortable into the future?[49] Or might the new economic elite and its business associations eventually enter their own post-communist "golden age" and gain independence and influence on a par with their counterparts elsewhere in Asia or Latin America? A scenario whereby civil society emerges easily and directly out of the process of economic reform has already been shown to be simplistic. A "disintegration" scenario also has been suggested by some observers. If the state were to face disintegration from pressures from either inside or outside the country, it is possible that economic elites could become an influential force for change, much as the chambers of commerce were at the end of Qing rule and during the May Fourth period. A contemporary example could be Russia, where the implosion of the Soviet state was followed by the opening of politics to include business elites. Indeed, some members of the new Russian business elite, who are very closely connected with state officials, have become powerful in that country's political system.[50] A disintegration scenario seems highly unlikely in China, however. Not only is China's central government too strong an international force to be seriously threatened with disintegration by outside powers, it also

49. This section does not attempt discussion of the overall likelihood of democratization in the PRC. As argued in ch. 1, any such analysis would have to consider forces outside of the new economic elite, particularly changes in the inclinations of the ruling elite. However, many of the reasons given below for the likely stasis of state-society relations in their current mode also are applicable to the broader question of democratization.

50. Erlanger (1995) and Stanley (1995). These elites were not at the forefront of the revolution, however. Indeed, they were relatively passive actors until after the Soviet Union ended in 1991; in other words, they did not bring about the revolution.

remains too potent domestically to face disintegration and, despite periodic displays of disaffection from intellectuals, retains relatively broadbased social support.[51]

That these extreme scenarios are unlikely does not mean, however, that we cannot imagine ways in which further liberalization of the political regime might occur, in part through the influence of the business elite. Given what we know about the foreign and private sectors in China, then, what is the "most plausible best case" to be made that China's new economic elite will help to usher in a significantly more liberal polity? Such a scenario has a number of possible components, and must account for the likely role to be played not only by societal actors but also by the state.[52] On the societal side of the equation, the seeds of greater independence that already exist could conceivably continue to grow. One component concerns the development of the business elite's ideology and group cohesiveness. If market forces deepen and the private and foreign sectors of the economy continue to be successful, the business elite may gain confidence in pressing its views in favor of extreme market reform and, often, political liberalization. It is possible to envision a number of scenarios wherein a major barrier present in the first decade and a half of reform—a practical disinterest and an unwillingness to be vocal, despite strongly held views—may erode. Members of the business elite could come to feel increasing friction from the limits imposed by partial marketization, and frustrated in their inability to bring about lasting changes through clientelist means. Or if the central government were to stumble in a major way in its handling of the economy, particularly such that business investments were severely threatened, leading to a crisis in performance legitimacy, then business pressures that had previously had less need to emerge might in fact find reason to do so.[53] This possibility may be especially pertinent to private entrepreneurs, who arguably have more of a stake in the political system

51. Zhang (1993) contrasts the PRC government's social support with that enjoyed by the Soviet state before its collapse.

52. The core components of this "most likely best case" scenario are extensions of two of the factors most likely to intervene in the relationship between economic and political reform—ideology and interests of societal actors and state actions—discussed previously.

53. Payne (1994, p. xv) finds that severe threats to business investments, combined with a sense of exclusion on the part of the business elite and the development of links to other sectors of society, can lead an otherwise inactive business elite to action on behalf of democratization.

because they do not possess the alternative means for pressure (foreign businesses) that foreign-sector managers do.

Organized pressure on the government for major systemic change would depend on the expansion of a more cohesive business elite. Processes of intra-elite circulation that are now quite weak could grow and enhance cohesion. In particular, the job mobility of members of the business elite could come to include the possibility of moving in and out of the government, or increasing their now very minor representation in people's congresses or the CPPCC.[54]

Functional associations, in which a very limited autonomy is already recognized in the corporatist strategy, could exercise a growing interest in serving their constituencies.[55] Here, Taiwan might be thought to provide a model. Taiwan's business sector was tightly controlled by the ruling Guomindang Party, but since the mid-1980s it has begun to exercise significant influence over economic policy. The government has attempted to engage business in the restructuring of the economy to be more internationally competitive. Business has begun to assert influence in part through existing corporatist business associations that had been established in the 1970s to maintain control over a business sector dominated by native Taiwanese. The Taiwanese business elite also has become deeply implicated in the electoral system, and indeed has gained significant influence over business matters through support of legislators to the increasingly powerful Legislative Yuan.[56]

Such an evolution in the PRC might, as it was in Taiwan, be stimulated by the government's recognition that further industrial development depends on a tightly coordinated effort to move the country in a new direction. This evolution would be more conceivable in the cases of CAEFI and ACFIC than in heavily state-dominated associations such as SELA. That CAEFI and ACFIC members have bases of authority in foreign companies and large private firms (hence outside of the state) and that they are funded primarily by membership dues suggest that they

54. It is possible, moreover, that both the blending of the business and government elite (intra-elite circulation) and growing pressure by business interests would create change in practice long before it is recognized in ideology or policy.

55. This scenario is depicted as quite likely in Chan (1993) and Unger and Chan (1995), who further argue that the activism of associations will evolve China toward societal corporatism rather than political democracy.

56. Chu (1994); Cheng, Haggard, and Kang (1995). Despite the rapid rise in business influence in the 1980s, however, the state still tends to dominate business in Taiwan.

would be more protected in any move toward greater independence, and have greater resources to put to the task. Such pressure is most likely to continue to come from the local levels of these organizations rather than the national level. Foreign managers involved in CAEFI could be a further impetus in this direction.[57]

We have already observed that China's new economic elites are unlikely to lead a challenge to the Party monopoly. It is plausible, however, that groups which are more naturally politicized than the business elite—students and intellectuals—may once again press the state for more drastic political change, as they did in the various political movements of the 1970s and 1980s. In those earlier movements, and particularly the 1989 Tiananmen movement, students and intellectuals failed to build effective bridges to those other sectors of society that might have lent the movement support.[58] Leaders of future movements might take such criticism to heart and actively build alliances with the economic elite. In such a "New May Fourth" setting, those in the leading-edge economic sectors could be mobilized to lend significant finances and prestige to support pressures on the state initiated elsewhere.

A "most plausible best case" scenario must also take into account the actions of the state. It is likely that the state will continue to use the institutions at its disposal to shape how state-society relations evolve. Corporatist institutions might facilitate further liberalization of the political system to the degree that reformist leaders may desire to see such change. Indeed, it could be in the context of corporatist structures that state officials' early learning about and comfort with contestation, a defining factor in democracy, could occur.[59] But the case of Taiwan reiterates, even for advocates of an optimistic vision of the future, that the participation of business elites in further liberalization in state-society relations is likely to lag behind actions on the part of others in the system, particularly by the state but also by other elements of society. In Taiwan it was, first, a decision on the part of the central leadership, and apparently on the part of Guomindang leader Chiang Ching-kuo, to

57. But expatriate managers, who generally try to be "good corporate citizens," are unlikely to press for changes in a way that would alienate officials. See Sklar (1976).

58. See, e.g., Perry (1992). The exception of the Stone Corporation is discussed in ch. 4.

59. Zhang (1994) argues that corporatist institutions make a country more conducive to successful negotiation of democratizing pacts. (He finds these lacking in China.) This view is consistent with Dahl's (1971) classic argument that contestation within an elite is more likely to lead to stable polyarchy than rapid and highly inclusive democratization.

open the political system to competition and, second, pressure from a constellation of middle-class Taiwanese and intellectuals on the state, that eventuated in liberalization.[60] The Taiwan case implies that in the PRC a rise in business influence will depend upon a "strategic opening" within the state combined with pressures from other sectors of society.

When speculating on the likelihood of such a "most plausible best case" scenario it is wise to bear in mind its limits. As the evidence provided in previous chapters suggests, there are reasons to expect continuing constraints on the willingness of business elites to act. Not only are the elites unlikely to be leaders of change, even their role as followers is problematic. The hybrid pattern of state-society relations that has grown up in the reform era serves the purposes of the business elite reasonably well, without posing the risks to the government of direct political action by the business elite. Indeed, it seems quite plausible that reliance upon personal ties could become institutionalized if the partial market system remains just that—partial. It is quite conceivable, moreover, that further change in the political environment could actually *harm* the interests of the new economic elite. Despite their expressed desires for political liberalization, uncertainties in the business environment that would be created by political upheaval could sap economic elites of reformist leanings. At the same time, members of the business elite could come to find in corporatist associations, if they were strengthened, a channel of effective contact with the state, and might therefore lose the incentive to seek other formal channels of influence. If the members of the business elite remain financially successful, and as the corporatist and clientelist institutions that keep them tied to the state become even more firmly entrenched, the business elite may be converted into a much more conservative political force. It is even conceivable that this elite could be absorbed, together with the former officials-turned-entrepreneurs and children of high-level cadres (*taizidang*), into a blended merchant-cum-official class analogous to that which existed during the late Qing and Nationalist eras.

Foreign-sector managers also may be prone to political conservatism in the future insofar as the foreign investors who back them will wish to

---

60. These explanations of Taiwan's democratization, which are reflected in various writings (e.g., Chu [1994]; Cheng and Haggard [1992]; and Tien [1989]), are largely consistent with the "transitions" theories described in ch. 1. Initiation of major change by the central leadership also was crucial in the Soviet Union, particularly Gorbachev's rescinding of the Soviet Constitution's Article 6 guaranteeing the Communist Party's monopoly.

see a stable investment environment, even one guaranteed by authoritarianism. And both foreign-sector managers and entrepreneurs may be prone to support a state that uses corporatist or even more authoritarian levers to ensure a docile labor force.[61] Their support for upheaval by other segments of society would be forthcoming only as long as the elites perceived that the movement was not disrupting the economic climate. Thus, a corporatist-clientelist hybrid that helps furnish access to government and to a stable environment in which to pursue business may be enough to snuff out any desire on the part of business to pursue civil society.

Limits on change are also imposed by the state's attempts to institutionalize its power in a new corporatist form. Even with a continuing decline in the Party-state's legitimacy, and even if the economic elite begins to form into a coherent "class for itself," the state can be expected to have the corporatist institutions it has established keep its own interests in the foreground, and to keep firm limits on the establishment of autonomous or competing associations. The pressure that arises out of such associations is therefore likely to be restricted to issues relevant to their functional areas, and to stop short of posing a fundamental threat to the state. Even if business elites or their associations do become more politically active on their own behalf, there is no guarantee that, absent major changes favoring liberalization elsewhere in the system, current institutions or counter-actions by the state will not be effective in rendering business pressure ineffective.

Ultimately, then, there is reason to be skeptical that the business elite in the PRC will either emerge as a strong independent force or that it will be at the center of a more progressive form of state-society relations. There is nothing obvious at work within the leading-edge sectors and their interaction with the state to suggest that a move away from the current pattern of state-society relations is likely, much less necessary. It is quite plausible that the contemporary business elite will continue for some time to cooperate closely with officials (particularly at the local level), and that its associations will retain a dualism characterized by elements of both state domination and independence. This group need move neither toward fuller liberalization nor toward monism. Such a stasis—the absence of a compulsion to resolve the tension between autonomy for society and continued domination by the state—would

61. The concern of business elites about social unrest, discussed in ch. 4, supports this view.

continue the deeply rooted pattern for state-society relations in China, and at the same time it finds a precedent in state corporatist regimes around the world.[62] The hybrid of socialist corporatism and clientelism is not necessarily an inexorable phase for socialist countries undergoing reform. But for China it is a logical situation in which to find itself, and one with staying power.

62. Stepan (1978, pp. 43–45) suggests with regard to organic statism that continuous tensions between autonomy and control are to be expected.

Foreign Direct Investment in China, 1979–1995

Year	Number of Projects Pledged	Value of Projects Pledged ($bil.)	Value of Projects Utilized ($bil.)	Utilized Value as % of Pledged
1979–82	922	4.61	1.77	38
1983	470	1.73	0.92	53
1984	1,856	2.65	1.42	54
1985	3,073	5.93	1.96	33
1986	1,498	2.83	2.25	80
1987	2,233	3.71	2.65	71
1988	5,945	5.30	3.74	71
1989	5,779	5.60	3.77	67
1990	7,273	6.60	3.41	52
1991	12,978	11.98	4.37	36
1992	48,764	58.12	11.00	19
1993	83,000	111.44	27.52	25
1994	47,490	81.41	33.79	42
1995	37,126	90.30	37.70	42
Total	258,407	392.21	136.27	35

SOURCES: MOFTEC, *Zhongguo Duiwai Jingji Maoyi Nianjian* [Yearbook of China's Foreign Economic Trade] (various years); "Investment Data," *China Business Review* 23, no. 3 (May–June, 1996), p. 40.

NOTE: Invariably a proportion of pledged investment is never actually absorbed, because deals fall apart. However, because there is a lag between the time contracts are pledged (signed) and when the capital is actually contributed (utilized), some capital not absorbed in the year of signing will be absorbed in later years.

APPENDIX 2

The Research Sample

The major source of data on the foreign-sector business elite is extended interviews conducted in 1991 and 1995 with fifty-one PRC nationals working in managerial positions in the elite segment of the foreign sector (defined in the introduction). Except that no interviews were conducted in Beijing in 1995, the composition of the 1995 interviewees (in terms of type of enterprise, foreign background, age, etc.) was quite similar, and the results were largely consistent with those from 1991. Where significant differences appeared between these two time frames, they are noted in the text. Interviewees were identified through contacts at foreign businesses, management programs operating in China, and miscellaneous personal contacts. The analysis in this book is also informed by interviews conducted with "old-line" Chinese JV managers and foreign investment officials during the mid-1980s, and by interviews with Hong Kong and other overseas Chinese business representatives with extensive investments in the PRC.[1] The discussion of business associations in chapter 5 is informed by interviews with officers of business associations in Beijing, Shanghai, and Guangzhou.

Although a set of standard questions concerning the central topics in the book broadly guided the interviews, the questions were open-ended.[2] This method facilitated a careful exploration of sensitive

1. Some of the results of earlier interviews with "old-line" PRC managers appear in Pearson (1991).
2. For an explanation of the open-ended interview method, see Walder (1986), pp. 255–269.

issues such as interviewees' political views. It also allowed the interview sessions to take unexpected turns when particularly interesting or new points were raised by an interviewee, thereby allowing new information to enter the research agenda.

To gain information on the foreign-sector managers' economic ideology (for chapter 3) and relationship with the state (chapter 4), I asked interviewees directly about their views on economic reform and the "open" policy. Questions focused on the relationship of their enterprises with the government, whether this relationship raised any problems that could be resolved by further reform, how managers are affected by various relevant economic policies (such as foreign exchange policy), and what sorts of market-oriented reforms would be inappropriate for China. Given the tension in the political atmosphere remaining from the events of 1989, during interviews conducted in early 1991 I was quite cautious in asking directly about foreign-sector managers' views on politics; I usually waited for the managers to express views on politics on their own, and then followed up with my own questions. Surprisingly, many of the foreign-sector managers interviewed readily volunteered views of politics and the need for political change, though, as I describe in chapter 3, their views were usually moderate.[3] In interviews conducted later in 1991 and especially in 1995, the more liberal political atmosphere made it easier to question managers directly about their views of political reform.

It can be difficult for foreign researchers to raise questions about politics in interviews with PRC citizens. Some of these difficulties were alleviated by virtue of the fact that interviewees from the foreign sector were accustomed to speaking with foreigners, more aware of the functions of university research and, on balance, not suspicious of my research motives. An alternative methodology for identifying and analyzing the ideology of foreign-sector managers would have been to examine public discourse in, for example, trade newspapers and association journals. There are two difficulties with using such materials in the case of Chinese foreign-sector managers, however. First, although some such materials exist (such as the business association journals, which I draw on in chapter 5), they are rather few, and so cannot be a major source of information. Second, those published materials that do exist are sponsored by organizations that have a not insignificant amount of governmental

---

3. The 1991 interviews were conducted prior to Deng Xiaoping's much-touted "southern journey" of early 1992, following which a strong push for further reform re-emerged at the expense of the more conservative thinking that had prevailed since the recession and political turmoil of the late 1980s.

control, and hence cannot be presumed to be wholly reflective of foreign-sector managers' views.

Consistent with the description of business elites given in the introduction, interviewees tended to be relatively young. The vast majority were in their late twenties (26%), thirties (35%), or forties (29%). Only 10% were in the more traditional fifties age cohort for middle and senior managers. A number of those in their mid-forties were part of the *laosanjie* group described in the introduction. The interviewees were predominantly male (84%). Their family backgrounds were in some respects varied, but the greatest proportion were from relatively privileged backgrounds. The largest category were children of intellectual parents (50%), three-quarters of whom did not work in the government, or were children of senior managerial or technical staff (12.5%). Others were children of government or Party officials (who did not have intellectual backgrounds) at senior (7.5%), medium (15%), or low levels (5%). A small portion was from peasant or worker families (10%). None were *taizidang*, i.e., children of the party's topmost officials.

As would be expected from this privileged group, they were almost uniformly well educated. Many reported that their upbringing emphasized education. All but one possessed a university degree. Most often these degrees were in technical fields (65%), usually engineering, although a number of the more recent graduates had training in economics or even liberal arts (23%).[4] Many interviewees had received B.A.s from less prestigious technical universities and institutes, or even in part-time evening programs (56%). A significant portion of the degree-holders, however, had been educated at China's premier universities (25%)—including Beijing, Qinghua, and Fudan—at the premier foreign-language institutes (8%), or at elite U.S. universities such as MIT and Harvard (8%). Some (not always those from premier universities) had received master's degrees in the PRC (12%), in foreign-supported M.B.A. programs in China (28%), or in other overseas M.A. programs (4%).[5]

The segment of interviewees who were not recruited directly from universities (i.e., were in their thirties or older) had prior work experience in state-owned enterprises, government bureaucracies (such as the former State Economic Commission), or quasi-governmental "investment corporations." Despite the frequency of their past work for the

4. This is consistent with the finding of Vermeer (1988, p. 55) that top-level executives tend to have university degrees in engineering, economics, or law.

5. Those who did not have M.B.A.s often received in-house management training from their employers.

government, the foreign-sector managers interviewed had not risen to the top of the government bureaucracy, and therefore lacked the strong connections of some higher-level cadres who had "jumped into the sea" (*xiahai*). Nor were most of them Party members (84%). The few who belonged to the Party were almost uniformly in their forties and fifties, which is to be expected given the relatively stronger appeal of the Party as a career path during the 1960s and early 1970s.

The level of management attained by foreign-sector managers in the sample was mixed, but was concentrated at senior and middle levels.[6] Despite their relative seniority, most had been at their jobs for less than five years, a figure that reflects the relative youth of both the managers and the foreign sector itself. Interviewees worked in a wide variety of industries typical of the foreign sector, including industry (43%), consumer goods and light manufacturing (14%), high-tech manufacturing (12%), finance and professional services (24%), and trading (8%). The managers worked in Beijing (29%), Shanghai (45%), and the Pearl Delta region (Guangzhou, Shenzhen Special Economic Zone, and Shekou Industrial Zone) (20%). Four of the 1995 interviews (6%) were conducted with PRC nationals working for foreign companies in Hong Kong, which was to be merged with the PRC two years hence.

In terms of *all* foreign investment, the sample of foreign-sector managers interviewed for this study overemphasizes foreign businesses in the two major metropolitan areas of Beijing and Shanghai at the expense of those located in Guangdong and the coastal and interior provinces.[7] However, as discussed in the introduction, the elite segment of foreign-sector managers tends to be located in Western and Japanese companies, and these in turn are more likely to be located in the major cities such as Shanghai rather than in rural areas or Guangdong (where Hong Kong investment is prevalent) or the coastal province of Fujian (where Taiwanese investment is concentrated). Representative offices, and particularly those in the emerging securities and professional services sectors, also tend to be located in Shanghai and Beijing.

In the sample, the largest proportion of managers worked for U.S. (43%) and European (35%) companies. About one-fifth (18%) worked

---

6. The senior managers were mostly in their thirties and forties, while middle managers were primarily in their twenties and thirties.

7. According to MOFTEC, the breakdown of foreign direct investment (therefore excluding representative offices) by region is as follows: coastal provinces, 37%; Guangdong Province, 29.9%; Shanghai, 6.3%; Beijing, 6.1%; interior provinces, 20.7%. "Investment Data" (1995).

for Hong Kong companies. The remainder (4%) worked for companies involving mixed-foreign backgrounds, including Japanese, Hong Kong, and U.S. In absolute terms, then, the sample is not representative of the universe of firms investing in China according to official statistics.[8] Nonetheless, the sample is appropriate for the purposes of this book for a number of reasons. The first reason concerns the fact, discussed in the introduction, that Hong Kong firms are a less likely venue for members of the foreign-sector business elite. Second, it has become clear that the dominance of Hong Kong firms in official statistics is overstated when the phenomenon of "false" (*jia*) foreign enterprises, which came to light in the early 1990s, is taken into account. To attract foreign capital the reformers have put in place powerful financial incentives—tax breaks, favorable financing, export and import privileges, etc.—to form joint ventures. Moreover, goods manufactured by foreign-backed firms often have better reputations than domestically made products. In response to these incentives, domestic companies have found ways to register as "foreign" enterprises. Typically, a PRC enterprise establishes a shell company in Hong Kong, which then, as a "foreign" firm, re-channels the funds back into the PRC under the label of "Hong Kong" investment. In addition, many PRC companies that operate abroad legitimately re-invest at home.[9] In some cases, foreign partners never invest any money but receive a fee for use of their name. Although precise figures of "false" foreign enterprises are not available, the World Bank has estimated that they constituted up to 25% of incoming foreign investment in 1992.[10] The phenomenon is widespread enough that the government closed down over 1,800 such ventures in 1994.[11]

It is also worth noting that, while the nationality of foreign investment remains a salient factor, the very concept of nationality is less clear-cut in the case of PRC investment than it might at first appear. This problem goes beyond the homily that many multi-national corporations are truly "multi-national," even if they are registered in just one country.

---

8. Difficulties in gaining access to managers at Japanese firms also has meant that these members of the business elite are underrepresented.

9. Most of these companies are located in Hong Kong. One survey indicates that over 90% of PRC companies operating overseas invest back in the PRC. See Dai (1993).

10. Harrold and Lall (1993), p. 24.

11. Xinhua (1995). Other reports on "false" joint ventures include Dai (1993); British Broadcasting Corporation Summary of World Broadcasts (1994); and "Registration of 7,500 Enterprises Canceled" (1994). Sabin (1994, pp. 957, 966) offers as a conservative estimate that 50% of all Sino-foreign JVs formed in 1992 were actually private PRC firms.

(Philips, formally of the Netherlands, is one such example.) A number of so-called "Hong Kong" firms that have invested in China are not really so. The phenomenon of false foreign investments originating in the PRC is only one aspect of the problem. Taiwan firms also may channel their monies through Hong Kong, thereby misrepresenting their origin. Other formally "Hong Kong" firms that are run by British nationals might as well be considered "European." The reverse of this problem also exists. Some firms that are not registered, or have de-registered, as Hong Kong firms—due to uncertainties over the transition to PRC rule in 1997—are actually Hong Kong firms in all but name.[12] American firms run by PRC-born but U.S.- or Canadian-naturalized citizens could be categorized as overseas Chinese as easily as Western. The firms with which the foreign-sector's business elites are associated are not immune to these issues of nationality.

12. Two such firms, with British Virgin Islands registry, are included in the sample under "Hong Kong" investments.

Bibliography

Abbreviations used:

CAEFI	China Association of Enterprises with Foreign Investment [Zhongguo Waishang Touzi Qiye Xiehui]
CND	*China News Digest* (on-line news service)
FBIS	Foreign Broadcast Information Service (Washington, D.C.)
MOFTEC	Ministry of Foreign Trade and Economic Cooperation
SAEFI	Shanghai Association of Enterprises with Foreign Investment [Shanghai Waishang Touzi Qiye Xiehui]
SFIEAJ	*Shanghai shi waishang touzi qiye xiehui huikan* [Shanghai Foreign Investment Enterprise Association Journal] (Shanghai Association of Enterprises with Foreign Investment)

Adams, Walter, and James Brock. 1993. *Adam Smith Goes to Moscow: A Dialogue on Radical Reform*. Princeton: Princeton University Press.

Agence France Presse. 1994. "A Brave Call for Private Banks" (22 May). Reported in CND, 24 May 1994.

Agence France Presse English Wire. 1994. "Chinese Economist Says: No Brake to Foreign Investment" (20 February). Reported in CND, 22 February 1994.

Amsden, Alice H. 1985. "The State and Taiwan's Economic Development." In *Bringing the State Back In*, edited by Peter Evans, Dietrich Rueschemeyer, and Theda Skocpol, pp. 78–106. Cambridge: Cambridge University Press.

———. 1989. *Asia's Next Giant: South Korea and Late Industrialization*. New York: Oxford University Press.

Anek Laothamatas. 1992. *Business Associations and the New Political Economy of Thailand: From Bureaucratic Polity to Liberal Corporatism*. Boulder, CO: Westview Press.

Arato, Andrew. 1981. "Civil Society against the State: Poland 1980–1981." *Telos* 47: 23–47.

Bangsberg, P. T. 1993. "45% of China's Economy Said to Be in Private Hands." *Journal of Commerce* (August 16). Reported in CND, 19 August 1993.

Becker, David G. 1983. *The New Bourgeoisie and the Limits of Dependency: Mining, Class, and Power in "Revolutionary" Peru.* Princeton: Princeton University Press.

———. 1990. "Business Associations in Latin America: The Venezuelan Case." *Comparative Political Studies* 23, no. 1: 114–138.

Beijing Youth News. 14 December 1993. Reported in CND, 16 December 1993.

Bennett, Douglas, and Kenneth Sharpe. 1985. *Transnational Corporations versus the State: The Political Economy of the Mexican Auto Industry.* Princeton: Princeton University Press.

Bergère, Marie-Claire. 1989. *The Golden Age of the Chinese Bourgeoisie, 1911–1937.* Translated by Janet Lloyd. Cambridge: Cambridge University Press.

Berle, Adolf Augustus, and Gardiner C. Means. 1932. *The Modern Corporation and Private Property.* New York: Macmillan.

Bian, Yanjie. 1994. *Work and Inequality in Urban China.* Albany: State University of New York Press.

Bianchi, Robert. 1984. *Interest Groups and Political Development in Turkey.* Princeton: Princeton University Press.

———. 1989. *Unruly Corporatism: Associational Life in Twentieth-Century Egypt.* New York: Oxford University Press.

Bjorkman, Ingmar. 1992. "A Preliminary Framework for Analyzing Role Perception and Behavior among Chinese Managers in Sino-Western Joint Ventures." Paper presented at the Conference on PRC Joint Ventures, University of Hong Kong Business School (June 16–19).

Blustein, Paul, and R. Jeffrey Smith. 1996. "Economic, Political Concerns Put Clinton on the Spot in China Policy." *Washington Post* (11 February): A26.

Bohlen, Celestine. 1993. "For Some 'Biznesmeni' in Politics, Democracy Is Flavored by Rubles." *New York Times* (6 December): A8.

Boisot, Max, and Guo Liangxing. 1991. "The Nature of Managerial Work in China." In *Advances in Chinese Industrial Studies.* Vol. 2, *The Changing Nature of Management in China,* edited by Nigel Campbell, Sylvain R. F. Plasschaert, and David H. Brown, pp. 39–46. Greenwich, CT: JAI Press.

Bonnin, Michael, and Yves Chevrier. 1991. "The Intellectual and the State: Social Dynamics of Intellectual Autonomy during the Post-Mao Era." *China Quarterly,* no. 127 (September): 569–593.

Borgonjon, Jan, and Wilfried R. Vanhonacker. 1992. "Modernizing China's Managers." *China Business Review* 19, no. 5 (September–October): 12–16.

Bova, Russell. 1991. "Political Dynamics of the Post-Communist Transition." *World Politics,* no. 44 (October): 113–138.

Bratton, Michael, and Nicolas Van De Walle. 1994. "Neopatrimonial Regimes and Political Transitions in Africa." *World Politics,* no. 46 (July): 453–489.

Brick, Andrew B. 1993. "China's Tide of Emigrants." *Wall Street Journal* (11 June).

British Broadcasting Corporation Summary of World Broadcasts. 1994. "Chinese Journal Says Foreign-Funded Firms Involved in 'Deceptive Practices'" (25 March). Reported in Nexis Library [On-line], Nexis File: INT'L, ASIAPC, item # FE/1955/G.

Brown, David H., and Michael R. Jackson. 1991. "Meeting the Challenge to Provide Effective Managers in the Changing Chinese Environment: A Systemically Structured Analysis of the Requirements for Management Education." In *Advances in Chinese Industrial Studies.* Vol. 2, *The Changing Nature of Management in China,* edited by Nigel Campbell, Sylvain R. F. Plasschaert, and David H. Brown, pp. 117–135. Greenwich, CT: JAI Press.

Brus, Wlodzimierz. 1983. "Political Pluralism and Markets in Communist Systems." In *Pluralism in the Soviet Union: Essays in Honor of H. Gordon Skilling,* edited by Susan Gross Solomon, pp. 108–130. New York: St. Martin's Press.

Bruun, Ole. 1995. "Political Hierarchy and Private Entrepreneurship in a Chinese Neighbourhood." In *The Waning of the Communist State: Economic Origins of Political Change in China and Hungary,* edited by Andrew G. Walder, pp. 184–212. Berkeley: University of California Press.

Bulman, Robin. 1994. "Beware the Wage Monster When Investing in China." Knight-Ridder/Tribune Business News (4 January). Reported in CND, 6 January 1994.

Bunce, Valerie, and John M. Echols III. 1980. "Soviet Politics in the Brezhnev Era: 'Pluralism' or 'Corporatism.'" In *Soviet Politics in the Brezhnev Era,* edited by Donald R. Kelley, pp. 1–26. New York: Praeger.

Burks, R. V. 1983. "The Political Implications of Economic Reform." In *Plan and Market: Economic Reform in Eastern Europe,* edited by Morris Bornstein, pp. 373–402. New Haven, CT: Yale University Press.

Burns, John P. 1987. "China's *Nomenklatura* System." *Problems of Communism* 36, no. 5: 36–51.

———. 1988. *Political Participation in Rural China.* Berkeley: University of California Press.

———. 1989. "China's Governance: Political Reform in a Turbulent Environment." *China Quarterly,* no. 119 (June): 481–518.

Bush, Richard C. 1982. *The Politics of Cotton Textiles in Kuomintang China, 1927–1937.* New York: Garland Publishing.

Business Week Editorial. 1994. "Chinese Dissidents Find Freedom—In Business." *Business Week* (21 March). Reported in CND, 14 April 1994.

CAEFI. 1987. "Zhongguo Waishang Touzi Qiye Xiehui" [China Association of Enterprises with Foreign Investment]. Beijing: CAEFI.

———. 1991. "Articles of the China Association of Enterprises with Foreign Investment." Article 4. Reprinted in *SFIEAJ,* no. 1 (10 February): 43–44.

Cai Hong. 1994. "Private Businesses Play a Subsidiary Role." *China Daily* (12 March): 4. In FBIS-CHI-94-050 (15 March): 58–59.

Cardoso, Fernando Henrique, and Enzo Faletto. 1978 (English edition). *Dependency and Development in Latin America.* Translated by Marjory Mattingly Urquidi. Berkeley: University of California Press.

Casati, Christine. 1991. "Satisfying Labor Laws—and Needs." *China Business Review* 18, no. 4 (July–August): 16–22.

Chamberlain, Heath B. 1987. "Party-Management Relations in China's Industries: Some Political Dimensions of Economic Reforms." *China Quarterly*, no. 112 (December): 631–661.

Chan, Anita. 1993. "Revolution or Corporatism? Workers and Trade Unions in Post-Mao China." *Australian Journal of Chinese Affairs*, no. 29 (January): 31–61.

Chan, Wellington. 1975. "Merchant Organizations in Late Imperial China: Patterns of Change and Development." *Journal of the Royal Asiatic Society* (Hong Kong Branch) 15: 28–42.

———. 1977. *Merchants, Mandarins and Modern Enterprise in Late Ch'ing China*. Cambridge, MA: Harvard University Press.

Chen Cui. 1992. "Entrepreneurs Staying in Shanghai to Make Money" *China Daily* (3 December): 6. In FBIS-CHI-92-234 (4 December 1992): 29.

Chen Jinluo and She Dehu. 1988. "Social Groups Are an Important Force for Building Socialist Democratic Politics." *Renmin ribao* (29 April). In FBIS-CHI-88-092 (30 April 1992): 27.

Chen Yaoxing. 1990. "Waishang touzi qiye laodong renshi guanli cunzai de wenti ji duice" [Problems of Labor and Personnel Management Existing in Foreign-Invested Enterprises and Their Countermeasures]. *Waiguo jingji yu guanli*, no. 6 (June): 2–5.

Chen Yulin. 1990. "Sanzi qiye laodong renshi guanli de tedian he zuofa" [The Special Points and Methods of Labor and Personnel Management in Foreign-Invested Enterprises]. *Waiguo jingji yu guanli* [Foreign Economics and Management] (Shanghai), no. 1 (January): 23–24.

Cheng, Tun-jen, and Stephan Haggard. 1992. "Regime Transformation in Taiwan: Theoretical and Comparative Perspectives." In *Political Change in Taiwan*, edited by Tun-jen Cheng and Stephan Haggard, pp. 1–29. Boulder, CO: Lynne Rienner Publishers.

Cheng, Tun-jen, Stephan Haggard, and David Kang. 1995. "Institutions, Economic Policy and Growth in Korea and Taiwan." Paper prepared for the UNCTAD Project on Economic Development in East Asia (unpublished manuscript).

Chevrier, Yves. 1990. "Micropolitics and the Factory Director Responsibility System, 1984–1987." In *Chinese Society on the Eve of Tiananmen: The Impact of Reform*, edited by Deborah Davis and Ezra F. Vogel, pp. 109–134. Cambridge, MA: Council on East Asian Studies, Harvard University.

Child, John. 1994. *Management in China during the Age of Reform*. Cambridge: Cambridge University Press.

Child, John, and Xu Xinzhong. 1991. "The Communist Party's Role in Enterprise Leadership at the High-Water of China's Economic Reform." In *Advances in Chinese Industrial Studies*. Vol. 2, *The Changing Nature of Management in China*, edited by Nigel Campbell, Sylvain R. F. Plasschaert, and David H. Brown, pp. 69–95. Greenwich, CT: JAI Press.

China Journal. 1995. No. 34 (July): 1–205. (Special issue on informal politics.)

China News Agency. 1993. "Jiangsu Province Develops Social Insurance System" (26 August). Reported in CND, 7 September 1993.

"China Pledges Reform to Join GATT." 1993. *Financial Times* (30 April). Reported in CND, 3 May 1993.

"China to Abolish City Hu-Kou (Two-Tier Registration) System." 1994. *Wall Street Journal* (26 April). Reported in CND, 27 April 1994.

China Youth Daily. 1995 (7 July). Reported in CND, 7 July 1995.

Chirot, Daniel. 1980. "The Corporatist Model and Socialism: Notes on Romanian Development." *Theory and Society* 9, no. 2: 363–381.

———. 1992. "What Happened in Eastern Europe in 1989?" In *Popular Protest and Popular Culture in Modern China: Learning from 1989*, edited by Jeffrey N. Wasserstrom and Elizabeth J. Perry, pp. 215–243. Boulder, CO: Westview Press.

Chu Yun-han. 1994. "The Realignment of Business-Government Relations and Regime Transition in Taiwan." In *Business and Government in Industrializing Asia*, edited by Andrew MacIntyre, pp. 113–141. Ithaca, NY: Cornell University Press.

Cleaves, Peter S., and Charles J. Stephens. 1991. "Businessmen and Economic Policy in Mexico." *Latin American Research Review* 26, no. 2:187–202.

Coble, Parks M., Jr. 1986 (second edition). *The Shanghai Capitalists and the Nationalist Government, 1927–1937*. Cambridge, MA: Council on East Asian Studies, Harvard University.

Cochran, Sherman. 1980. *Big Business in China: Sino-Foreign Rivalry in the Cigarette Industry, 1890–1930*. Cambridge, MA: Harvard University Press.

Cohen, Youssef, and Franco Pavoncello. 1987. "Corporatism and Pluralism: A Critique of Schmitter's Typology." *British Journal of Political Science* 17, no. 1 (January): 117–122.

Comisso, Ellen, and Paul Marer. 1986. "The Economics and Politics of Reform in Hungary." In *Power, Purpose, and Collective Choic*, edited by Ellen Comisso and Laura D'Andrea Tyson, pp. 245–278. Ithaca, NY: Cornell University Press.

Dahl, Robert A. 1971. *Polyarchy: Participation and Opposition*. New Haven, CT: Yale University Press.

Dai Zigeng. 1993. "What We Should Say About 'False Joint Ventures.'" *Guangming ribao*, 4 April. In FBIS-CHI-93-084 (1993): 30.

Dalton, Gregory R. 1990. "Training China's Business Elite." *China Business Review* 17, no. 5 (September–October): 46–48.

Davis, Deborah. 1989. "Chinese Social Welfare: Policies and Outcomes." *China Quarterly*, no. 119 (September): 577–597.

———. 1990. "Urban Job Mobility." In *Chinese Society on the Eve of Tiananmen: The Impact of Reform*, edited by Deborah Davis and Ezra F. Vogel, pp. 85–108. Cambridge, MA: Council on East Asian Studies, Harvard University.

———. 1992. "Job Mobility in Post-Mao Cities: Increases on the Margins." *China Quarterly*, no. 132 (December): 1062–1085.

"Debate on Political Rights Reopened in China." 1993. *Christian Science Monitor* (29 January). Reported in CND, 31 January 1993.

Deyo, Frederic C. 1987. "Coalitions, Institutions, and Linkage Sequencing— Toward a Strategic Capacity Model of East Asian Development." In *The*

Political Economy of New Asian Industrialism, edited by Frederic Deyo, pp. 227–247. Ithaca, NY: Cornell University Press.

———. 1990. "Economic Policy and the Popular Sector." In *Manufacturing Miracles: Paths of Industrialization in Latin America and East Asia*, edited by Gary Gereffi and Donald L. Wyman, pp. 179–204. Princeton: Princeton University Press.

Ding Xueliang. 1995. *The Decline of Communism in China: Legitimacy Crisis, 1977–1989*. Cambridge: Cambridge University Press.

Dittmer, Lowell. 1987. "Public and Private Interests and the Participatory Ethic in China." In *Citizens and Groups in Contemporary China*, edited by Victor C. Falkenheim, pp. 18–23. Ann Arbor: Center for Chinese Studies, University of Michigan.

Dixon, Chris, and David Drakakis-Smith. 1993. *Economic and Social Development in Pacific Asia*. London: Routledge.

Djilas, Milovan. 1959. *The New Class: An Analysis of the Communist System*. New York: Praeger.

Doner, Richard F. 1991. "Limits of State Strength: Toward an Institutionalist View of Economic Development." *World Politics*, no. 44 (April): 398–431.

———. 1992. "Approaches to the Politics of Economic Growth in Southeast Asia." *Journal of Asian Studies* 50, no. 4 (November): 835–836.

Dore, Ronald. 1986. *Flexible Rigidities*. Stanford: Stanford University Press.

Eastman, Lloyd E. 1984. "New Insights into the Nature of the Nationalist Regime." *Republican China* 9, no. 2 (February): 8–18.

Eckstein, Alexander. 1977. *China's Economic Revolution*. Cambridge: Cambridge University Press.

Eckstein, Harry. 1975. "Case Study and Theory in Political Science." In *Handbook of Political Science*. Vol. 7, *Strategies of Inquiry*, edited by Fred Greenstein and Nelson Polsby, pp. 79–137. Reading, MA: Addison-Wesley.

"$82.68 Billion Foreign Investments Approved Last Year." 1995. (10 April). Reported in CND, 12–13 April 1995.

Elvin, Mark. 1973. *The Pattern of the Chinese Past: A Social and Economic Interpretation*. Stanford: Stanford University Press.

Engardio, Peter. 1993. "Motorola in China: A Great Leap Forward." *Business Week* (17 May): 59.

Erlanger, Steven. 1995. "A Corrupt Tide in Russia from State-Business Ties." *New York Times* (3 July): 1, 5.

Evans, Peter. 1979. *Dependent Development: The Alliance of Multinational, State, and Local Capital in Brazil*. Princeton: Princeton University Press.

———. 1995. *Embedded Autonomy: States and Industrial Transformation*. Princeton: Princeton University Press.

Faison, Seth. 1995. "A Business Deal Makes a Point for China." *New York Times* (16 July): 6.

Falkenheim, Victor C., ed. 1987. *Citizens and Groups in Contemporary China*. Ann Arbor: Center for Chinese Studies, University of Michigan.

FBIS-CHI-93-094. 1993. 18 May: 37.

Feuerwerker, Albert. 1976. *The Foreign Establishment in China in the Early Twentieth Century*. Ann Arbor: Center for Chinese Studies, University of Michigan.

Fewsmith, Joseph. 1984. "Responses to Eastman." *Republican China* 9, no. 2 (February): 19–27.

———. 1985. *Party, State, and Local Elites in Republican China: Merchant Organizations and Politics in Shanghai, 1890–1930*. Honolulu: University of Hawaii Press.

———. 1991. "The Dengist Reforms in Historical Perspective." In *Contemporary Chinese Politics in Historical Perspective*, edited by Brantly Womack, pp. 23–52. New York: Cambridge University Press.

Friedheim, Daviel V. 1993. "Bringing Society Back into Democratic Transition Theory after 1989: Pact Making and Regime Collapse." *East European Politics and Societies* 7, no. 3 (Fall): 482–512.

Friedrich, Carl J., and Zbigniew K. Brzezinski. 1961. *Totalitarian Dictatorship and Autocracy*. New York: Praeger.

Frisbie, John. 1992. "Housing Local Employees." *China Business Review* 19, no. 5 (September–October): 26–27.

Frisbie, John, and Richard Brecher. 1992. "FIE Labor Practices." *China Business Review* 19, no. 5 (September–October): 25.

Gardner, John. 1969. "The Wu-fan Campaign in Shanghai: A Study in the Consolidation of Urban Control." In *Chinese Communist Politics in Action*, edited by A. Doak Barnett, pp. 477–539. Seattle: University of Washington Press.

Gerlach, Michael L. 1992. *Alliance Capitalism: The Social Organization of Japanese Business*. Berkeley: University of California Press.

Gernet, Jacques. 1973. *Daily Life in China on the Eve of the Mongol Invasion, 1250–1276*, pp. 86–88. Stanford: Stanford University Press.

Giesert, Bradley Kent. 1979. "Power and Society: The Kuomintang and Local Elites in Kiangsu Province, China, 1924–1937." Ph.D. diss., University of Virginia.

Glassman, Ronald M. 1991. *China in Transition: Communism, Capitalism, and Democracy*. New York: Praeger.

Gold, Thomas B. 1985. "After Comradeship: Personal Relations in China since the Cultural Revolution." *China Quarterly*, no. 104: 657–675.

———. 1986. *State and Society in the Taiwan Miracle*. Armonk, NY: M. E. Sharpe.

———. 1989. "Urban Private Business in China." *Studies in Comparative Communism* 21, nos. 2/3 (Summer/Autumn): 187–201.

———. 1990. "Party-State versus Society in China." In *Building a Nation-State: China at Forty*, edited by Joyce K. Kallgren, pp. 125–151. Berkeley: Institute of East Asian Studies, University of California.

———. 1990a. "Urban Private Business and Social Change." In *Chinese Society on the Eve of Tiananmen: The Impact of Reform*, edited by Deborah Davis and Ezra Vogel, pp. 157–178. Cambridge, MA.: Council on East Asian Studies, Harvard University.

Goldman, Marshall I., and Merle Goldman. 1987–1988. "Soviet and Chinese Economic Reform." *Foreign Affairs* 66, no. 3: 551–573.

Goldstein, Steven M. 1995. "China in Transition: The Political Foundations of Incremental Reform." *China Quarterly*, no. 144 (December): 1105–1131.

Goodman, Bryna. 1992. "New Culture, Old Habits: Native-Place Organization and the May Fourth Movement." In *Shanghai Sojourners*, edited by Frederic Wakeman, Jr., and Wen-hsin Yeh, pp. 76–107. Berkeley: Institute of East Asian Studies, University of California.

Goodman, David S. G., ed. 1984. *Groups and Politics in the People's Republic of China*. Armonk, NY: M. E. Sharpe.

Granick, David. 1990. *Chinese State Enterprises: A Regional Property Rights Analysis*. Chicago: University of Chicago Press.

"Guanyu caiwu qingkuang de baogao" [Report on Financial Affairs]. 1991. *SFIEAJ*, no. 1 (10 February): 52.

Guojia Jingji Tizhi Gaige Weiyuanhui [State Commission on Reforming the Economic System]. 1994. *Zhongguo jingji tizhi gaige, 1993 nianjian* [China Economic Systems Reform Yearbook, 1993]. Beijing: Gaige Chubanshe [Reform Publishing House].

Habermas, Jurgen. 1989. *The Structural Transformation of the Public Sphere: An Inquiry into a Category of Bourgeois Society*. Cambridge, MA: MIT Press.

Haggard, Stephan. 1990. *Pathways from the Periphery: The Politics of Growth in the Newly Industrializing Countries*. Ithaca, NY: Cornell University Press.

Haggard, Stephan, Byung-kook Kim, and Chung-in Moon. 1991. "The Transition to Export-Led Growth in South Korea: 1954–1966." *Journal of Asian Studies* 50, no. 4 (November): 850–873.

Haggard, Stephan, and Chung-in Moon. 1983. "The South Korean State in International Economy: Liberal, Dependent, or Mercantile?" In *The Antinomies of Interdependence*, edited by John Ruggie, pp. 131–190. New York: Columbia University Press.

Halpern, Nina C. 1989. "Economic Reform and Democratization in Communist Systems: The Case of China." *Studies in Comparative Communism* 22, nos. 2/3 (Summer/Autumn): 139–152.

———. 1992. "Information Flows and Policy Coordination in the Chinese Bureaucracy." In *Bureaucracy, Politics and Decision-Making in Post-Mao China*, edited by David M. Lampton and Kenneth Lieberthal, pp. 125–148. Berkeley: University of California Press.

Hao, Yen-p'ing. 1970. *The Comprador in Nineteenth Century China: Bridge between East and West*. Cambridge, MA: Harvard University Press.

———. 1986. *The Commercial Revolution in Nineteenth-Century China: The Rise of Sino-Western Mercantile Capitalism*. Berkeley: University of California Press.

Harding, Harry. 1981. *Organizing China: The Problem of Bureaucracy, 1949–1976*. Stanford: Stanford University Press.

Harrold, Peter, and Rajiv Lall. 1993. *China: Reform and Development in 1992–1993*. World Bank Discussion Paper no. 215. Washington, D.C.: World Bank.

He Guanghui. 1990. "Deepen the Enterprise Reform and Steadily Develop the Economy." *Zhongguo jingji tizhi gaige* [Reform of China's Economic System], no. 1 (23 January): 6–9, 40. In FBIS-CHI-90-031 (14 February 1990): 19–23.

Henriot, Christian. 1993. *Shanghai, 1927–1937: Municipal Power, Locality, and Modernization.* Translated by Noël Castelino. Berkeley: University of California Press.

Hough, Jerry, and Merle Fainsod. 1977. *How the Soviet Union Is Governed.* Cambridge, MA.: Harvard University Press.

Huang Yasheng. 1990. "Web of Interests and Patterns of Behaviour of Chinese Local Economic Bureaucracies and Enterprises during Reforms." *China Quarterly* 123 (September): 431–458.

———. 1996. *Inflation and Investment Controls in China: The Political Economy of Central-Local Relations during the Reform Era.* New York: Cambridge University Press.

Huntington, Samuel. 1992. "How Countries Democratize." *Political Science Quarterly* 106, no. 4 (Winter): 579–616.

Hwang, Kuang-kuo. 1987. "Face and Favor: The Chinese Power Game." *American Journal of Sociology* 92, no. 4 (January): 944–974.

Implementing Act for the Law of the People's Republic of China on Joint Ventures Using Chinese and Foreign Investment [*Zhonghua renmin gongheguo zhong wai hezi jingying qiye fa shishi tiaoli*]. 1983. Translated in *Beijing Review*, no. 4 (10 October 1983): 1–6.

Interim Provisions Concerning Ideological and Political Work for Chinese Staff and Workers in Chinese-Foreign Equity and Cooperative Joint Ventures. Promulgated 11 August 1987. Translated by Paul, Weiss, Rifkind, Wharton, and Garrison.

"Investment Data." 1995. *China Business Review* 22, no. 3 (May–June): 32.

Janos, Andrew C. 1979. "Interest Groups and the Structure of Power: Critique and Comparisons." *Studies in Comparative Communism* 12, no. 1 (Spring): 6–20.

Jefferson, Gary. 1992. "The Chinese Economy: Moving Forward." In *China Briefing, 1992,* edited by William Joseph, pp. 35–54. Boulder, CO: Westview Press.

Jiang Shaogao and Li Jie. 1992. "Enterprise Management Association, Entrepreneurs' Association Say Change in Government Function May Gear Enterprises to Market." *Renmin ribao* (12 April): 4. In FBIS-CHI-92-085 (1 May 1992): 25–26.

Johnson, Chalmers A. 1982. *MITI and the Japanese Miracle: The Growth of Industrial Policy, 1925–1975.* Stanford: Stanford University Press.

———. 1987. "Political Institutions and Economic Performance: The Government-Business Relationship in Japan, South Korea, and Taiwan." In *The Political Economy of the New Asian Industrialism,* edited by Frederic Deyo, pp. 136–164. Ithaca, NY: Cornell University Press.

Jones, Leroy P., and Il Sakong. 1980. *Government, Business, and Entrepreneurship in Economic Development: The Korean Case.* Cambridge, MA: Harvard University Press.

Jowitt, Kenneth. 1975. "Inclusion and Mobilization in European Leninist Regimes." *World Politics* 28, no. 1 (October): 69–96.

Kang, David. 1995. "Profits of Doom: Transaction Costs, Rent-Seeking, and Development." Ph.D. diss., University of California, Berkeley.

Karl, Terry Lynn. 1990. "Dilemmas of Democratization in Latin America." *Comparative Politics* 23, no. 1 (October): 1–21.

Karmel, Solomon M. 1994. "Emerging Securities Markets in China: Capitalism with Chinese Characteristics." *China Quarterly*, no. 140 (December): 1105–1120.

Keane, John. 1988. "Despotism and Democracy: The Origins and Development of the Distinction between Civil Society and the State, 1750–1850." In *Civil Society and the State*, edited by John Keane, pp. 35–77. London: Verso Publishers.

Kirby, William C. 1989. "Technocratic Organization and Technological Development in China: The Nationalist Experience and Legacy, 1928–1953." In *Science and Technology in Post-Mao China*, edited by Denis Fred Simon and Merle Goldman, pp. 23–43. Cambridge, MA: Council on East Asian Studies, Harvard University.

———. 1995. "China Unincorporated: Company Law and Business Enterprise in Twentieth-Century China." *Journal of Asian Studies* 54, no. 1 (February): 43–63.

Koo, Hagen. 1987. "The Interplay of State, Social Class, and World System in East Asian Development: The Cases of South Korea and Taiwan." In *The Political Economy of the New Asian Industrialism*, edited by Frederic Deyo, pp. 165–181. Ithaca, NY: Cornell University Press.

Kraus, Willy. 1991. *Private Business in China: Revival between Ideology and Pragmatism*. Translated by Eric Holz. Honolulu: University of Hawaii Press.

Kristof, Nicholas D. 1992. "Entrepreneurs in China Attain the Age of Greed." *New York Times* (30 August): 3.

———. 1993. "China Applauds as Its Officials Plunge into Profit." *New York Times* (6 April): A6.

Krugman, Paul. 1994. "The Myth of Asia's Miracle." *Foreign Affairs* (November–December): 62–78.

Kyodo News Service. 1995. "Zhu Rongji Confidant Appointed Shanghai Mayor." Japan Economic Newswire (24 February). Reported in Nexis Library [On-line], Nexis File: INT'L, ASIAPC.

Lam, Willy Wo-Lap. 1992. "Firms to Be Given Greater Powers." *South China Morning Post* (October 23): 12. Reported in Nexis Library [On-line], Nexis File: INT'L, ASIAPC.

Lampton, David M., and Kenneth Lieberthal, eds. 1992. *Bureaucracy, Politics and Decision-Making in Post-Mao China*. Berkeley: University of California Press.

Lardy, Nicholas. 1992. *Foreign Trade and Economic Reform in China, 1978–1990*. New York: Cambridge University Press.

———. 1995. "The Role of Foreign Trade and Investment in China's Eco-

nomic Transformation." *China Quarterly*, no. 144 (December):
1065–1082.

Lee, Edmond. 1991. "A Bourgeois Alternative? The Shanghai Arguments for a Chinese Capitalism: The 1920s and 1980s." In *Contemporary Chinese Politics in Historical Perspective*, edited by Brantly Womack, pp. 90–128. New York: Cambridge University Press.

Lee, Hong Yung. 1991. *From Revolutionary Cadres to Party Technocrats in Socialist China*. Berkeley: University of California Press.

Lee, Peter Nan-shong. 1991. "The Chinese Industrial State in Historical Perspective: From Totalitarianism to Corporatism." In *Contemporary Chinese Politics in Historical Perspective*, edited by Brantly Womack, pp. 153–179. New York: Cambridge University Press.

Lenin, V. I. 1939. *Imperialism, the Highest Stage of Capitalism: A Popular Outline*. New York: International Publishers.

Levine, Daniel H. 1988. "Paradigm Lost: Dependence to Democracy." *World Politics* 25, no. 3 (April): 377–394.

Levy, Daniel, and Gabriel Szekely. 1987. *Mexico: Paradoxes of Stability and Change* (second edition). Boulder, CO: Westview Press.

Lew, Seok-jin. 1992. "Bringing Capital Back In: A Case Study of South Korean Automobile Industrialization." Ph.D. diss., Yale University.

Li Zheng. 1990. "Pluralization and Liberalization." *Guangming ribao* (10 April). In FBIS-CHI-90-090 (9 May 1990): 22.

Li Zongbo. 1992. "Industry Federation Promotes Self-Run Enterprises." Zhongguo Xinwen She [China News Agency] (16 December). In FBIS-CHI-92-245 (21 December 1992): 42.

Liang Fuqiang. 1990. "Pay Close Attention to Ideological and Political Work in Joint-Venture Enterprises." *Gongren ribao* (25 October): 4. In FBIS-CHI-90-196 (10 October 1990): 36–37.

Liao, Kuang-sheng. 1984. *Antiforeignism and Modernization in China, 1860–1980*. Hong Kong: Chinese University of Hong Kong Press.

Lin, Nan, and Yanjie Bian. 1991. "Getting Ahead in Urban China." *American Journal of Sociology* 97, no. 3 (November): 657–688.

Lindblom, Charles. 1977. *Politics and Markets*. New York: Basic Books.

Ling Wenli, Shao Daosheng, Feng Bailin, Zhang Jiatang, Fang Liluo, Liu Dawei, and Zhang Liye. 1993. "Zhong-ri hezi qiye zhongguo yuangong dui riben guanlizhe ji suozai qiye de pingjia" [An Assessment of Sino-Japanese Joint Venture Chinese Staff and Workers of Japanese Management and Their Enterprises]. *Zhongguo shehui kexue* [Social Sciences in China], no. 1: 214–215.

Lipset, Seymour Martin. 1981. *Political Man* (expanded edition). Baltimore: Johns Hopkins University Press.

Liu Donghua and Niu Changzheng. 1993. "Industry, Commerce Federation Congress Closes." Xinhua radio (17 October). In FBIS-CHI-93–205 (26 October): 27.

Liu, Drew. 1995. "The Rise of Neo-Conservatism in China." *China Focus* 3, no. 1 (January): 1–2.

Liu, Ya-ling. 1992. "Reform from Below: The Private Economy and Local Politics in the Rural Industrialization of Wenzhou." *China Quarterly*, no. 130 (June): 293–316.

Luo Rongxing, Zhu Huaxin, and Cao Huanrong. 1987. "Different Interest Groups under Socialism." *Beijing Review* (30 November–6 December): 18–19.

Ma Shu-yun. 1994. "The Chinese Discourse on Civil Society." *China Quarterly*, no. 137 (March): 180–193.

Maibach, Michael. 1995. "Hi-Tech Tradeoffs with China." *Asia-Pacific Economic Review* 3, no. 3: 10.

Manion, Melanie. 1992. "Politics and Policy in Post-Mao Cadre Retirement." *China Quarterly*, no. 129 (March): 1–25.

Mann, Susan. 1987. *Local Merchants and the Chinese Bureaucracy, 1750–1950*. Stanford: Stanford University Press.

Mao Zedong. 1967. "On New Democracy." In *Selected Works of Mao Tse-tung* 2, pp. 339–384. Peking: Foreign Languages Press.

———. 1969. "On the People's Democratic Dictatorship." In *Selected Works of Mao Tse-tung* 4, pp. 411–424. Peking: Foreign Languages Press.

Martin, Brian G. 1995. "The Green Gang and the Guomindang State: Du Yuesheng and the Politics of Shanghai, 1927–1937." *Journal of Asian Studies* 54, no. 1 (February): 64–92.

Marx, Karl. 1958. "The German Ideology." In *Selected Works*. Moscow: Foreign Languages Publishing House.

McCormick, Barrett, and David Kelly. 1994. "The Limits of Anti-Liberalism." *Journal of Asian Studies* 53, no. 3 (October): 804–831.

McEwen, Susan. 1994. "New Kids on the Block." *China Business Review* 21, no. 3 (May–June): 35–39.

McGregor, James. 1991. "Foreign Firms in China Upset by Added Tax." *Wall Street Journal* (15 April): A1.

———. 1993. "Changes in China Lure Chinese Back Home." *Wall Street Journal*, 20 June. Reported in *CND Books and Journal Review* (4 July 1993).

McMillan, John, and Barry Naughton. 1992. "How to Reform a Planned Economy: Lessons from China." *Oxford Review of Economic Policy* 8, no. 1 (Spring): 130–143.

Migdal, Joel S. 1988. *Strong Societies and Weak States: State Society Relations and State Capabilities in the Third World*. Princeton: Princeton University Press.

MOFTEC. n.d. *Zhongguo duiwai jingji maoyi nianjian* [Yearbook of China's Foreign Economic Trade]. Reported in "Investment Data." *China Business Review* 22, no. 3 (May–June 1995): 32.

Moore, Barrington. 1966. *Social Origins of Dictatorship and Democracy*. Boston: Beacon Press.

Murphy, Rhoads. 1970. *The Treaty Ports and China's Modernization: What Went Wrong?* Ann Arbor: Center for Chinese Studies, University of Michigan.

Nathan, Andrew J. 1973. "A Factionalism Model for CCP Politics," *China Quarterly*, no. 53 (January–March): 34–66.

———. 1985. *Chinese Democracy.* New York: Alfred Knopf.

———. 1989. "Chinese Democracy in 1989: Continuity and Change." *Problems of Communism* 38 (September–October): 16–29.

Nathan, Andrew J., and Tianjian Shi. 1993. "Cultural Requisites for Democracy in China: Findings from a Survey." *Daedalus* 122, no. 2(Spring): 95–124.

National Council for U.S.-China Trade (NCUSCT). 1987. *U.S. Joint Ventures in China: A Progress Report.* Washington, D.C.: NCUSCT.

Naughton, Barry. 1994. "What Is Distinctive about China's Economic Transition? State Enterprise Reform and Overall System Transformation." *Journal of Comparative Economics* 18, no. 3 (June): 470–490.

Nee, Victor. 1989. "Theory of Market Transition: From Redistribution to Market in State Socialism." *American Sociological Review*, no. 54 (October): 663–681.

Nee, Victor, and Su Sijin. 1990. "Institutional Change and Economic Growth in China: The View from the Villages." *Journal of Asian Studies*, no. 49: 3–25.

Nevitt, Christopher Earle. 1994. "Private Business Associations in China: Civil Society or Tools of Local Government Autonomy." Paper prepared for the Summary Conference of the UCSD/UC Irvine/Tianjin Academy of Social Sciences Collaborative Research Project.

O'Brien, Kevin J. 1992. "Bargaining Success of Chinese Factories." *China Quarterly*, no. 132 (December): 1086–1100.

Odgaard, Ole. 1992. "Entrepreneurs and Elite Formation in Rural China." *Australian Journal of Chinese Affairs*, no. 28 (July): 89–108.

O'Donnell, Guillermo. 1973. *Modernization and Bureaucratic Authoritarianism.* Berkeley: University of California Press.

O'Donnell, Guillermo, and Philippe C. Schmitter. 1986. *Transitions from Authoritarian Rule: Tentative Conclusions about Uncertain Democracy.* Baltimore: Johns Hopkins University Press.

Oi, Jean C. 1985. "Communism and Clientelism: Rural Politics in China." *World Politics* 37, no. 2 (January): 238–266.

———. 1992. "Fiscal Reform and the Economic Foundations of Local State Corporatism in China." *World Politics* 45, no. 1 (October): 99–126.

———. 1992a. "Private and Local State Entrepreneurship: The Shandong Case." Paper presented at the Forty-Fourth Annual Meeting of the Association for Asian Studies, Washington, D.C. (April 5).

Okimoto, Daniel I. 1989. *Between MITI and the Market: Japanese Industrial Policy for High Technology.* Stanford: Stanford University Press.

Onis, Ziya. 1991. "The Logic of the Developmental State." *Comparative Politics* 24, no. 1 (October): 109–126.

Ost, David. 1989. "Towards a Corporatist Solution in Eastern Europe: The Case of Poland." *East European Politics and Society* 3, no. 1 (Winter): 152–174.

Ostergaard, Clemens Stubbe. 1989. "Citizens, Groups, and a Nascent Civil Society in China: Towards an Understanding of the 1989 Student Demonstrations." *China Information* 4, no. 2 (Autumn): 28–41.

"Over 13,000 Foreign Enterprises Established." 1993. *Zhongguo xinwen she* (Beijing, 26 June). In FBIS-CHI-93-123 (29 June 1993): 50.

Palma, Gabriel. 1978. "Dependency: A Formal Theory of Underdevelopment or a Methodology for the Analysis of Concrete Situations of Underdevelopment?" *World Development* 6 (July–August): 881–924.

Panagariya, Arvind. 1991. *Unraveling the Mysteries of China's Foreign Trade Regime: A View from Jiangsu Province.* World Bank Policy Research Working Paper Series no. 801 (November). Washington, D.C.: World Bank.

Park, Moon Kyo. 1987. "Interest Representation in South Korea." *Asian Survey* 27, no. 8 (August): 903–917.

"Party to Increase Profile in Joint Ventures." 1990. *South China Morning Post* (4 August): 10. In FBIS-CHI-90-152 (7 August 1990): 23–24.

Payne, Leigh A. 1994. *Brazilian Industrialists and Democratic Change.* Baltimore: Johns Hopkins University Press.

Pearson, Margaret M. 1990. "Party and Politics in Joint Ventures." *China Business Review* 17, no. 6 (November–December): 38–40.

———. 1991. *Joint Ventures in the People's Republic of China: The Control of Foreign Direct Investment under Socialism.* Princeton: Princeton University Press.

———. 1992. "Breaking the Bonds of 'Organized Dependence': Managers in China's Foreign Sector." *Studies in Comparative Communism* 25, no. 1 (March): 57–77.

———. 1994. "Foreign Trade and Investment." In *China Briefing, 1994,* edited by William A. Joseph, pp. 55–86. Boulder, CO: Westview Press.

Pelczynski, Z. A. 1988. "Solidarity and 'The Rebirth of Civil Society' in Poland, 1976–1981." In *Civil Society and the State,* edited by John Keane, pp. 361–380. London: Verso Publishers.

Perry, Elizabeth J. 1989. "State and Society in Contemporary China." *World Politics* 41, no. 4 (July): 579–591.

———. 1992. "Casting a Chinese 'Democracy' Movement: The Roles of Students, Workers, and Entrepreneurs." In *Popular Protest and Political Culture in Modern China,* edited by Jeffrey N. Wasserstrom and Elizabeth J. Perry, pp. 146–164. Boulder, CO: Westview Press.

Przeworski, Adam. 1991. *Democracy and Markets: Political and Economic Reforms in Eastern Europe and Latin America.* New York: Cambridge University Press.

Pye, Lucian W. 1967. *The Spirit of Chinese Politics.* Cambridge, MA: MIT Press.

Rankin, Mary Backus. 1986. *Elite Activism and Political Transformation in China.* Stanford: Stanford University Press.

———. 1990. "The Origins of a Chinese Public Sphere: Local Elites and Community Affairs in the Late Imperial Period." *Etudes Chinoises* 9, no. 2 (Autumn): 13–60.

Redding, Gordon. 1995. "Overseas Chinese Networks: Understanding the Enigma." *Long Range Planning* 28, no. 1: 61–69.

"Registration of 7,500 Enterprises Canceled." 1994. *South China Morning*

Post (4 August): 4. Reported in Nexis Library [On-line], Nexis File: INT'L, ASIAPC.

"Regulations Issued on Social Organizations." 1989. *China Daily* (1 November). In FBIS-CHI-89-210 (1 November 1989): 20

Remer, Carl F. 1933. *A Study of Chinese Boycotts.* Baltimore: Johns Hopkins University Press.

Robinson, Pearl T. 1991. "Niger: Anatomy of a Neotraditional Corporatist State." *Comparative Politics* 24, no. 1 (October): 1–20.

Rowe, William T. 1984. *Hankow, Commerce and Society in a Chinese City, 1796–1889.* Stanford: Stanford University Press.

———. 1990. "The Public Sphere in Modern China: A Review Article." *Modern China* 16, no. 2 (July): 309–329.

Sabin, Lora. 1994. "The Growth of Non-State Sector Employment." *China Quarterly*, no. 140 (December): 944–999.

SAEFI. 1991. "Guanyu xiugai zhangcheng de shuoming" [Explanation of the Amendments to the Articles of Association]. *SFIEAJ*, no. 1 (10 February): 50.

Sautman, Barry. 1992. "Sirens of the Strongman: Neo-Authoritarianism in Recent Chinese Political Theory." *China Quarterly*, no. 129 (March): 72–102.

Schmidt, Steffen W., James C. Scott, Carl Lande, and Laura Guasti, eds. 1977. *Friends, Followers, and Factions: A Reader in Political Clientelism.* Berkeley: University of California Press.

Schmitter, Philippe C. 1974. "Still the Century of Corporatism?" In *The New Corporatism: Social-Political Structures in the Iberian World*, edited by Fredrick B. Pike and Thomas Stritch, pp. 93–94. Notre Dame, IN: University of Notre Dame Press.

Schoppa, R. Keith. 1982. *Chinese Elites and Political Change: Zhejiang Province in the Early Twentieth Century.* Cambridge, MA: Harvard University Press.

Schurmann, Franz. 1968 (second edition). *Ideology and Organization in Communist China.* Berkeley: University of California Press.

Sears, Katherine Elizabeth. 1985. "Shanghai's Textile Capitalists and the State: The Nationalization Process in China." Ph.D. diss., University of Michigan.

Seymour, James D. 1987. *China's Satellite Parties.* Armonk, NY: M. E. Sharpe.

"Shanghai's Richest." 1993. *China Focus* 1, no. 4 (May): 7.

Shen Jueren. 1991. "Bi mu ci" [Closing Speech]. *SFIEAJ*, no. 1 (10 February): 30.

Shi Xianmin. 1993. "Beijing's Privately Owned Small Businesses: A Decade's Development." *Social Sciences in China*, no. 114 (Spring): 153–164.

Shils, Edward. 1991. "The Virtue of Civil Society." *Government and Opposition* 26, no. 1: 3–20.

Shirk, Susan. 1993. *The Political Logic of Economic Reform.* Berkeley: University of California Press.

Shue, Vivienne. 1988. *The Reach of the State: Sketches of the Chinese Body Politic*. Stanford: Stanford University Press.

Skilling, H. Gordon, and Franklin Griffiths. 1971. *Interest Groups in Soviet Politics*. Princeton: Princeton University Press.

Sklar, Richard L. 1976. "Postimperialism." *Comparative Politics* 9, no. 1: 75–92

Solinger, Dorothy J. 1984. *Chinese Business under Socialism: The Politics of Domestic Commerce, 1949–1980*. Berkeley: University of California Press.

———. 1991. "The Floating Population as a Form of Civil Society?" Paper prepared for the panel on "Civil Society in People's China" at the Forty-Third Annual Meeting of the Association for Asian Studies, New Orleans (11–14 April).

———. 1992. "Urban Entrepreneurs and the State: The Merger of State and Society." In *State and Society in China: The Consequences of Reform*, edited by Arthur Lewis Rosenbaum, pp. 121–141. Boulder, CO: Westview Press.

Stanley, Alessandra. 1995. "To Russia's New Elite, Politics Is Good Business." *New York Times* (4 July): 3.

Stepan, Alfred B. 1978. *The State and Society: Peru in Comparative Perspective*. Princeton: Princeton University Press.

Stranahan, Patricia. 1992. "Strange Bedfellows: The Communist Party and Shanghai's Elite in the National Salvation Movement." *China Quarterly*, no. 129 (March): 26–51.

Strand, David. 1990. "Protest in Beijing: Civil Society and Public Sphere in China." *Problems of Communism* 39 (May–June): 1–19.

Sun Ping. 1984. "Individual Economy under Socialism." *Peking Review* 27, no. 33 (13 August): 26.

Suttmeier, Richard P. 1987. "Riding the Tiger: The Political Life of China's Scientists." In *Citizens and Groups in Contemporary China*, edited by Victor C. Falkenheim, pp. 123–158. Ann Arbor: Center for Chinese Studies, University of Michigan.

Szelenyi, Ivan. 1988. *Socialist Entrepreneurs: Embourgeoisement in Rural Hungary*. Madison: University of Wisconsin Press.

———. 1989. "Eastern Europe in an Epoch of Transition: Toward a Socialist Mixed Economy?" In *Remaking the Economic Institutions of Socialism: China and Eastern Europe*, edited by Victor Nee and David Stark, pp. 208–231. Stanford: Stanford University Press.

Tan Hongkai. 1992. "Private Firms in Need of Support and Open Mind." *China Daily* (6 September): 4. In FBIS-CHI-92-194 (6 October): 48–49.

———. 1993. "Officials Turned Entrepreneurs Centre of Dispute." *China Daily* (27 January): 4. In FBIS-CHI-93-018 (29 January 1993): 35–36.

Tan Hongkai and Zhang Xiaogang. 1991. "Protection for Private Businesses." *China Daily* (28 February): 4.

Thompson, Thomas N. 1979. *China's Nationalization of Foreign Firms: The Politics of Hostage Capitalism, 1949–1957*. Baltimore: School of Law, University of Baltimore.

Tien, Hung-mao. 1989. *The Great Transition: Political and Social Change in the Republic of China*. Stanford: Hoover Institution Press.

———. 1992. "Transformation of an Authoritarian Party State: Taiwan's Development Experience." In *Political Change in Taiwan*, edited by Tun-jen Cheng and Stephan Haggard, pp. 33–55. Boulder, CO: Lynne Rienner Publishers.

Townsend, James. 1967. *Political Participation in Communist China*. Berkeley: University of California Press.

Treacy, Lisa Jacobson. 1988. "The Managerial Elite." *China Business Review* 15, no. 6 (November–December): 38–42.

Unger, Jonathan, and Anita Chan. 1995. "China, Corporatism, and the East Asian Model." *Australian Journal of Chinese Affairs*, no. 33 (January): 29–53.

United Press International. 1993. "Government to Ease on Job Moves, Tighten on Transients" (13 July). Reported in CND, 15 July 1993.

———. 1995. "Chinese Workers Yearn for Their Own Businesses" (27 January). Reported in Nexis Library [On-line], Nexis File: INT'L, ASIAPC.

Vermeer, Eduard B. 1988. "Chinese Management Training Programmes: A Review." *China Information* 3, no. 2 (August): 51–62.

Wade, Robert. 1990. *Governing the Market: Economic Theory and the Role of Government in East Asian Industrialization*. Princeton: Princeton University Press.

———. 1992. "East Asia's Economic Success: Conflicting Perspectives, Partial Insights, Shaky Evidence." *World Politics* 44, no. 2 (January): 270–320.

Wakeman, Frederic, Jr. 1993. "The Civil Society and Public Sphere Debate: Western Reflections on Chinese Political Culture." *Modern China* 19 (April): 108–138.

Walder, Andrew G. 1983. "Organized Dependence and Cultures of Authority in Chinese Industry." *Journal of Asian Studies* 43, no. 1 (November): 51–76.

———. 1986. *Communist Neo-Traditionalism: Work and Authority in Chinese Industry*. Berkeley: University of California Press.

———. 1989. "Factory and Manager in an Era of Reform." *China Quarterly*, no. 118 (June): 242–264.

———. 1991. "Workers, Managers, and the State: The Reform Era and the Political Crisis of 1989." *China Quarterly*, no. 127 (September): 467–492.

———. 1991a. "A Reply to Womack." *China Quarterly*, no. 126 (June): 333–339.

———. 1994. "The Decline of Communist Power: Elements of a Theory of Institutional Change." *Theory and Society*, no. 23 (April): 297–323.

Wang Lingling. 1985. "Gongye hangye guanli gaige de chutan" [An Initial Exploration into the Reform of Trade and Industry Management]. *Beijing ribao* (6 May): 3.

Wang Yihe, Xu E, and Zhou Jianping. 1984. *Zhong wai hezi jingying qiye* [Chinese-Foreign Joint Venture Enterprises]. Shanghai: Shanghai Shehui Kexue Yuan Chubanshe [Shanghai Academy of Social Sciences Publishers].

Wank, David L. 1991. "Merchant Entrepreneurs and the Development of Civil Society: Some Social and Political Consequences of Private Sector Expansion in a Southeast Coastal City." Paper prepared for the Forty-

Third Annual Meeting of the Association for Asian Studies, New Orleans (11–14 April).

———. 1992. "Symbiotic Alliance of Entrepreneurs and Officials: The Logics of Private Sector Expansion in a South China City." Paper prepared for the conference on "The Political Consequences of Departures from Central Planning." Arden House, Harriman, New York (25–30 August).

———. 1995. "Private Business, Bureaucracy, and Political Alliance in a Chinese City." *Australian Journal of Chinese Affairs*, no. 33 (January): 55–71.

———. 1995a. "Bureaucratic Patronage and Private Business: Changing Networks of Power in Urban China." In *The Waning of the Communist State: Economic Origins of Political Change in China and Hungary*, edited by Andrew G. Walder, pp. 153–183. Berkeley: University of California Press.

Weber, Max. 1947. *The Theory of Social and Economic Organization*. New York: Oxford University Press.

Wei Yuming. 1991. "Jiaqiang fuwu, kaituo jinqu, chongfen fahui xiehui de zuoyong—diyi jie lishihui de huiwu gongzuo baogao" [Rendering Better Service and Forging Ahead in a Pioneering Spirit to Bring the Association into Full Play—Report on the Work of the First Session of the Council]. *SFIEAJ*, no. 1 (10 February): 34.

White, Gordon. 1987. "The Impact of Economic Reforms in the Chinese Countryside: Towards the Politics of Social Capitalism." *Modern China* 13, no. 4 (October): 411–440.

———. 1993. *Riding the Tiger: The Politics of Economic Reform in Post-Mao China*. Stanford: Stanford University Press.

———. 1993a. "Prospects for Civil Society in China." *Australian Journal of Chinese Affairs*, no. 29 (January): 63–88.

White, Lynn T., III. 1987. "Leadership and Participation: The Case of Shanghai's Managers." In *Citizens and Groups in Contemporary China*, edited by Victor C. Falkenheim, pp. 189–211. Ann Arbor: Center for Chinese Studies, University of Michigan.

Whiting, Susan. 1991. "The Politics of NGO Development in China." *Voluntas* 2, no. 2 (November): 16–48.

Whyte, Martin King. 1992. "Prospects for Democratization in China." *Problems of Communism* (May–June): 58–70.

———. 1992a. "Urban China: A Civil Society in the Making?" In *State and Society in China: The Consequences of Reform*, edited by Arthur Lewis Rosenbaum, pp. 77–101. Boulder, CO: Westview Press.

Whyte, Martin King, and William L. Parish. 1984. *Urban Life in China*. Chicago: University of Chicago Press.

Winckler, Edwin. 1992. "Taiwan Transition?" In *Political Change in Taiwan*, edited by Tun-jen Cheng and Stephan Haggard, pp. 221–254. Boulder, CO: Lynne Rienner Publishers.

Woo, Jung-en. 1991. *Race to the Swift: State and Finance in Korean Industrialization*. New York: Columbia University Press.

Wright, Erik Olin. 1985. *Classes*. London: Verso Publishers.

Wright, Tim. 1988. "'The Spiritual Heritage of Chinese Capitalism': Recent Trends in the Historiography of Chinese Enterprise Management." *Australian Journal of Chinese Affairs*, no. 19/20: 185–214.

Xi Weihang. 1991. *"Jingcheng Bailing"* ["The Capital City's White Collar"]. *Beijing Ribao* (27 April): 2.

Xinhua. 1987. "Rise of Horizontal Business Associations" (12 April.) Reported in Nexis Library [On-line], Nexis File: INT'L, ASIAPC, item #0412072.

———. 1988. "Federation of Industry and Commerce Revises Constitution" (30 November). Reported in Nexis Library [On-line], Nexis File: INT'L, ASIAPC.

———. 1989. "Business Guilds Make a Dramatic Comeback" (1 December). In FBIS-CHI-89-234 (7 December 1989): 32–33.

———. 1990. "Foreign-Funded Enterprise Association Formed." In FBIS-CHI-90-143 (25 July): 60.

———. 1991. "Self-Employed People in Shenzhen Profiled" (24 December). In FBIS-CHI-91-250 (28 December 1991): 56.

———. 1992. "Association to Set Up Foreign Investors Center" (10 November). In FBIS-CHI-92-220 (13 November 1992): 46.

———. 1992a. "Children of Private Entrepreneurs Troublesome." Xinhua radio (11 June). In FBIS-CHI-92-014 (22 January): 31.

———. 1992b. "Industry Federation to Guide Non-public Economy" (6 January). In FBIS-CHI-92-010 (15 January): 41.

———. 1992c. "Tian Jiyun and Ding Guangen Urge Support for Private Economy" (11 January). In BBC Summary of World Broadcasts, FB/1276/B2/1 (13 January 1992). Reported in Nexis Library [On-line], Nexis File: INT'L, ASIAPC.

———. 1993. "Beijing Commends 1,117 Foreign-Funded Enterprises" (6 July). In FBIS-CHI-93-131 (12 July 1993): 44.

———. 1994. "Beijing Forms First Self-Employed Workers CYL Committee" (5 April). In FBIS-CHI-94-073 (15 April): 19.

———. 1994a. "Federation to Promote Nonstate-Owned Economy" (3 February). In FBIS-CHI-94-024 (4 February): 28.

———. 1994b. "Industry-Commerce Group Support Economic Reforms" (18 March). In FBIS-CHI-94-057 (24 March): 55.

———. 1994c. "Xinhua Reports More Young Scientists Becoming Entrepreneurs." Xinhua radio (21 March). In FBIS-CHI-94-058 (25 March): 59–60.

———. 1995. "China Recorfunded [sic] Funds" (10 January 1995). Reported in Nexis Library [On-line], Nexis File: INT'L, ASIAPC, item #0110032.

Yang, Mayfair Mei-hui. 1986. "The Art of Social Relationships and Exchange in China." Ph.D. diss., University of California, Berkeley.

———. 1989. "Between State and Society: The Construction of Corporateness in a Chinese Socialist Factory." *Australian Journal of Chinese Affairs*, no. 22 (July): 31–60.

———. 1989a. "The Gift Economy and State Power in China." *Comparative Studies in Society and History* 31, no. 1: 25–54.

Yeung, Chris. 1991. "Capital Way of Getting to the Top of the Heap." *South China Morning Post* (8 April): 8.

Young, Susan. 1991. "Wealth but Not Security: Attitudes towards Private Business in China in the 1980s." *Australian Journal of Chinese Affairs*, no. 25 (January): 115–137.

Zeigler, Harmon. 1988. *Pluralism, Corporatism, and Confucianism: Political Association and Conflict Regulation in the United States, Europe, and Taiwan.* Philadelphia: Temple University Press.

Zeng Hua. 1995. "Xu Kuangdi, How Will You Act as Shanghai Mayor?" *Ta Kung Pao* (22 March): B1. In BBC Summary of World Broadcasts, FE/2266/G (31 March 1995).

Zhang Baohui. 1993. "Institutional Aspects of Reforms and the Democratization of Communist Regimes." *Communist and Post-Communist Studies* 26, no. 2 (June): 165–181.

———. 1994. "Corporatism, Totalitarianism, and Transitions to Democracy." *Comparative Political Studies* 27, no. 1 (April): 108–136.

Zhao Ziyang. 1987. "Advance along the Road of Socialism with Chinese Characteristics." Report delivered at the Thirteenth National Congress of the Communist Party of China. *Beijing Review* (20 December): 18.

———. 1987a. "On Separating Party from Government." *Beijing Review* (14–20 December): 18–20.

Zhongguo geti laodongzhe xiehui zhangcheng [Constitution of the China Individual Laborers Association], 5 December 1986.

Zhongguo gongshangye lianhehui zhangcheng [Constitution of the All-China Federation of Industry and Commerce],—16 November 1993.

Zhongguo Xinwen She [China News Agency]. 1994. "Shenzhen Opens Party Branch for Individual Entrepreneurs" (8 June). In FBIS-CHI-94-111 (9 June): 51.

Zweig, David. 1991. "Internationalizing China's Countryside: The Political Economy of Exports from Rural Areas." *China Quarterly*, no. 128 (December): 716–741.

Index

ACFIC (All-China Federation of Industry and Commerce): as channel for political change, 161; foreign-sector membership, 130n36; institutional continuity, 63; and interlocking structure among organizations, 124; as mass organization, 59; as *minjian* organization, 119–20, 121, 131; organized after 1949, 58–59; representation of private sector, 131–32; Tianjin branch, 132; ties to state, 132, 135

Africa, 26

Agriculture, 45

All-China Federation of Industry and Commerce. *See* ACFIC

All-China Federation of Scientific Societies, 59n43

All-China Federation of Trade Unions, 133n47

Amakudari, 148, 155, 156

Amsden, Alice, 152n30

Anti-corruption campaigns, 153n33. *See also* Corruption

Anti-pornography campaign, 128

Anti-Rightist campaign, 59n43

"Anti–spiritual pollution" campaigns, 114, 114n30

Arato, Andrew, 27n16

Artisans (*gong*), 45

Association for the Preparation of Constitutionalism, 52n24

Autonomy: of associations, 120, 120n12,

129; defined, 66; in East Asia, 148, 148n21, 154; embedded, 154–55, 154n37; of foreign-sector managers, 8, 66, 67, 86, 99, 137; ideological, 65n1, 87–99; of merchants, 53, 117; in private sector, 8, 99; and socialist corporatism, 39–40, 129; of state enterprises, 66, 122, 145; structural, 4, 65n1, 65–87, 96–97, 99

Banker's Weekly, 54

Bank of China, 111n19

Banks, 53n26, 127, 132

Beijing, 79, 86, 128, 169, 172, 172n7

Beijing Autonomous Students' Union, 120

Beijing Institute for Research in the Social and Economic Sciences, 120

Beijing ribao, 119

Beijing Spring, 120

Benefits: and dossier system, 68, 69, 75–76; in foreign sector, 83–86, 137; in joint ventures, 82–83; in private sector, 96, 137; retirement, 76, 81, 84, 96; in state sector, 81–82

Benevolent halls, 45n3

Bergère, Marie-Claire, 49n15, 53, 54n29, 62

Bian, Yanjie, 82n39

Biaoxian (display of correct behavior), 81, 83

"Black money," 18n46

Examination system, 46

Exclusion Act (U.S.), 49–50n17

Expatriate managers, 11, 11n23, 16n38, 108n12, 109, 162n57

Export associations, 125n28

Exports, 90, 146, 146n18, 152, 158; Taiwan, 147n20

Factory managers, 37n46

"False" joint ventures, 10n18, 17n43, 173–74

Fatuan (trade associations), 45

Federal Assembly (Russia), 111

Federation of Chambers of Commerce, 55

Federation of Korean Industry (FKI), 147, 149

FESCO (Foreign Employee Service Corporation): held in disdain by Chinese employees, 84n44, 91; hiring of personnel through, 74, 75, 79, 80, 91; informal cohesiveness in, 109; personnel dossiers held at, 74, 76; political study sessions at, 72, 83; salaries and benefits paid by, 83–84, 84n45, 85

Fewsmith, Joseph, 37n47, 57n38, 64

Finance sector, 17

Floating population, 79n32, 85n46

Foreign direct investment: breakdown by region, 172n7; 1979–1995, 167

Foreign Employee Service Corporation. *See* FESCO

Foreigners, role in change, 103, 104. *See also* Expatriate managers

Foreign exchange, 66, 90, 90n55, 127, 128, 170

Foreign investment, 10, 66, 158, 169; CAEFI service center for investors, 126–27; duplication of, 156n42; nationality of firms, 13n29, 173–74; and preference for domestic sales, 90, 90n54. *See also* Joint ventures; Wholly foreign-owned enterprises

Foreign sector: attraction of employment in, 15; defined, 10–11; early years, 65–66; as escape from "politics," 16; establishment of, 10; Party role in, 69; relative autonomy in, 66. *See also* Joint ventures; Representative offices; Wholly foreign-owned enterprises

Foreign-sector managers (FSMs): apoliti-

cal posture of, 101–2, 138, 139; autonomy of, 8, 67, 86, 99, 137; in business elite, 13–15; Chinese and foreign, 11–12; defined, 3; focus on narrow problems, 90–91, 92; future political conservatism of, 163–64; in Hong Kong and Taiwan firms, 12–13; hostility toward, 106n9; ideology of, 99, 137, 140; lack of horizontal ties, 108–9, 139; number of, 13, 13n28; "old-line," 12, 13n28, 14; past political activity of, 101; personnel dossiers of, 73–77, 137; salaries of, 15; view of state-sector managers, 91–92, 92n57; views about economic reform, 88–92; views of Party, 92–93; views on political change, 93–94, 137; views of student movement, 97–98. *See also* Business elite

Foreign trade: under communist regime, 60; corporations, 90, 90n56; in late Qing, 48

Former officials, 9, 9n17, 10, 18n48, 123, 163

Fourteenth Party Congress, 111, 122

Fragmentation of authority, 153

Friedheim, Daniel V., 30n26

Fujian Province, 88n51, 172

Functional associations, 40, 161

Gambling, 18n46

Gentry-merchants, 50

Germany, 89, 94; East, 28, 30

Geti (individual) businesses, 16–17; number of, 17n43

Geti entrepreneurs: associations of, 118, 133; conspicuous consumption among, 98; distinguished from *siying* entrepreneurs, 97n67, 114; support for demonstrators in 1989, 110; ties to state, 113n27, 133; views on economic reform, 96–97. *See also* SELA

Gifts to officials, 107, 108, 111, 113n27

"Golden age" of bourgeoisie, 52–55, 61, 62, 63, 109, 117, 139

Goldstein, Steven M., 158n48

Gong (public) activities: and CAEFI, 126; in Ming and Qing, 44, 46–47, 49, 116

Gong (public) realm: and civil society, 46, 47, 47n11; criticism of, 47n11; and Maoist ideology, 58; and merchant networks, 62; and state co-optation, 47n9, 63, 117

Index: Susan Stone
Composition: Braun-Brumfield
Text: 10/13 Galliard
Display: Galliard
Printing and binding: Braun-Brumfield